EXERCISES IN ENGLISH

☆ GRAMMAR FOR LIFE ☆

TEACHER'S EDITION

LEVEL H

LOYOLAPRESS

CHICAGO

The Complete Grammar Program with Character

Enhancing Grammar with Grade-Level Science, Social Studies, Language Arts, and Character Education

- **Instruction** and **practice** in every area of modern grammar, usage, and mechanics help students build comprehensive, lifelong skills.

- **Grade-level science**, **social studies**, and **language arts** content reinforces learning in other subject areas.

- **Character education** enriches students' lives through profiles of multicultural role models.

EXERCISES IN ENGLISH
★ GRAMMAR FOR LIFE ★

LEVEL D

EXERCISES IN ENGLISH
★ GRAMMAR FOR LIFE ★

LEVEL E

EXERCISES IN ENGLISH
★ GRAMMAR FOR LIFE ★

ED'S

EXERC
IN EN
★ GRAMMAR F

LEVEL F

ERCISES
ENGLISH
MMAR FOR LIFE ★

LEVEL G

A Six-Level Program

Carefully sequenced Student Editions for grades 3–8 provide thorough teaching of all modern grammar concepts.

Easy-to-use Teacher's Editions offer clear, concise answers to exercises.

Introductory Review section, starting at Level D, helps students get back on track at the beginning of the year.

Self-teaching student lessons optimize class time.

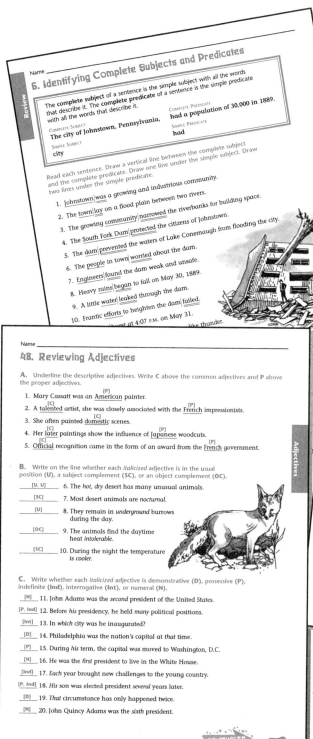

Review

Name _____

6. Identifying Complete Subjects and Predicates

The **complete subject** of a sentence is the simple subject with all the words that describe it. The **complete predicate** of a sentence is the simple predicate with all the words that describe it.

COMPLETE SUBJECT
The city of Johnstown, Pennsylvania,

COMPLETE PREDICATE
had a population of 30,000 in 1889.

SIMPLE SUBJECT
city

SIMPLE PREDICATE
had

Read each sentence. Draw a vertical line between the complete subject and the complete predicate. Draw one line under the simple subject. Draw two lines under the simple predicate.

1. Johnstown | was a growing and industrious community.
2. The town | lay on a flood plain between two rivers.
3. The growing community | narrowed the riverbanks for building space.
4. The South Fork Dam | protected the citizens of Johnstown.
5. The dam | prevented the waters of Lake Conemaugh from flooding the city.
6. The people in town | worried about the dam.
7. Engineers | found the dam weak and unsafe.
8. Heavy rains | began to fall on May 30, 1889.
9. A little water | leaked through the dam.
10. Frantic efforts to heighten the dam | failed.
   ... burst at 4:07 P.M. on May 31. ... like thunder.

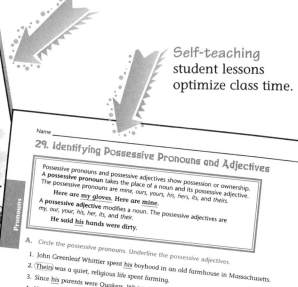

Pronouns

Name _____

29. Identifying Possessive Pronouns and Adjectives

Possessive pronouns and possessive adjectives show possession or ownership.
A **possessive pronoun** takes the place of a noun and its possessive adjective.
The possessive pronouns are *mine, ours, yours, his, hers, its,* and *theirs.*
   Here are **my** gloves. Here are **mine.**
A **possessive adjective** modifies a noun. The possessive adjectives are
my, our, your, his, her, its, and *their.*
   He said **his** hands were dirty.

A. Circle the possessive pronouns. Underline the possessive adjectives.

1. John Greenleaf Whittier spent his boyhood in an old farmhouse in Massachusetts.
2. Theirs was a quiet, religious life spent farming.
3. Since his parents were Quakers, Whittier is called the Quaker poet.
4. His poems celebrated our New England country life.
5. His was not just a life spent dreaming about the beauties of rural life.
6. His work against slavery is well known.
7. My history book describes him as an abolitionist.
8. Yours might mention his term in the Massachusetts legislature.
9. Is that copy of *Snow-Bound* ours?
10. I'll give you mine as long as you return it.

B. Replace the *italicized* word(s) with a possessive. Write **A** on the line if the possessive is an adjective and **P** if it is a pronoun.

[Its, A] 1. The *Monterey Bay Aquarium's* otters are a popular attraction.
[his, A] 2. Have you read *Roy Nickerson's* book on otters?
[Its, A] 3. *California's* laws now ban the use of gill nets.
[their, A] 4. The laws protect otters from being caught in *fishermen's* nets.
[Its, A] 5. A *gill net's* victim might include a harbor porpoise.
[theirs, P] 6. These laws were one of *Friends of the Sea Otters* accomplishments.
[Their, A] 7. *Oil tankers'* spilled oil also endangers otters.
[her, P] 8. The otter relocation idea was *a woman's* idea.
[Its, A] 9. Being playful and fun to watch is *an otter's* attraction.
[ours, P] 10. An otter's need for clean and safe water is like *our* need.

32

Name _____

48. Reviewing Adjectives

A. Underline the descriptive adjectives. Write **C** above the common adjectives and **P** above the proper adjectives.

1. Mary Cassatt was an American[P] painter.
2. A talented[C] artist, she was closely associated with the French[P] impressionists.
3. She often painted domestic[C] scenes.
4. Her later[C] paintings show the influence of Japanese[P] woodcuts.
5. Official[C] recognition came in the form of an award from the French[P] government.

B. Write on the line whether each *italicized* adjective is in the usual position (**U**), a subject complement (**SC**), or an object complement (**OC**).

[U, U] 6. The *hot, dry* desert has many unusual animals.
[SC] 7. Most desert animals are *nocturnal.*
[U] 8. They remain in *underground* burrows during the day.
[OC] 9. The animals find the daytime heat *intolerable.*
[SC] 10. During the night the temperature is *cooler.*

C. Write whether each *italicized* adjective is demonstrative (**D**), possessive (**P**), indefinite (**Ind**), interrogative (**Int**), or numeral (**N**).

[N] 11. John Adams was the *second* president of the United States.
[P, Ind] 12. Before *his* presidency, he held *many* political positions.
[Int] 13. In *which* city was he inaugurated?
[D] 14. Philadelphia was the nation's capital at *that* time.
[P] 15. During *his* term, the capital was moved to Washington, D.C.
[N] 16. He was the *first* president to live in the White House.
[Ind] 17. *Each* year brought new challenges to the young country.
[P, Ind] 18. *His* son was elected president *several* years later.
[D] 19. *That* circumstance has only happened twice.
[N] 20. John Quincy Adams was the *sixth* president.

Adjectives

CONTINUED **53**

Section reviews offer regular assessment opportunities.

Features that set us apart...

Clear definitions and examples
help students easily understand concepts.

Nouns

When two or more people own something together, it is called joint possession. To show joint possession, use 's after the last noun only.

John and Jack's hardware store

When two or more people each own a separate thing, it is called separate possession. To show separate possession, use 's after each noun.

John's and Jack's tools

A. Write whether the possessive nouns express separate or joint ownership.

[separate] 1. Arthur's and Henry's songs were well performed.
[joint] 2. It was a good start to North High and South High's art fair.
[separate] 3. Julia's and Roy's sculptures both used found objects this year.
[separate] 4. We visited the art exhibit at North's and South's art rooms.

Pronouns

An object pronoun can be used as the direct or indirect object of a verb or as the object of a preposition.

A. Circle the correct pronoun in each sentence. Write on the line whether the pronoun is used as a subject (S), a subject complement (SC), or an object (O).

[S] 1. Because myths are handed down by word of mouth, (they) them) have no correct form.
[O] 2. Myths provide (us) we) with explanations of natural phenomena.
[SC] 3. In the story of Persephone, it is (she) her) who is abducted.
[O] 4. Pluto, god of the underworld, keeps (her) she) for part of each year.
[S] 5. When (he) him) gives her back, Earth returns to spring and summer.
[S] 6. Do (we) us) think this is the explanation for the seasons?
[O] 7. Maybe not, but myths give (us) we) insights into the beliefs of other cultures.
[S] 8. (They) Them) were used to explain creation, religion, and the meaning of life.
[O] 9. Older people often told myths to the youth to teach (them) they) about the supernatural.
[O] 10. The myth of Pandora's box gave (them) they) an explanation for good and evil.

B. Circle the pronoun in each sentence. Write whether it is used as a subject (S), a subject complement (SC), a direct object (DO), an indirect object (IO), or the object of a preposition (OP).

[S] 1. (He) had magnificent physical strength.
[IO] 2. The gods gave (him) special gifts.
[DO] 3. Hercules' mother put (him) to bed one night.
[DO] 4. Two snakes attacked (him) and a brother.
[S, DO] 5. Hercules grasped the creatures by their throats, and (he) strangled (them).
[SC] 6. It was (he) who killed a lion at the age of eighteen.
[OP] 7. Hercules had to accomplish many labors—twelve of (them).
[IO] 8. In the twelfth labor Pluto gave (him) permission to bring Cerberus, the three-headed dog, up from Hades.
[DO] 9. Hercules carried (it) to Earth but eventually returned Cerberus to Hades.
[OP] 10. Many other great deeds were performed by (him) after the last labor.

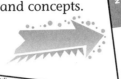

Grade-level content
provides enrichment and reinforcement of what is being studied in science, social studies, and language arts.

Character education lessons
offer students information on multicultural role models on a consistent basis.

[interrogative] 3. Why didn't he live with his mother [?]
[declarative] 4. His mother had to work long hours in the cornfields [.]
[exclamatory] 5. Goodness, that's a horrible situation [!]
[declarative] 6. When he was eight years old, Frederick was sent to live in Baltimore [.]
[declarative] 7. His owner's wife, Sophia Auld, taught him the alphabet [.]
[declarative] 8. Sophia's husband made her stop [.]
[declarative] 9. It was illegal to teach slaves to read [.]
[interrogative] 10. How did Frederick finally learn to read and write [?]
[declarative] 11. He bribed some neighborhood boys to teach him [.]
[declarative] 12. As a teenager, Frederick had to work as a field hand [.]
[declarative] 13. He was whipped unmercifully [.]
[exclamatory] 14. Oh, my, his life was terrible [!]
[declarative] 15. At the age of twenty, Frederick dressed up as a sailor and escaped [.]
[exclamatory] 16. What a brave young man he was [!]
[declarative] 17. Frederick became a lecturer and a newspaper publisher [.]
[declarative] 18. He worked for justice and opportunity for black people and for women [.]
[interrogative] 19. Where can you learn more about Frederick Douglass [?]
[imperative] 20. Find out about his relationship with Abraham Lincoln [.]

Frederick Douglass used the power of language to create positive change. Give an example of how you can use language to change things for the better.

4

30. Once threatened with extinction, blue whales now exist in (greater) greatest) numbers.

F. Complete each sentence with *fewer* or *less*.

31. If you eat poorly, you will have [less] energy.
32. Vegetables have [fewer] calories than junk food.
33. But junk food provides [fewer] vitamins.
34. The [less] you exercise, the [fewer] calories you will burn.
35. The [less] junk food you eat, the better you will feel.

Try It Yourself
On a separate sheet of paper, write five sentences that describe an exciting event in your life. Use adjectives correctly.

Check Your Own Work
Choose a piece of writing from your portfolio or journal, a work in progress, an assignment from another class, or a letter. Revise it, applying the skills you have learned in this chapter. The checklist will help you.

✔ Have you included appropriate adjectives?
✔ Have you used the comparative forms of adjectives correctly?
✔ Have you chosen adjectives that create a clear picture for your reader?
✔ Have you used your thesaurus?

Writing in context
allows students to practice and use what they have learned.

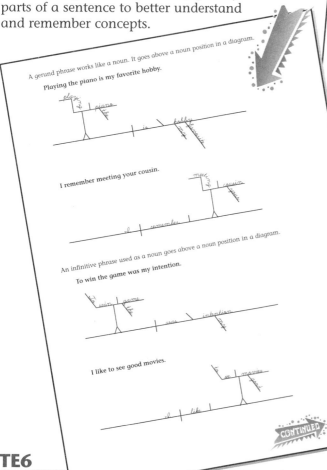

136. Deciding Which Internet Site to Use

Name _____

When you use a search engine to locate information on the Internet, it is important to know what kind of Web site it has taken you to. The organization or group that sets up a Web site is called a host. The hostname domain, the three letters that end each address, will tell you what kind of site you are looking at. The seven hostname domains in common use are:

.com — Businesses and individuals use .com.

.edu — All educational institutions, which may include museums, use this ending.

.gov — These letters signify that the address belongs to a government agency.

.org — Addresses for nonprofit groups such as United Way end in .org.

.mil — The armed forces use these letters.

.net — This means a networking organization such as netscape.net.

.int — International organizations such as the International Red Cross use these letters.

A search engine is a handy tool for finding information. But sometimes you may wish you knew the URL (Uniform Resource Locator), or address, for a specific place like the Smithsonian Institution or the White House. It would save time if there were a giant directory of Web addresses, but none exists. Following are a few addresses that may be useful to you in doing research online.

For information on the federal government

- FedWorld is a gateway to links to federal government departments.
  http://www.fedworld.gov:80

- The White House Web site provides information on the activities of the current president and the executive branch of government.
  http://www.whitehouse.gov

- Each house of Congress has its own Web site. To reach the home page of a particular senator or representative, type his or her last name after the slash in the appropriate URL.
  - U.S. Senators: http://www.senate.gov/
  - House of Representatives: http://www.house.gov/

- Thomas, maintained by the Library of Congress, has links to the House, Senate, Congressional Record, and other federal departments.
  http://thomas.loc.gov

CONTINUED 151

Research Skills — *vertical tab*

Research Skills section provides teaching and practice with tools such as the Internet and atlases. Students learn to combine grammar and writing in projects for other classes.

Handbook of Terms helps students refresh and expand their knowledge of grammar points.

A subject pronoun can replace a noun used as a subject complement.

A pronoun may be used as the direct object of a verb. The object pronouns are *me, you, him, her, it, us, them.*

An object pronoun may be used as the object of a preposition.

A pronoun that follows the conjunction *than* or *as* must be a subject pronoun if the word with which it is compared is a subject: John (subject) is happier than *I* (subject). It must be an object pronoun if the word with which it is compared is an object.

When a sentence contains a negative, such as *not* or *never*, use *anyone* or *anything* rather than *no one* or *nothing.*

See also **contraction, possessive pronoun,** and **reflexive pronoun.**

Q

question mark A punctuation mark (?) used at the end of a question: What time is it?

quotation marks Punctuation marks (" ") used before and after every direct quotation and every part of a divided quotation: "Let's go shopping," said Michiko. "I can go with you," Father said, "after I have eaten lunch."
Quotation marks enclose titles of short stories, poems, magazine articles, television shows, and radio programs. Titles of books, magazines, newspapers, movies, and works of art are usually printed in *italics* or are underlined.

R

reflexive pronoun A reflexive pronoun ends in *–self* or *–selves.* The reflexive pronouns are *myself, yourself, himself, herself, itself, ourselves, yourselves,* and *themselves.* A reflexive pronoun often refers to the subject of the sentence: She saw *herself* in the mirror.
A reflexive pronoun can also be used to show emphasis: I *myself* cooked the entire dinner.

relative pronoun A pronoun that connects a dependent clause to the person, place, or thing it modifies: Hal, *who* grew up in Indonesia, now lives in Boston.
The relative pronouns are *who, whom, whose, which,* and *that.* Use *who* if the pronoun is the subject of the dependent clause: Sue, *who* helped me, is my cousin. Use *whom* if the pronoun is the object of the dependent clause: Sue, *whom* you know, helps me study.

S

semicolon A punctuation mark (;) used as follows:
- to separate the clauses of a compound sentence when they are not separated by a conjunction: The bicycle was broken; the wheel was damaged.

(continued on next page)

Handbook of Terms — *vertical tab*

175

Sentence Diagramming section, starting at Level D, helps students visually portray the parts of a sentence to better understand and remember concepts.

A gerund phrase works like a noun. It goes above a noun position in a diagram.

Playing the piano is my favorite hobby.

I remember meeting your cousin.

An infinitive phrase used as a noun goes above a noun position in a diagram.

To win the game was my intention.

I like to see good movies.

Sentence Diagrams — *vertical tab*

CONTINUED 161

Plus

- **Flexible format** allows use of the books at multiple grade levels.

- **Perforated student pages** facilitate grading and inclusion in student portfolios.

- **Easy-to-grade exercises** are always divisible by five.

- **Sentence Analysis section** in the Teacher's Edition provides extra tools for daily oral grammar activities.

Exercises in English—Scope and Sequence

SENTENCES	C	D	E	F	G	H
The Four Kinds of Sentences	✔	✔	✔	✔	✔	✔
Subjects and Predicates	✔	✔	✔	✔	✔	✔
Simple Subjects and Predicates		✔		✔	✔	✔
Compound Subjects and Predicates		✔	✔	✔	✔	✔
Direct Objects		✔	✔	✔	✔	✔
Complete Subjects and Predicates			✔	✔	✔	✔
Natural and Inverted Order in Sentences			✔	✔	✔	✔
Indirect Objects				✔	✔	✔
Compound Sentences				✔	✔	✔
Complex Sentences					✔	✔
Compound Complex Sentences						✔
NOUNS	**C**	**D**	**E**	**F**	**G**	**H**
Proper and Common Nouns	✔	✔	✔	✔	✔	✔
Singular and Plural Nouns	✔	✔	✔	✔	✔	✔
Possessive Nouns	✔	✔	✔	✔	✔	✔
Nouns Used as Subjects		✔	✔	✔		
Nouns Used as Objects		✔	✔	✔	✔	✔
Nouns Used as Subject Complements			✔	✔	✔	
Nouns Used in Direct Address			✔	✔		
Nouns Used as Objects of Prepositions			✔	✔	✔	
Appositives				✔	✔	
Collective Nouns				✔	✔	✔
Concrete and Abstract Nouns				✔	✔	✔
Words Used as Nouns and Verbs				✔		✔
Nouns Used as Object Complements						✔
VERBS	**C**	**D**	**E**	**F**	**G**	**H**
Regular and Irregular Verbs	✔	✔	✔	✔	✔	✔
Present Tense	✔	✔	✔	✔	✔	✔
Progressive Tenses	✔	✔	✔	✔	✔	✔
Past Tense	✔	✔	✔	✔	✔	✔
Future Tenses	✔	✔	✔	✔	✔	✔
Action Verbs	✔	✔	✔			
Verbs of Being	✔	✔	✔			
Helping Verbs	✔	✔				
Forms of *Bring*	✔					
Forms of *Buy*	✔					

	C	D	E	F	G	H
Forms of *Come*	✔					
Forms of *Eat*	✔					
Forms of *Go*	✔		✔			
Forms of *See*	✔		✔			
Forms of *Sit* and *Set*	✔		✔	✔		
Forms of *Take*	✔		✔			
Forms of *Write*	✔					
Forms of *To Be*	✔	✔	✔			
Forms of *Begin*		✔				
Forms of *Break*		✔	✔			
Forms of *Choose*		✔	✔			
Forms of *Do*		✔				
Verb Phrases		✔	✔	✔	✔	
Intransitive Verbs (Linking Verbs)		✔	✔	✔	✔	✔
There Is and *There Are*		✔		✔	✔	
Subject-Verb Agreement			✔	✔	✔	✔
Transitive Verbs			✔	✔	✔	✔
Doesn't and *Don't*			✔	✔	✔	✔
Let and *Leave*			✔	✔		
Teach and *Learn*			✔			
Lie and *Lay*			✔	✔		
Rise and *Raise*				✔		
Perfect Tenses				✔	✔	
Words Used as Nouns and Verbs					✔	
Active and Passive Voice					✔	✔
Modal Auxiliary Verbs					✔	✔
You Are and *You Were*					✔	
Compound Tenses						✔
Emphatic Verb Forms						✔
PRONOUNS	C	D	E	F	G	H
Singular and Plural Pronouns	✔	✔	✔			
Subject Pronouns	✔	✔	✔	✔	✔	✔
Possessive Pronouns	✔	✔	✔	✔	✔	✔
I and *Me*	✔	✔				
Pronouns Used as Subject Complements	✔		✔	✔	✔	✔
Pronouns Used as Direct Objects		✔	✔	✔	✔	✔
The Person of Pronouns		✔	✔	✔		
The Gender of Pronouns			✔			
We and *Us*		✔				
Pronouns Used as Objects of Prepositions			✔	✔		

Pronouns Used in Contractions			✔	✔		
Reflexive Pronouns			✔	✔	✔	
Interrogative Pronouns				✔	✔	✔
Indefinite Pronouns				✔	✔	✔
Double Negatives				✔		
Pronouns Used as Indirect Objects					✔	✔
Who and *Whom*					✔	✔
Pronouns Used after *Than* and *As*					✔	✔
Relative Pronouns					✔	✔
Demonstrative Pronouns					✔	✔
Nothing and *Anything*					✔	
Pronouns Used as Objects of Prepositions						✔
Intensive Pronouns			✔			✔

ADJECTIVES	C	D	E	F	G	H
Descriptive Adjectives	✔			✔	✔	
Adjectives That Tell How Many	✔	✔	✔	✔		
Indefinite and Definite Articles	✔	✔	✔	✔	✔	
Demonstrative Adjectives	✔	✔	✔	✔	✔	✔
Comparative Forms of Adjectives	✔	✔	✔	✔	✔	✔
Possessive Adjectives		✔	✔	✔		
Common and Proper Adjectives		✔	✔			✔
Good and *Bad*		✔				
The Position of Adjectives			✔	✔	✔	✔
Superlative Forms of Adjectives			✔	✔	✔	✔
Adjectives Used as Subject Complements				✔		
Words Used as Adjectives or Nouns				✔	✔	✔
Those and *Them*				✔		
Interrogative Adjectives				✔		
Fewer and *Less*					✔	

ADVERBS	C	D	E	F	G	H
Adverbs of Time	✔	✔	✔	✔		
Adverbs of Place	✔	✔	✔	✔		
Good and *Well*	✔	✔	✔			
Comparative Adverbs		✔	✔	✔	✔	✔
Adverbs of Manner		✔	✔	✔		
No, Not, and *Never*		✔	✔	✔		
Superlative Adverbs			✔	✔		
Real and *Very*			✔			
Their and *There*			✔	✔		
To, Too, and *Two*			✔	✔		

	C	D	E	F	G	H
Adverbs and Adjectives				✔	✔	✔
There, *Their*, and *They're*					✔	
Farther and *Further*					✔	✔
Interrogative Adverbs					✔	✔
Adverbial Nouns					✔	✔
As . . . As, *So . . . As*, and *Equally*						✔

PUNCTUATION, CAPITALIZATION, ABBREVIATIONS	C	D	E	F	G	H
End Punctuation	✔	✔	✔	✔	✔	✔
Periods after Abbreviations, Titles, and Initials	✔	✔				
Capital Letters	✔	✔	✔	✔	✔	
Titles of Books and Poems	✔		✔	✔	✔	
Commas Used in Direct Address	✔	✔	✔	✔		
Punctuation in Direct Quotations	✔	✔	✔	✔		
Apostrophes		✔	✔			
Commas after *Yes* and *No*		✔	✔	✔		
Commas Separating Words in a Series		✔	✔	✔		
Commas after Parts of a Letter			✔	✔		
Commas in Dates and Addresses			✔	✔		
Commas in Geographical Names			✔			
Commas Used with Appositives				✔		
Commas Used in Compound Sentences				✔		
Semicolons and Colons				✔	✔	✔
Apostrophes, Hyphens, and Dashes				✔	✔	✔
Commas and Semicolons						✔

PREPOSITIONS, CONJUNCTIONS, INTERJECTIONS	C	D	E	F	G	H
Prepositions and Prepositional Phrases			✔	✔	✔	✔
Interjections			✔	✔	✔	✔
Between and *Among*			✔	✔		
From and *Off*			✔			
Adjectival Phrases			✔			
Adverbial Phrases			✔			
Coordinate Conjunctions			✔			
Words Used as Prepositions and Adverbs				✔	✔	✔
At and *To*				✔		
Beside and *Besides*, *In* and *Into*				✔		
Coordinate and Correlative Conjunctions					✔	
Conjunctive Adverbs					✔	

					G	H
Subordinate Conjunctions					✔	✔
Without and *Unless, Like, As,* and *As If*					✔	✔

PHRASES, CLAUSES	C	D	E	F	G	H
Adjectival Phrases				✔	✔	
Adverbial Phrases				✔	✔	
Adjectival Clauses					✔	✔
Adverbial Clauses					✔	✔
Restrictive and Nonrestrictive Clauses					✔	
Noun Clauses						✔

PARTICIPLES, GERUNDS, INFINITIVES	C	D	E	F	G	H
Participles						✔
Dangling Participles						✔
Gerunds						✔
Infinitives						✔
Hidden and Split Infinitives						✔

WORD STUDY SKILLS	C	D	E	F	G	H
Synonyms	✔	✔	✔	✔		
Antonyms	✔	✔				
Homophones	✔	✔	✔			
Contractions	✔	✔				
Compound Words		✔				

PARAGRAPH SKILLS	C	D	E	F	G	H
Using Colorful Adjectives	✔		✔			
Combining Subjects, Verbs, and Sentences	✔					
Finding the Exact Word		✔				
Using Similes		✔				
Expanding Sentences		✔				
Rewriting Rambling Sentences		✔	✔			
Revising		✔				
Proofreading		✔				
Recognizing the Exact Meaning of Words			✔			

LETTER WRITING	C	D	E	F	G	H
Friendly Letters	✔	✔				
Invitations	✔					
Letters of Acceptance	✔					
Thank-You Letters	✔			✔		
E-Mail Messages	✔	✔		✔		

TE11

Envelopes	✔	✔				
Forms	✔	✔				
Business Letters				✔		
RESEARCH	**C**	**D**	**E**	**F**	**G**	**H**
Computer Catalog	✔					
Dictionary	✔	✔				
Encyclopedia	✔		✔			
Thesaurus		✔				
Internet		✔	✔	✔	✔	✔
Almanac			✔			
Atlas			✔		✔	
Guides to Periodicals				✔		
Biographical Information				✔		
The Dewey Decimal System				✔		
Books of Quotations					✔	
Books in Print					✔	
The Statistical Abstract of the United States						✔
Research Tools						✔

Sentence Analysis

Purpose

Sentence analysis is a classroom-tested strategy designed to aid students in the understanding of a sentence through the study of its grammatical components and their relationship to one another.

Sentence analysis begins with a careful and thoughtful reading of the sentence to determine that it does contain a complete thought. Students then determine the *use* of the sentence (for example, declarative). Next, they identify the subject and the predicate. They can then go on to analyze the details in the sentence.

It is often useful to conduct a sentence analysis as an oral exercise. Each student responds to one point in the analysis in some predetermined order—by row, by group, or by number. Keep the responses moving at a fairly fast pace to hold students' interest. Five minutes at the beginning of each grammar period will focus the students on the task. Prolonging the activity may make it a chore rather than a challenge.

Give each student a copy of the Sentence Analysis Chart (page TE16) or place a blown-up version where all students can see it. Select a sentence from this or another book and write it on the board for analysis.

Ideally, you should act as an observer during the activity, allowing students to perform the analysis without assistance. The students' performance will indicate their grasp of grammar and help you identify areas that need review.

Consistent practice in identifying grammatical concepts will ensure that students arrive at an understanding of how the English language is structured and how they can use its patterns to express their own thoughts.

Procedure

Display the Sentence Analysis Chart (page TE16) or distribute a copy to each student. Choose a sentence that contains the aspects of grammar recently taught or reviewed and write it on the board. The first few times you do the activity, you may also want to display or distribute the Sentence Analysis Questions (page TE15) to help students complete the task.

Now have students use the chart to work through the steps of analysis, identifying each part of the sentence.

1. Sentence

Have the sentence read aloud. You may want to have the class read as a whole or ask an individual to read. Students should recognize that a sentence has a subject and a predicate and forms a complete thought.

EXAMPLE SENTENCE: **Yesterday the happy children played drums noisily.**

2. Use

Students should be able to recognize that a sentence is declarative, interrogative, imperative, or exclamatory. In selecting sentences for analysis, vary your choice among the four types.

According to *use*, the example sentence is declarative because it makes a statement.

Note: You may want to have students practice steps 1 and 2 several times before moving on to step 3. Once the students are comfortable identifying sentences, add the following steps one at a time, practicing them in short sessions each day.

3. Predicate

The predicate is the part of a sentence that contains a verb. Because the verb is the focal point of the thought, it should be identified first. The verb expresses action or being.

The verb in the example sentence is *played*.

4. Subject

The verb tells what the subject does or is. The subject can be determined by asking *who* or *what* before the verb.

The subject of the example sentence is *children*.

5. Object/Complement

Sometimes the predicate verb is completed by a direct object or a subject complement. They answer the questions *whom, who,* or *what* after the verb.

The direct object of the example sentece is *drums*.

6. Modifiers

Adverbs modify verbs. Adverbs answer the questions *how, when,* or *where.*

In the example sentence, the adverb *yesterday* tells when the children played, and the adverb *noisily* tells how the children played.

Adjectives modify nouns or pronouns. Adjectives answer the questions *what, what kind, how many,* or *whose.* An article is an adjective that points out a noun.

In the example sentence, the article *the* points out the noun *children*, and the adjective *happy* tells what kind of children.

7. Parts of Speech

To close the activity, ask the students to name the part of speech of each word in the sentence, beginning with the first and moving through the sentence in order.

In the example sentence, *yesterday* is an adverb, *the* is an article, *happy* is an adjective, *children* is a noun, *played* is a verb, *noisily* is an adverb.

Sentence Analysis Questions

1. Sentence
Does the group of words form a complete thought with a subject and a predicate? (If it does, it's a sentence.)

2. Use
Is the sentence *declarative* (makes a statement), *interrogative* (asks a question), *imperative* (gives a command), or *exclamatory* (shows surprise or emotion)?

3. Predicate
The predicate of a sentence contains a *verb*. A verb shows action or being. What is the verb in the sentence? (The verb includes the main verb and any helping verbs: *swam/had swum, goes/is going.*)

4. Subject
The *subject* is a noun or a pronoun. The verb tells what the subject does or is. To find the subject, ask *who* or *what* before the verb.

5. Object/Complement
The direct object or subject complement complete the verb. To find them ask *whom, who,* or *what* after the verb.

6. Modifiers
Adverbs tell more about verbs. To find the adverbs, ask *how, when,* or *where* the action or being took place.

Adjectives describe nouns or pronouns. To find the adjectives, ask *what, what kind, how many,* or *whose* about each noun or pronoun. An article is an adjective that points out a noun.

7. Parts of Speech
- Which words name persons, places, or things? (Those words are *nouns.*)
- Which words take the place of nouns? (Those words are *pronouns.*)
- Which words express action or being? (Those words are *verbs.*)
- Which words tell more about verbs? (Those words are *adverbs.*)
- Which words describe nouns? (Those words are *adjectives.*)

Sentence Analysis Chart

Sentence

Use

Predicate

Subject

Object/Complement

Modifiers

Parts of Speech

EXERCISES IN ENGLISH

☆ GRAMMAR FOR LIFE ☆

LEVEL H

LOYOLAPRESS.

CHICAGO

Consultants
Therese Elizabeth Bauer
Martina Anne Erdlen
Anita Patrick Gallagher
Patricia Healey
Irene Kervick
Susan Platt

Linguistics Advisor
Timothy G. Collins
National-Louis University

Series Design: Karen Christoffersen
Cover Design: Vita Jay Schweighart
Cover Art: Jody Lepinot/prairiestudio.com
Cover Photoshop: John Petroshius/prairiestudio.com
Interior Art: Dan Hatala/munrocampagna.com
Character Education Portraits: Jim Mitchell
Back Cover Text: Ted Naron

0-8294-2021-5 ★

0-8294-1752-4 ★

03 04 05 06 07 08 QuebD ★ 10 9 8 7 6 5 4 3 2

03 04 05 06 07 08 QuebD ★ 10 9 8 7 6 5 4 3 2 1

Table of Contents

v

Name _____

1. Identifying Sentences

A **sentence** is a group of words that expresses a complete thought.
A sentence has a **subject** and a **predicate**. The subject is who or what
the sentence is about. The predicate tells what the subject is or does.
Every sentence begins with a capital letter.

SUBJECT	PREDICATE
The solar system	contains nine major planets.
All the planets in the solar system	orbit the sun.

A. Read each sentence. Write **S** on the line if the words form a sentence.
Put a period at the end of each sentence.

_[S]_   1. All the planets move in elliptical orbits [.]

_[S]_   2. The orbits of Earth and Venus are almost circular [.]

_____   3. Mercury and Pluto

_[S]_   4. Jupiter's diameter is 11 times larger than Earth's diameter [.]

_____   5. Only a tenth the diameter of the sun

B. Read each sentence. Draw a line between
the subject and the predicate.

1. Neptune | is the eighth planet from the sun.
2. A hollowed-out Neptune | could hold nearly 60 Earths.
3. One orbit of the sun | takes Neptune 165 years.
4. A day on Neptune | is about 16 hours long.
5. The spaceship *Voyager* | discovered six of Neptune's eight moons.
6. Methane gas | gives Neptune its blue color.
7. Several large dark spots | can be seen on the surface of Neptune.
8. The largest of these spots | is about the size of Earth.
9. *Voyager* | saw long bright clouds high in Neptune's atmosphere.
10. These clouds | cast shadows on the cloud decks below.
11. The strongest winds on any planet | are on Neptune.
12. Winds on Neptune | blow up to 1,200 miles per hour.
13. Neptune | has a narrow, faint set of rings.
14. The four rings of Neptune | are made of dust particles.
15. Scientists all over the world | are studying this fascinating planet.

2. Identifying Declarative and Interrogative Sentences

A **declarative sentence** makes a statement. A declarative sentence ends with a period.

Levi Strauss was born in Bavaria in 1829.

An **interrogative sentence** asks a question. An interrogative sentence ends with a question mark.

What is Levi Strauss famous for?

Decide whether each sentence is declarative or interrogative. Write your answer on the line. Add the correct end punctuation.

[declarative] 1. Levi Strauss moved to San Francisco in 1850 [.]

[interrogative] 2. What was his reason for moving [?]

[declarative] 3. He wanted to strike it rich in the Gold Rush [.]

[interrogative] 4. Did he look for gold [?]

[declarative] 5. Strauss had trained to be a tailor [.]

[declarative] 6. He planned to manufacture tents for the forty-niners [.]

[declarative] 7. Business was not very good [.]

[interrogative] 8. What did he decide to do then [?]

[declarative] 9. Strauss had brought heavy canvas to make the tents [.]

[declarative] 10. He decided to use the canvas to make pants for the miners [.]

[declarative] 11. The pants were very sturdy [.]

[declarative] 12. Miners found the pants perfect for their work [.]

[declarative] 13. Strauss opened a factory in San Francisco [.]

[interrogative] 14. Did he change the pants in any way [?]

[declarative] 15. He added rivets at stress points in the pants [.]

[declarative] 16. A heavy blue denim material was substituted for the canvas [.]

[declarative] 17. Levi Strauss's company is still in business [.]

[declarative] 18. The pants he made are still called Levi's [.]

[declarative] 19. Levi Strauss died in San Francisco in 1902 [.]

[interrogative] 20. Have you ever worn a pair of Levi's [?]

3. Identifying Imperative and Exclamatory Sentences

> An **imperative sentence** gives a command or makes a request. An imperative sentence ends with a period.
>
> **Investigate the law of gravity.**
>
> An **exclamatory sentence** expresses a strong emotion. An exclamatory sentence ends with an exclamation point.
>
> **That's incredible!**

A. Underline the sentences that are imperatives.

1. Get some modeling clay, a marble or ball bearing, a ruler, and a cookie sheet.
2. Mold the modeling clay into a flat rectangle.
3. Place the clay on a cookie sheet.
4. Drop the marble or ball bearing into the clay.
5. The object will make a dent in the clay.
6. Drop the object from different heights.
7. Measure the size of the dent each time.
8. Record your results.
9. What happens as you drop the object from greater heights?
10. Objects that fall farther are traveling faster when they hit the ground.

B. Decide whether each sentence is imperative or exclamatory. Write your answer on the line. Add the correct end punctuation.

[imperative] 1. Use a heavy ball bearing, a marble, and a cookie sheet [.]

[imperative] 2. Put the cookie sheet on the floor [.]

[imperative] 3. Stand on a chair [.]

[exclamatory] 4. Careful; don't fall [!]

[imperative] 5. Be sure you don't lose your balance [.]

[imperative] 6. Hold the ball bearing in one hand and the marble in the other [.]

[imperative] 7. Raise your hands over your head [.]

[imperative] 8. Drop the two objects at the same time [.]

[imperative] 9. Listen for when they hit the cookie sheet [.]

[exclamatory] 10. Yikes, they missed the cookie sheet [!]

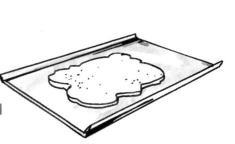

Review

4. Identifying the Four Kinds of Sentences

A sentence can be declarative, interrogative, imperative, or exclamatory.

Decide whether each sentence is declarative, interrogative, imperative, or exclamatory. Write your answer on the line. Add the correct end punctuation.

[declarative] 1. Frederick Douglass was born into slavery in 1818 [.]

[declarative] 2. As a small child, Frederick lived with his grandmother [.]

[interrogative] 3. Why didn't he live with his mother [?]

[declarative] 4. His mother had to work long hours in the cornfields [.]

[exclamatory] 5. Goodness, that's a horrible situation [!]

[declarative] 6. When he was eight years old, Frederick was sent to live in Baltimore [.]

[declarative] 7. His owner's wife, Sophia Auld, taught him the alphabet [.]

[declarative] 8. Sophia's husband made her stop [.]

[declarative] 9. It was illegal to teach slaves to read [.]

[interrogative] 10. How did Frederick finally learn to read and write [?]

[declarative] 11. He bribed some neighborhood boys to teach him [.]

[declarative] 12. As a teenager, Frederick had to work as a field hand [.]

[declarative] 13. He was whipped unmercifully [.]

[exclamatory] 14. Oh, my, his life was terrible [!]

[declarative] 15. At the age of twenty, Frederick dressed up as a sailor and escaped [.]

[exclamatory] 16. What a brave young man he was [!]

[declarative] 17. Frederick became a lecturer and a newspaper publisher [.]

[declarative] 18. He worked for justice and opportunity for black people and for women [.]

[interrogative] 19. Where can you learn more about Frederick Douglass [?]

[imperative] 20. Find out about his relationship with Abraham Lincoln [.]

Frederick Douglass used the power of language to create positive change. Give an example of how you can use language to change things for the better.

4

5. Identifying Simple Subjects and Predicates

A sentence has a subject and a predicate. The **simple subject** is the noun or pronoun that names the person, place, or thing the sentence is about. The **simple predicate** is the verb that tells what the subject does or is.

SIMPLE SUBJECT

People

Native people

Native people of the Northwest coast

SIMPLE PREDICATE

celebrate.

celebrated social occasions.

celebrated social occasions with potlatches.

A. Write the simple subject and simple predicate of each sentence in the correct column.

SIMPLE SUBJECT	SIMPLE PREDICATE	
[potlatch]	[marked]	1. A potlatch often marked an event in a family's life.
[family]	[celebrated]	2. The family celebrated a birth, a marriage, or a death.
[family]	[made]	3. The host family made elaborate preparations.
[preparations]	[included]	4. The lavish preparations included huge amounts of food.
[Dishes]	[contained]	5. Dishes at a potlatch often contained fish or seal meat.
[individuals]	[ate]	6. High-ranking individuals ate the choicest dishes.
[Diners]	[dipped]	7. Diners dipped the food in seal oil.
[Guests]	[received]	8. Guests at the potlatch received extravagant gifts.
[Potlatches]	[featured]	9. Potlatches also featured speeches, singing, and dancing.
[event]	[highlighted]	10. Every event highlighted the host's wealth and status.

B. Read each sentence. Draw one line under the simple subject. Draw two lines under the simple predicate.

1. Parties are still important events for native people of the Northwest coast.

2. A family often spends a whole year planning for a family celebration.

3. Hundreds of people gather together over a weekend.

4. The host family provides the food, snacks, and beverages.

5. Honored guests receive cash and other gifts.

6. Identifying Complete Subjects and Predicates

The **complete subject** of a sentence is the simple subject with all the words that describe it. The **complete predicate** of a sentence is the simple predicate with all the words that describe it.

COMPLETE SUBJECT
The city of Johnstown, Pennsylvania,

COMPLETE PREDICATE
had a population of 30,000 in 1889.

SIMPLE SUBJECT
city

SIMPLE PREDICATE
had

Read each sentence. Draw a vertical line between the complete subject and the complete predicate. Draw one line under the simple subject. Draw two lines under the simple predicate.

1. Johnstown | was a growing and industrious community.

2. The town | lay on a flood plain between two rivers.

3. The growing community | narrowed the riverbanks for building space.

4. The South Fork Dam | protected the citizens of Johnstown.

5. The dam | prevented the waters of Lake Conemaugh from flooding the city.

6. The people in town | worried about the dam.

7. Engineers | found the dam weak and unsafe.

8. Heavy rains | began to fall on May 30, 1889.

9. A little water | leaked through the dam.

10. Frantic efforts to heighten the dam | failed.

11. The dam | burst at 4:07 P.M. on May 31.

12. Inhabitants of the city | heard a roar like thunder.

13. Twenty million tons of water | rushed through Johnstown.

14. The wall of floodwater | rose to 60 feet high.

15. The huge wave | crashed down the valley at 40 miles per hour.

16. The flood | destroyed most of the major buildings in the city.

17. The raging water | carried everything with it—trees, animals, and people.

18. More than 2,200 people | died.

19. Thousands of other people | suffered injuries.

20. The Johnstown Flood | was the worst flood in American history.

Name _____

7. Forming Sentences

> A sentence has a subject and a predicate.

A. Make sentences by matching the complete subjects in Column A
with the complete predicates in Column B. Write the correct letter on the
line. Use each letter once.

COLUMN A

___[c]___ 1. Diamond

___[f]___ 2. The formation of diamonds

___[i]___ 3. Pits of boiling magma

___[a]___ 4. Heat and pressure in the pits

___[h]___ 5. Explosive volcanic eruptions

___[j]___ 6. Twenty tons of earth

___[d]___ 7. Only one diamond out of four

___[e]___ 8. Various kinds of industry

___[g]___ 9. The difficulty of finding diamonds

___[b]___ 10. The diamonds people wear today

COLUMN B

a. transformed carbon into diamonds.

b. are more than 100 million years old.

c. is the hardest natural substance on Earth.

d. is good enough to make jewelry.

e. use three-fourths of all diamonds.

f. took place over billions of years.

g. makes them expensive.

h. brought the diamonds to the surface.

i. bubbled 150 km below Earth's surface.

j. must be dug up to find one diamond.

B. Choose the best simple predicate to complete each sentence.
Use each word once.

displays   is   measures   received   weighs

1. The Hope Diamond _____[received]_____ its name
   from an owner, Henry Philip Hope.

2. The Hope _____[is]_____ a flawless,
   dark blue diamond.

3. It [weighs] _____ 45.52 carats (more
   than 9 grams).

4. The stone _____[measures]_____ 25.6 mm in length,
   21.78 mm in width, and 12 mm in depth.

5. The Smithsonian Institution _____[displays]_____ this fabulous gem.

7

8. Identifying Compound Subjects and Predicates

> A **compound subject** consists of more than one simple subject.
>   <u>People</u> and <u>animals</u> eat plants.
> A **compound predicate** consists of more than one simple predicate.
>   Food from plants <u>satisfies</u> hunger and <u>provides</u> nutrients.

A. Each sentence has a compound subject or predicate. Draw a vertical line between the subject and the predicate. Underline the compound subject or predicate.

1. <u>People</u> and <u>animals</u> | have lived together for thousands of years.

2. The earliest peoples | <u>hunted</u> and <u>killed</u> animals for food.

3. Then they | <u>domesticated</u> some animals and <u>began</u> to raise them.

4. <u>Cattle</u>, <u>sheep</u>, and <u>goats</u> | provided people with meat and milk.

5. <u>Sheep</u> and <u>goats</u> | also provided wool for clothing.

B. Read each sentence. Underline the simple subject(s). Circle the simple predicate(s).

1. Today many <u>people</u> (own) and (care) for pets.

2. More than 52 million pet <u>dogs</u> and almost 60 million pet <u>cats</u> (live) in the United States.

3. However, some <u>dogs</u> and <u>cats</u> (care) for their owners.

4. Service <u>animals</u> and therapy <u>animals</u> (assist) people with disabilities.

5. Guide <u>dogs</u> (navigate) for sightless people and (lead) them around obstacles.

6. Signal <u>dogs</u> (listen) for sounds and (alert) their deaf owners.

7. Both <u>cats</u> and <u>dogs</u> (act) as therapy animals.

8. Therapy <u>animals</u> (visit) hospitals and (interact) with the patients.

9. The <u>patients</u> (pet) the animals and (play) with them.

10. The <u>animals</u> (cheer) the patients up and (make) them feel better.

8

Name _____

9. Identifying Direct Objects

> The **direct object** is the noun or pronoun that completes the action of the verb. Many sentences need direct objects to complete their meaning. To find the direct object of a sentence, ask *whom* or *what* after the verb. A direct object may be compound.
>
> | SUBJECT | VERB | DIRECT OBJECT |
> |---|---|---|
> | The children | are studying | Navaho arts and culture. |
> | They | found | information on the Internet. |

A. Circle the direct object in each sentence.

1. The earliest Navaho used (deerskins) to make clothing.

2. Later the men wore cotton or velvet (shirts) (breeches), and (moccasins).

3. Women wore (dresses) made of plain, dark cloth.

4. The Navaho built round (houses) of logs, brush, and earth.

5. The doors of these hogans always faced the (east).

6. They welcomed the morning (sun).

7. Navaho artists created beautiful (blankets) and (jewelry).

8. Sand painting played a major (role) in ceremonies.

9. Most sand paintings required many (hours) and much (skill) to create.

10. Some ceremonies included eight or nine different sand (paintings).

B. Complete each sentence by writing one or more direct objects. **[Sample answers are given.]**

1. Every day I use _____[the computer]_____.

2. At school I often write _____[stories]_____.

3. At home I often play _____[computer games]_____.

4. I know how to make _____[banana splits]_____.

5. On the weekends I sometimes buy _____[ice cream]_____.

10. Identifying Indirect Objects

Some sentences have two objects—the direct object and the indirect object. The **indirect object** is the noun or pronoun that tells *to whom* or *for whom* the action is done. An indirect object may be compound.

The artist sold the picture.
The artist sold Alice the picture.

Alice bought the picture.
Alice bought her mother and father the picture.

A. Read each sentence. Circle the indirect object. The direct object is in *italics*.

1. The principal promised the (students) a spring *party*.

2. The children sent their (parents) and (friends) *invitations*.

3. The teachers showed the (students) the *schedule* of athletic events.

4. The coach told the (athletes) the *rules*.

5. The music teacher taught the (orchestra) and (chorus) a new *song*.

6. She gave each (member) a *copy* of the music.

7. The merchant sold the (girls) and (boys) *supplies* to make posters.

8. He also offered (them) his *help*.

9. Some of the parents bought the (school) *refreshments*.

10. The committee wrote (everyone) a thank-you *note*.

B. Read each sentence. Underline the direct object. Circle the indirect object.

1. The reporter asked the factory (owner) a <u>question</u> about pollution.

2. The owner didn't give the (reporter) a very clear <u>answer</u>.

3. The reporter showed the (men) and (women) in the audience a court <u>order</u>.

4. The order denied (observers) <u>access</u> to the property.

5. The factory owner promised (everyone) a complete <u>explanation</u>.

11. Reviewing Sentences

A. Decide whether each sentence is declarative, interrogative, imperative, or exclamatory. Write your answer on the line. Add the correct end punctuation.

__[declarative]__ 1. The hoatzin is the national bird of Guyana [.]

__[imperative]__ 2. Look in the encyclopedia for a picture of a hoatzin [.]

__[declarative]__ 3. It looks like a pheasant with a large golden crest [.]

__[declarative]__ 4. Hoatzins live in large, flat unlined nests [.]

__[declarative]__ 5. The babies have claws on the tips of their wings [.]

__[exclamatory]__ 6. Gosh, what a strange baby that is [!]

__[interrogative]__ 7. What do they use the claws for [?]

__[declarative]__ 8. Very shortly after birth, young hoatzins wander out of the nest [.]

__[declarative]__ 9. They use the claws on their wings to climb branches [.]

__[declarative]__ 10. They don't learn to fly until they're 60 or 70 days old [.]

__[exclamatory]__ 11. That's amazing [!]

__[interrogative]__ 12. What else is unusual about the hoatzin [?]

__[declarative]__ 13. It's the only tree-dwelling bird that eats leaves [.]

__[interrogative]__ 14. Why is that unusual [?]

__[declarative]__ 15. Leaves are a low-energy food source [.]

__[declarative]__ 16. It takes a lot of energy to fly [.]

__[declarative]__ 17. Bacteria in the hoatzin's crop and esophagus ferment the leaves [.]

__[declarative]__ 18. The hoatzin's digestive system is something like that of a cow [.]

__[declarative]__ 19. The fermentation provides energy but produces a very bad smell. [.]

__[declarative]__ 20. The hoatzin is sometimes called the stinky pheasant [.]

CONTINUED

Review

B. Read each sentence. Underline the simple subject(s). Circle the simple predicate(s).

1. Grasslands (cover) about 15 percent of North America.

2. Before the 1860s the grasslands (were) America's frontier.

3. Buffalo, elk, and other wildlife (grazed) on the abundant vegetation.

4. Apache, Arapaho, Comanche, and other Indian tribes (lived) and (hunted) there.

5. By 1890 six million settlers (had moved) to the grasslands and (changed) everything.

6. Ranchers, soldiers, and railroad workers (had) almost (eliminated) the buffalo.

7. Farmers (settled) on the prairie and (plowed) vast stretches of land.

8. The incessant winds (picked up) the dry soil and (blew) it around like snow.

9. Texas, Oklahoma, Nebraska, and nearby states (were covered) by a dust cloud 20,000 feet high.

10. Between 1936 and 1940, millions of people (fled) the Dust Bowl.

C. Read each sentence. Underline the direct object. Circle the indirect object.

1. Grasslands provide many (animals) food and shelter.

2. Prairie dogs dig their (families) elaborate burrows in the earth.

3. Mother coyotes teach their (cubs) hunting skills among the grasses.

4. The tall grass offers (quail) and other (birds) hiding places.

5. Mature buffalos show (calves) the best water holes.

Try It Yourself
On a separate sheet of paper, write four sentences about an animal you are familiar with. Be sure each sentence is complete. Use correct punctuation.

Check Your Own Work
Choose a piece of writing from your portfolio or journal, a work in progress, an assignment from another class, or a letter. Revise it, applying the skills you have reviewed. The checklist will help you.

✔ Does each sentence express a complete thought?

✔ Does each sentence start with a capital letter?

✔ Does each sentence end with the correct punctuation mark?

12. Identifying Common and Proper Nouns

> A **noun** is a name word. A **proper noun** names a particular person, place, or thing. A **common noun** names any member of a group of persons, places, or things. Proper nouns are capitalized.
>
> COMMON NOUNS
> **explorer, ocean, merchant ship**
>
> PROPER NOUNS
> **John Smith, Jamestown, the Virginia Company**

A. Circle all the common nouns. Underline all the proper nouns.

1. The Virginia Company helped establish the colony called Jamestown.

2. Three ships sailed up the James River in 1607.

3. The English on board included craftsmen, laborers, and four small boys.

4. The sailors landed far upstream.

5. Away from the shore, the settlers thought they would be safe from the Spanish.

6. The first winter was difficult.

7. Drinking water was salty, and food was scarce.

8. Rats ate grain the settlers had stored.

9. Capt. John Smith was a leader at Jamestown.

10. Jamestown was the first capital of Virginia.

B. Write one common noun and one proper noun related to each noun listed. **[Sample answers are given.]**

	COMMON	PROPER
1. person	[governor]	[Colin Powell]
2. place	[seashore]	[Point Reyes Lighthouse]
3. thing	[cabin]	[the White House]
4. reference book	[dictionary]	[World Book Encyclopedia]
5. way to travel	[bicycle]	[Cadillac]
6. document	[letter]	[Declaration of Independence]
7. body of water	[sea]	[Pacific Ocean]
8. landform	[mountain]	[Mount Rainier]
9. group of people	[team]	[Chicago Bears]
10. animal	[lizard]	[Komodo dragon]

13. Identifying Collective, Concrete, and Abstract Nouns

A **collective noun** names a group of persons, places, or things considered as one. A collective noun usually takes a singular verb.

   crew, herd, fleet

A **concrete noun** names a person, place, or thing that can be seen or touched. An **abstract noun** names a quality, a condition, or a state of mind.

CONCRETE NOUNS	ABSTRACT NOUNS
sister, river, ship	**bravery, hardship, idea**

A. Identify the *italicized* word in each sentence as a collective noun, a concrete noun, or an abstract noun.

[abstract]	1. Early settlers endured great *hardships*.
[abstract]	2. Today, immigrants come to the United States for different *reasons*.
[concrete]	3. Immigrants first came by *ship* from England.
[collective]	4. An English *colony* was started on the East Coast.
[collective]	5. Colonists raised *flocks* of ducks for food.
[concrete]	6. They grew crops of *tobacco*.
[abstract]	7. Later colonists had *ideas* about self-government.
[collective]	8. Settlers built an *army* and fought the British.
[abstract]	9. They won the war and started a *government*.
[abstract]	10. People associate the United States with freedom and *justice*.

B. Underline the abstract noun or nouns in each sentence.

1. Susan B. Anthony achieved <u>fame</u> for her <u>work</u> in obtaining for women the <u>right</u> to vote in the United States.

2. When she was born in 1820, women had few legal <u>rights</u>.

3. In most states they did not possess the <u>freedom</u> to vote.

WORKING WOMEN DEMAND THE VOTE

4. As a Quaker, Susan believed in the <u>equality</u> of men and women.

5. She was willing to suffer for her <u>beliefs</u>.

6. In 1872 her <u>courage</u> was tested when she dared to vote and was arrested and fined.

7. She had great <u>hope</u> that the constitution would be amended to allow women to vote.

8. Susan Anthony, however, did not live to see her <u>dream</u> come true.

9. After she died, her <u>perseverance</u> was rewarded, and the Constitution was amended.

10. She has the <u>honor</u> of having a school named after her.

Name _____

14. Identifying Words Used as Nouns and Verbs

A noun is a name word. A verb expresses action or being. Many words can be used as nouns or verbs.

I collect rocks. She rocks the boat.

A. Identify the *italicized* word in each sentence as a noun or a verb.

__[noun]__   1. Rocks show a geologic *record* of the age of the earth.

__[verb]__   2. Geologists *mine* rock for clues about the composition of the crust.

__[noun]__   3. The rock *cycle* is just one process you'll study in Earth science class.

__[noun]__   4. The *labor* required to collect useful specimens is difficult.

__[verb]__   5. Workers must be careful because rock walls can *collapse*.

__[verb]__   6. Huge drills *drive* deep into rock surfaces.

__[noun]__   7. Tremendous *pressure* changes limestone into marble.

__[noun]__   8. As a literature buff, I am a late *convert* to science.

__[verb]__   9. Usually my parents *return* from their searches without any fossils.

__[noun]__   10. We watched hours of *film* showing rock formations.

B. Write sentences using each word as a noun and then as a verb. [Sample answers are given.]

1. star   (noun) __[A binary star is actually two stars revolving around each other.]__

          (verb) __[My cousin Alex will star in a play on Broadway.]__

2. orbit   (noun) __[In its orbit, Earth makes one complete revolution around the sun.]__

          (verb) __[A planet can orbit another body more than one time in a year.]__

3. plant   (noun) __[A plant produces its own food by means of photosynthesis.]__

          (verb) __[Plant your feet firmly in front of the base and swing.]__

4. marvel   (noun) __[The pyramid was a marvel of design and planning at any age.]__

          (verb) __[Any child would marvel at the new merry-go-round.]__

5. cover   (noun) __[The cover of the book identified both the author and the illustrator.]__

          (verb) __[The gardener will cover the tender seedlings at night.]__

15. Identifying Singular and Plural Nouns

> A singular noun refers to one person, place, or thing. A plural noun refers to more than one person, place, or thing.

A. Write the singular and plural for each noun. Use a dictionary to check your spelling.

	SINGULAR	PLURAL
1. ranch	[ranch]	[ranches]
2. berries	[berry]	berries]
3. sisters-in-law	[sister-in-law]	[sisters-in-law]
4. barrel	[barrel]	[barrels]
5. heroes	[hero]	[heroes]
6. journeys	[journey]	[journeys]
7. knife	[knife]	[knives]
8. potatoes	[potato]	[potatoes]
9. bus	[bus]	[buses]
10. scarf	[scarf]	[scarves]

B. Complete each sentence with the plural form of the noun at the left. Use a dictionary to check your answers.

device
1. A science laboratory includes timing _____[devices]_____.

inquiry
2. Students must have a wide range of tools for their _____[inquiries]_____.

computer
3. _____[Computers]_____ are used to tabulate and compare results.

change
4. In the lab, students can manipulate _____[changes]_____ in materials.

system
5. Students can study the behavior of physical _____[systems]_____.

Name _____

process   6. Complicated _____[processes]_____ can be simulated in a lab.

instrument   7. Students have access to sophisticated _____[instruments]_____.

dish   8. Biology students can grow cultures in petri _____[dishes]_____.

microscope   9. They can observe cells with high-powered _____[microscopes]_____.

technology   10. The _____[technologies]_____ in labs have improved science education.

C. Write **S** above the *italicized* word if it is singular or **P** if it is plural.
Use a dictionary to check your answers.

1. There was *popcorn* scattered all over the floor.
   [S]

2. *Salmon* swim upstream to spawn.
   [P]

3. My favorite meal is grilled *salmon* with rice pilaf.
   [S]

4. That big *squash* isn't ripe yet.
   [S]

5. Each of those baskets will hold a dozen *squash*.
   [P]

D. Write the plural form of each word. Use a dictionary to check your spelling.

1. tornado   _____[tornadoes)_____

2. hurricane   _____[hurricanes]_____

3. nor'wester   _____[nor'westers]_____

4. thunderstorm   _____[thunderstorms]_____

5. flurry   _____[flurries]_____

6. cloudburst   _____[cloudbursts]_____

7. gale   _____[gales]_____

8. breeze   _____[breezes]_____

9. downpour   _____[downpours]_____

10. easterly   _____[easterlies]_____

16. Working with Nouns

Nouns

A noun can be the **subject** of a sentence, a **subject complement,** or an **appositive.** A subject tells what the sentence is about. A subject complement is a noun that follows a verb of being and renames or describes the subject. An appositive is a noun that follows another noun. It renames or describes the noun it follows.

NOUN AS THE SUBJECT OF A VERB   **Colonists waged a war.**

NOUN AS A SUBJECT COMPLEMENT   **The war was the beginning of a new nation.**

NOUN AS AN APPOSITIVE   **Samuel Adams, a patriot, argued for war.**

A noun used in direct address names the person spoken to.

Paul Revere, will you ride tonight?

Write whether each underlined noun is a subject (**S**), a subject complement (**SC**), an appositive (**App**), or a noun in a direct address (**Add**). Write the abbreviation on the line at the left.

[Add] 1. History students, take note! Benjamin Franklin had a fascinating career.

[App] 2. Franklin, a man interested in many topics, served his country in politics, science, and civic matters.

[S] 3. Born in Boston, Franklin became a printer and moved to Philadelphia.

[App] 4. His newspaper, the *Philadelphia Gazette,* became quite popular.

[S] 5. His wise sayings, published in *Poor Richard's Almanac,* are still quoted today.

[SC] 6. A library and a fire department were two of Franklin's improvements for Philadelphia.

[S] 7. Having a passion for the exploration of unanswered questions, Franklin joined the Leather Apron Club.

[S] 8. Experimenting with a kite, Franklin discovered that electricity and lightning were the same.

[SC] 9. The Franklin stove was his invention.

[App] 10. Soon Franklin, a thinker, became interested in the politics of our young nation.

[SC, SC] 11. Benjamin Franklin was both a writer and a signer of the Declaration of Independence.

[S] 12. After the Revolutionary War began, Franklin went abroad to forge an alliance with France.

[Add] 13. Mr. Franklin, did you enjoy your visit to Paris?

[S] 14. At the age of 81, Franklin helped write the U.S. Constitution.

[Add] 15. What a wide range of interests you had, Ben!

Benjamin Franklin shared his talents by inventing things that helped people in daily life and by participating in civic life. Give an example of how you can help others by sharing one of your talents.

17. Using Possessive Nouns

The **possessive form** of a noun expresses possession, ownership, or connection.
Add *'s* to most singular nouns and to plural nouns that do not end in *s* to form the possessive forms.

> cat's paws, women's shoes

Add *'* (but not an *s*) to plural nouns that end in *s*.

> students' papers, hostesses' job

A. Write the singular possessive and the plural possessive of each word.

	SINGULAR POSSESSIVE	PLURAL POSSESSIVE
1. son-in-law	[son-in-law's]	[sons-in-law's]
2. hero	[hero's]	[heroes']
3. man	[man's]	[men's]
4. pilot	[pilot's]	[pilots']
5. writer	[writer's]	[writers']
6. secretary	[secretary's]	[secretaries']
7. child	[child's]	[children's]
8. judge	[judge's]	[judges']
9. actress	[actress's]	[actresses']
10. officer	[officer's]	[officers']

B. Complete each sentence with the possessive of the noun at the left.

sister-in-law 1. My ____[sister-in-law's]____ watch is very valuable.

David 2. What happened to ____[David's]____ pen?

Mr. Enley 3. ____[Mr. Enley's]____ explanation about the lost items was easy.

police officers 4. The ____[police officers']____ opinion was different.

men 5. All the ____[men's]____ jewelry was gone.

Sally 6. We looked in the drawer for ____[Sally's]____ silver.

weeks 7. Mr. King donated two ____[weeks']____ free ad space for the notice.

readers 8. The ____[readers']____ papers carried news of the thefts.

culprit 9. The ____[culprit's]____ motive was uncovered.

Ms. Alexis 10. ____[Ms. Alexis's]____ detective work paid off.

18. Identifying Nouns That Show Separate and Joint Possession

> When two or more people own something together, it is called joint possession. To show joint possession, use 's after the last noun only.
>
> **John and Jack's hardware store**
>
> When two or more people each own a separate thing, it is called separate possession. To show separate possession, use 's after each noun.
>
> **John's and Jack's tools**

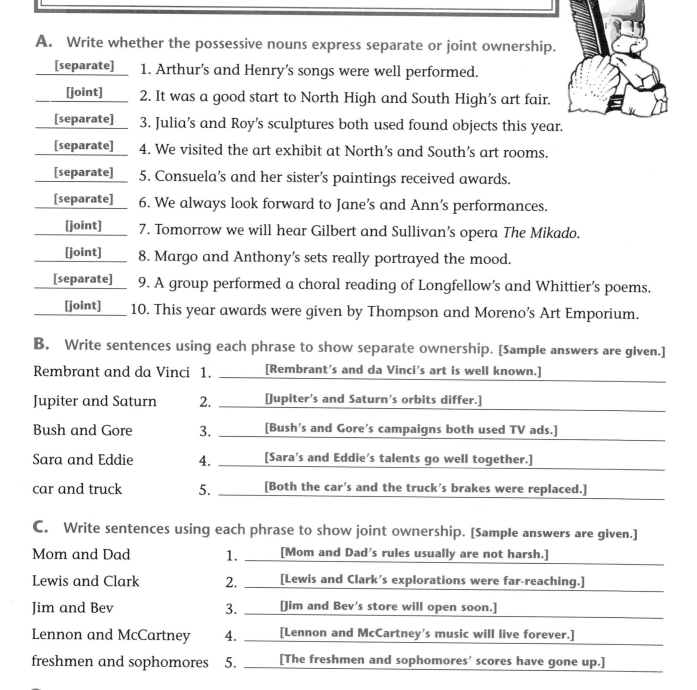

A. Write whether the possessive nouns express separate or joint ownership.

___[separate]___ 1. Arthur's and Henry's songs were well performed.

___[joint]___ 2. It was a good start to North High and South High's art fair.

___[separate]___ 3. Julia's and Roy's sculptures both used found objects this year.

___[separate]___ 4. We visited the art exhibit at North's and South's art rooms.

___[separate]___ 5. Consuela's and her sister's paintings received awards.

___[separate]___ 6. We always look forward to Jane's and Ann's performances.

___[joint]___ 7. Tomorrow we will hear Gilbert and Sullivan's opera *The Mikado*.

___[joint]___ 8. Margo and Anthony's sets really portrayed the mood.

___[separate]___ 9. A group performed a choral reading of Longfellow's and Whittier's poems.

___[joint]___ 10. This year awards were given by Thompson and Moreno's Art Emporium.

B. Write sentences using each phrase to show separate ownership. [Sample answers are given.]

Rembrant and da Vinci 1. _____ [Rembrant's and da Vinci's art is well known.]

Jupiter and Saturn 2. _____ [Jupiter's and Saturn's orbits differ.]

Bush and Gore 3. _____ [Bush's and Gore's campaigns both used TV ads.]

Sara and Eddie 4. _____ [Sara's and Eddie's talents go well together.]

car and truck 5. _____ [Both the car's and the truck's brakes were replaced.]

C. Write sentences using each phrase to show joint ownership. [Sample answers are given.]

Mom and Dad 1. _____ [Mom and Dad's rules usually are not harsh.]

Lewis and Clark 2. _____ [Lewis and Clark's explorations were far-reaching.]

Jim and Bev 3. _____ [Jim and Bev's store will open soon.]

Lennon and McCartney 4. _____ [Lennon and McCartney's music will live forever.]

freshmen and sophomores 5. _____ [The freshmen and sophomores' scores have gone up.]

19. Using Nouns as Objects

A noun can be used as the direct object of a verb, an indirect object of a verb, or the object of a preposition. A direct object answers the question *whom* or *what* after a verb. The indirect object tells to whom or for whom the action was done. A noun that follows a preposition in a prepositional phrase is called the object of the preposition.

Noun as Direct Object	The clerk sold the bicycle.
Noun as Indirect Object	The clerk sold Amy the bicycle.
Noun as Object of a Preposition	Amy rode the bicycle with excitement.

A direct or indirect object can have an appositive.

We saw Amy, a teenager, on her way to school.

A. Underline the nouns that are used as objects. Write above each whether it is a direct object (**DO**), an indirect object (**IO**), the object of a preposition (**OP**), or an appositive (**App**).

1. History gives us many puzzles [DO], such as the story of Amelia Earhart [OP], an extraordinary pilot [App].

2. From an early age [OP], flying gave Amelia [IO] a sense [DO] of excitement [OP].

3. Flying offered Amelia [IO], a woman [App], unique opportunities [DO] with new challenges [OP].

4. She set many records [DO] for solo and nonstop flights [OP] before she accepted aviation's greatest challenge [DO], a flight [App] around the world [OP].

5. Amelia Earhart's tragic disappearance during that trip [OP], her last flight [App], gives historians [IO] reason [DO] to wonder.

B. Rewrite each sentence. Use the noun as an indirect object.

workers   1. Employers should pay a just salary.
[Employers should pay workers a just salary.]

grandma   2. Dad may buy a new motorcycle.
[Dad may buy grandma a new motorcycle.]

the cast   3. The director gave a party after the final performance.
[The director gave the cast a party after the final performance.]

C. Complete each sentence with an appositive. Circle the noun it explains.

the mayor   4. We shall ask (Mr. Taylor) about the toll.
[We shall ask Mr. Taylor, the mayor, about the toll.]

my brother   5. Our neighbor, Mr. Provasnik, teaches (Charles) how to drive.
[Our neighbor, Mr. Provasnik, teaches Charles, my brother, how to drive.]

20. Identifying Object Complements

A noun can be used as an object complement. An object complement follows a direct object. The object complement renames or describes the noun it follows.

They elected George Bush president.

A. If the *italicized* word is an object complement, write **OC** above it. If it is not an object complement, write **N.**

1. They considered the evening meal a *disaster.* [OC]

2. The sun is ninety-three million *miles* from Earth. [N]

3. Sharon and Hamad named their daughter *Grace.* [OC]

4. Sue calls her florist shop *Love in Bloom.* [OC]

5. Christine and Mari hiked a ten-mile *hike.* [N]

6. At the memorial service Arturo gave the first *reading.* [N]

7. In art class, the students made black-and-white abstract *drawings.* [N]

8. The organizers of the parade appointed the mayor *grand marshal.* [OC]

9. Many Southerners call the Civil War the *War Between the States.* [OC]

10. The physics committee named Dr. Ernst Ruska the 1986 Nobel Prize *winner.* [OC]

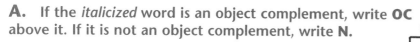

B. Use an appropriate noun phrase from Column 2 as an object complement to complete each sentence.

COLUMN 1	COLUMN 2
The school board designated the first Monday in May	the Fun Run
The organizing committee called our fund-raising event	a good sport
Once again, the principal named Neil	Activity Day
Although she lost her race, the other athletes consider May	the official meeting place
Neil made the local soda fountain	chairperson for the event

1. _____ [The school board designated the first Monday in May Activity Day.]

2. _____ [The organizing committee called our fund-raising event the Fun Run.]

3. _____ [Once again, the principal named Neil chairperson for the event.]

4. _____ [Although she lost her race, the other athletes consider May a good sport.]

5. _____ [Neil made the local soda fountain the official meeting place.]

21. Reviewing Nouns

A. Identify each *italicized* word. On the first line write **A** if the word is a common noun or **B** if it is a proper noun. On the second line write **C** if the word is a collective noun, **D** if it is an abstract noun, or **E** if it is a concrete noun.

[A]   [D]   1. It took much *effort* to overcome the disastrous first winter.

[B]   [E]   2. *Jamestown* is located in what is now Virginia.

[A]   [D]   3. Our family visited the site during Christmas *vacation.*

[A]   [C]   4. A *flock* of chickens wanders free there.

[B]   [E]   5. An old *Bible* is on view.

B. Write the number of the *italicized* noun in each sentence. Write **S** for singular or **P** for plural.

[S]   6. Astronomers are discovering much about the *planet.*

[P]   7. We, the *scientists,* are thrilled with the news.

[S]   8. *Mars* might have had life forms.

[P]   9. What do you think of that, *students?*

[S]   10. *Water* has been shown to be trapped between the rocks on Mars.

C. Identify the way each *italicized* noun is used. Use **S** for subject, **SC** for subject complement, **App** for appositive, and **Add** for direct address.

[S]   11. At least fifty times a year the *Empire State Building* is struck by lightning.

[App]   12. Hippocrates, the *Father of Medicine,* applied logic to medicine.

[Add]   13. *Lois,* please turn down that station!

[S]   14. *Triskaidekaphobia* is the fear of the number thirteen.

[SC]   15. One major tourist attraction is the *Great Wall of China.*

[App]   16. Robinson Crusoe, a marooned *sailor,* was on an island twenty-eight years.

D. Write whether the possessive nouns express separate or joint ownership.

[joint]   17. Last week we celebrated Joan and Henry's wedding anniversary.

[separate]   18. Michael's and Dan's gifts were the same.

[separate]   19. Whitney Houston's and Elton John's CDs are still popular.

[joint]   20. We watched Ann and Jack's dance steps at the reception.

 CONTINUED

Nouns

E. Write the singular possessive and plural possessive of each word.

		SINGULAR POSSESSIVE	PLURAL POSSESSIVE
21.	brother-in-law	[brother-in-law's]	[brothers-in-law's]
22.	deer	[deer's]	[deer's]
23.	woman	[woman's]	[women's]
24.	hostess	[hostess's]	[hostesses']
25.	ox	[ox's]	[oxen's]

F. The *italicized* nouns are used as objects. Write whether each is a direct object (**DO**), an indirect object (**IO**), or the object of a preposition (**OP**).

[DO] 26. Henry Ford began his motor *company* in 1903.

[OP] 27. He employed twelve workers and made his cars in a *factory*.

[OP] 28. Soon Ford ran out of *money*.

[IO] 29. A friend's sister gave *Ford* a loan.

[DO] 30. Now many people wanted *Model Ts*.

[IO] 31. The company offered *Ford* a way to become wealthy.

G. Write whether each *italicized* noun is used as an appositive (**App**) or an object complement (**OC**).

[OC] 32. The basketball team chose Patrick *captain*.

[App] 33. Have you seen Christie's new horse, *Midnight?*

[App] 34. I cheered for my favorite team, *the Yankees*.

[OC] 35. The Bulls called their mascot *Benny*.

Try It Yourself

On a separate sheet of paper, write four sentences about a person or a place. Be sure to use nouns correctly.

Check Your Own Work

Choose a piece of writing from your portfolio or journal, a work in progress, an assignment from another class, or a letter. Revise it, applying the skills you have learned. The checklist will help you.

✔ Have you used the correct spellings of plural nouns?

✔ Have you used nouns in a variety of ways?

✔ Have you used possessive nouns correctly?

Name _____

22. Identifying Personal Pronouns

A **pronoun** is a word that takes the place of a noun. A personal pronoun shows the speaker *(first person)*; the person spoken to *(second person)*; or the person, place, or thing spoken about *(third person)*.

FIRST PERSON: **I, mine, me, we, ours, us**
SECOND PERSON: **you, yours**
THIRD PERSON: **he, she, it, his, hers, its, him, her, they, theirs, them**

A. Underline the personal pronouns in each sentence. Write **1** above each pronoun in the first person, **2** above each pronoun in the second person, and **3** above each pronoun in the third person.

          [2]
1. Do <u>you</u> enjoy reading fables?
                [1]
2. My sister and <u>I</u> went to the library to look for some folktales.
  [1]
3. <u>We</u> learned that Walt Disney wrote many fables.
 [3]   **[3]**
4. <u>He</u> told <u>them</u> in comic strips and animated cartoons.

5. In the 1950s a new kind of American fable appeared. <u>It</u> was **[3]**

   in the form of newspaper comic strips.
                [3]
6. Animals played a large part in <u>them</u>.
 [1]
7. <u>We</u> went to the computer database

   to find other fables.
 [1]
8. <u>We</u> borrowed books from the library
     [3]   **[1]**
   for <u>her</u> and <u>me</u>.

9. In "The Fox and the Lion," a fox is
            [3]
   terrified when <u>it</u> meets a lion.
  [2]
10. <u>You</u> should try to write your own fable.

B. Complete each sentence with the correct personal pronoun. The person and number are given.

Third person, singular   1. Since _____**[it]**_____ was first semester, I helped students discover the pleasure of writing.

First person, singular   2. The students and _____**[I]**_____ explored the writing process.

Third person, plural   3. _____**[They]**_____ would have a good chance of learning about themselves through writing.

First person, plural   4. _____**[We]**_____ worked to discover new ideas and reshape old ones.

First person, plural   5. The activity of engaging in peer response was new for most of _____**[us]**_____ .

Name _____

23. Identifying Pronouns Used as Subjects

A personal pronoun can be used as the subject of a sentence.
The subject pronouns are *I, we, you, he, she, it,* and *they.*

A. Circle the correct pronoun in parentheses.

1. Ellen and (I me) are good friends.
2. (We Us) are all going camping this weekend.
3. (Us We) girls have prepared the food pack.
4. Have Juan and (him he) returned with the camp stove?
5. Was (he him) given the necessary camping permit?
6. (He Him) and (I me) are partners in the first aid project.
7. Leo and (him he) quit and joined the rock-climbing class.
8. Neither (he him) nor (she her) has ever been hiking at Starved Rock.
9. (She Her) and her friends have promised to go on Memorial Day weekend.
10. Where have Rosa and (she her) put the tents?
11. (We Us) should help with packing.
12. My brother and (I me) read an exciting book about winter camping.
13. You and (me I) will go and stay in the lodge!
14. (She Her) and (I me) are not going.
15. (We Us) have too much homework.

B. On the line, write a pronoun that can replace the *italicized* word or words.

_____[They]_____ 1. *The students* began to plan a class trip.

_____[He/She]_____ 2. *Their teacher* suggested going to Washington, D.C.

_____[We]_____ 3. "*You and I* will want to see the Air and Space Museum," she said.

_____[He/She]_____ 4. *The class secretary* called the bus company.

_____[It/They]_____ 5. *The company* charged $350 for the bus rental.

_____[He]_____ 6. *Mr. Zimmerman* gave Sara seventy-five dollars to spend on the trip.

_____[She]_____ 7. *Sara* packed her own snacks to save money for souvenirs.

_____[It]_____ 8. *The White House* was the first stop.

_____[They]_____ 9. *Dana and Zeke* climbed to the top of the Washington Monument.

_____[It]_____ 10. *The trip* was a huge success.

24. Identifying Pronouns Used as Subject Complements

A subject pronoun can replace a noun used as a subject complement. A subject complement follows a linking verb and refers to the same person or thing as the subject of the sentence.

Mom thought it was I who called.

The pronoun must agree in person (first, second, or third) and number (singular or plural) with the subject. The third person singular must also agree in gender.

A. Circle the correct pronoun in parentheses.

1. Was it (she) her) who missed the bus?

2. I am not sure if it is (her (she)).

3. Mr. Fisher said that it could have been (them (they)).

4. No one would have believed it was (I) me).

5. Jim said it was (him (he)) who called.

6. Cheryl thinks it was (I) me) who called her.

7. It wasn't (they) them) who go to early morning choir.

8. Mindy could not believe it was (we) us) on the bus that early.

9. Last year the route scheduler was (she) her).

10. Did you know that the algebra winner was (he) him)?

B. Complete each sentence with an appropriate pronoun. Write the person, number, and gender of your pronoun on the line at the left. [**Sample answers are shown.**]

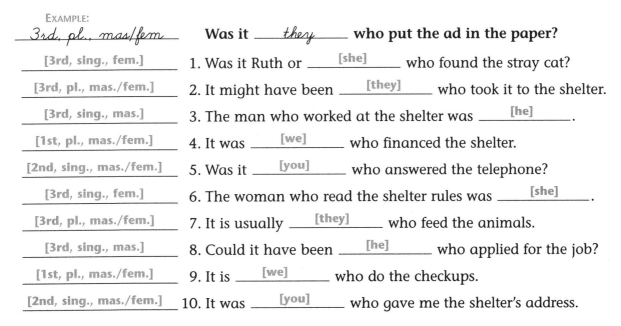

EXAMPLE:

3rd., pl., mas/fem	Was it ___they___ who put the ad in the paper?
[3rd, sing., fem.]	1. Was it Ruth or ___[she]___ who found the stray cat?
[3rd, pl., mas./fem.]	2. It might have been ___[they]___ who took it to the shelter.
[3rd, sing., mas.]	3. The man who worked at the shelter was ___[he]___.
[1st, pl., mas./fem.]	4. It was ___[we]___ who financed the shelter.
[2nd, sing., mas./fem.]	5. Was it ___[you]___ who answered the telephone?
[3rd, sing., fem.]	6. The woman who read the shelter rules was ___[she]___.
[3rd, pl., mas./fem.]	7. It is usually ___[they]___ who feed the animals.
[3rd, sing., mas.]	8. Could it have been ___[he]___ who applied for the job?
[1st, pl., mas./fem.]	9. It is ___[we]___ who do the checkups.
[2nd, sing., mas./fem.]	10. It was ___[you]___ who gave me the shelter's address.

25. Identifying Pronouns Used as Direct Objects

A personal pronoun can be used as the direct object of a verb. The object pronouns are *me, us, you, him, her, it,* and *them.*

The bell startled us.

A. Circle the correct pronoun in parentheses.

1. Our chemistry teacher surprised (we (us)) last week.

2. The lesson on the periodic table of the elements interested ((us) we).

3. The periodic table arranges (they (them)) in rows called periods.

4. Mr. Gonzalez, the teacher, praised Steve and ((me) I)
   for our report on element 104.

5. The teacher invited (she (her)) to chemistry club.

6. All the members wanted ((them) they) on the science team.

7. A science reporter interviewed (he (him)) about the atom model.

8. The newspaper will help ((them) they) with money for more study.

9. The field of chemistry excited (I (me)) after that.

10. The chemistry teacher warned (we (us)) about the work involved.

B. Write the pronoun that correctly replaces the underlined word or words.

___[him]___ 1. Did you meet Larry at the movie?

___[them]___ 2. Grace invited Steve and Ben to the discussion afterwards.

___[us]___ 3. The speaker informed the group and me about movie making.

___[him]___ 4. Have you met Jeremy Black, the *Tribune's* new reviewer?

___[her]___ 5. His opinions sometimes infuriate Sheila.

___[it]___ 6. We saw the movie *Castaway* on Saturday.

___[us]___ 7. Call Jean and me when you are ready to see it.

___[her]___ 8. After the lecture Mom expected Mai to come right home.

___[them]___ 9. Instead she joined our friends at the coffee shop.

___[him]___ 10. They were busy criticizing the speaker about his latest review.

26. Identifying Pronouns Used as Indirect Objects or Objects of Prepositions

> An object pronoun can be used as the indirect object of a verb.
> **The secretary read <u>them</u> the minutes.**
> An object pronoun can be used as the object of a preposition.
> **The president made copies for <u>her</u>.**

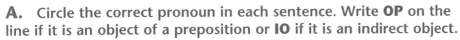

A. Circle the correct pronoun in each sentence. Write **OP** on the line if it is an object of a preposition or **IO** if it is an indirect object.

[IO]　　1. Jan showed (we (us)) her report about Dorothy Day.

[IO]　　2. It certainly gave (I (me)) something to think about.

[IO]　　3. One historian called (she (her)) one of the most significant, interesting, and influential women in America.

[IO]　　4. During the Great Depression, Day established houses of hospitality for the less fortunate, which gave ((them) they) food and shelter and hope.

[OP]　　5. The shelters served meals to about 5,000 of ((them) they) every day.

B. Rewrite the following sentences, substituting pronouns for the *italicized* words.

1. In 1933 Day started a newspaper for Catholic workers with *Peter Maurin*.

   [In 1933 Day started a newspaper for Catholic workers with him.]

2. This monthly newspaper provided *the workers* with information on peaceful change.

   [This monthly newspaper provided them with information on peaceful change.]

3. During the 1960s, Day showed her support for *activists* by fasting for ten days.

   [During the 1960s, Day showed her support for them by fasting for ten days.]

4. Mother Teresa gave *Day* a special cross.

   [Mother Teresa gave her a special cross.]

5. My mother handed *my brother* an article about *Dorothy Day*.

   [My mother handed him an article about her.]

Dorothy Day worked to improve the lives of those less fortunate. She spoke out in favor of peace and nonviolent change. Give an example of how you can work for peace and fairness in your daily life.

27. Reviewing Pronouns Used as Subjects and Objects

> A subject pronoun can be used as the subject or subject complement of a sentence. An object pronoun can be used as the direct or indirect object of a verb or as the object of a preposition.

A. Circle the correct pronoun in each sentence. Write on the line whether the pronoun is used as a subject **(S)**, a subject complement **(SC)**, or an object **(O)**.

[S] 1. Because myths are handed down by word of mouth, (they them) have no correct form.

[O] 2. Myths provide (us we) with explanations of natural phenomena.

[SC] 3. In the story of Persephone, it is (she her) who is abducted.

[O] 4. Pluto, god of the underworld, keeps (her she) for part of each year.

[S] 5. When (he him) gives her back, Earth returns to spring and summer.

[S] 6. Do (we us) think this is the explanation for the seasons?

[O] 7. Maybe not, but myths give (us we) insights into the beliefs of other cultures.

[S] 8. (They Them) were used to explain creation, religion, and the meaning of life.

[O] 9. Older people often told myths to the youth to teach (them they) about the supernatural.

[O] 10. The myth of Pandora's box gave (them they) an explanation for good and evil.

B. Circle the pronoun in each sentence. Write whether it is used as a subject **(S)**, a subject complement **(SC)**, a direct object **(DO)**, an indirect object **(IO)**, or the object of a preposition **(OP)**.

[S] 1. (He) had magnificent physical strength.

[IO] 2. The gods gave (him) special gifts.

[DO] 3. Hercules' mother put (him) to bed one night.

[DO] 4. Two snakes attacked (him) and a brother.

[S, DO] 5. Hercules grasped the creatures by their throats, and (he) strangled (them).

[SC] 6. It was (he) who killed a lion at the age of eighteen.

[OP] 7. Hercules had to accomplish many labors—twelve of (them).

[IO] 8. In the twelfth labor Pluto gave (him) permission to bring Cerberus, the three-headed dog, up from Hades.

[DO] 9. Hercules carried (it) to Earth but eventually returned Cerberus to Hades.

[OP] 10. Many other great deeds were performed by (him) after the last labor.

Pronouns

28. Identifying the Pronouns to Use After <u>Than</u> and <u>As</u>

The conjunctions *than* and *as* can be used to compare a noun and a pronoun or two pronouns. If the noun with which the pronoun is compared is a subject or a subject complement, the pronoun following the conjunction must be a subject pronoun. Sometimes words are left out of sentences that make comparisons; figuring out what words are missing will help you decide if the pronoun is used as a subject or as an object.

> **Bill is as tall as <u>he</u> (is).**

If the noun with which the pronoun is compared is an object, the pronoun following the conjunction must be an object pronoun.

> **She takes Wanda to the movies more often than (she takes) <u>me</u>.**

A. Circle the pronoun in parentheses that agrees correctly with the *italicized* word.

1. In the office *Claire* is as efficient as (she⃝ her).
2. The trainer gave *Lanette* fewer pointers on phone use than (me⃝ I).
3. *Luce* wrote a more realistic business plan than (he⃝ him).
4. Because we took a long break, *we* were later getting our assignment than (they⃝ them).
5. The girls had seen *Keith* more than (she her⃝) at the copy machine.
6. At the computer help desk more requests came to *me* than (he him⃝).
7. The *bosses* are as happy as (we⃝ us).
8. My father admires *the owners* more than (they them⃝).
9. Sam offered *Sean* as well as (he him⃝) a full-time job.
10. *Brian* was more excited at the prospect of working than (I⃝ me).

B. Underline the word with which the *italicized* pronoun is compared.

1. <u>Christine</u> is older than *I.*
2. Gramps praised <u>Ellen</u> as well as *her.*
3. My Aunt Joe pointed to <u>him</u> as well as *me.*
4. In the final inning <u>Johann</u> played as well as *they.*
5. Uncle Will did not throw so many curves to <u>Josie</u> as to *me.*
6. Ed told <u>Piku</u> the secret as well as *me.*
7. In the first game <u>Dad</u> scored better than *I.*
8. Mick gave <u>Ozzie</u> a bigger piece than *me.*
9. Is <u>Jan</u> as short as *she?*
10. Do you know <u>his brother</u> better than *him?*

29. Identifying Possessive Pronouns and Adjectives

> Possessive pronouns and possessive adjectives show possession or ownership.
> A **possessive pronoun** takes the place of a noun and its possessive adjective.
> The possessive pronouns are *mine, ours, yours, his, hers, its,* and *theirs.*
>
> **Here are <u>my gloves</u>. Here are <u>mine</u>.**
>
> A **possessive adjective** modifies a noun. The possessive adjectives are
> *my, our, your, his, her, its,* and *their.*
>
> **He said <u>his</u> hands were dirty.**

A. Circle the possessive pronouns. Underline the possessive adjectives.

1. John Greenleaf Whittier spent <u>his</u> boyhood in an old farmhouse in Massachusetts.

2. (Theirs) was a quiet, religious life spent farming.

3. Since <u>his</u> parents were Quakers, Whittier is called the Quaker poet.

4. <u>His</u> poems celebrated <u>our</u> New England country life.

5. (His) was not just a life spent dreaming about the beauties of rural life.

6. <u>His</u> work against slavery is well known.

7. <u>My</u> history book describes him as an abolitionist.

8. (Yours) might mention <u>his</u> term in the Massachusetts legislature.

9. Is that copy of *Snow-Bound* (ours)?

10. I'll give you (mine) as long as you return it.

B. Replace the *italicized* word(s) with a possessive. Write **A** on
the line if the possessive is an adjective and **P** if it is a pronoun.

_____[Its, A]_____ 1. *The Monterey Bay Aquarium's* otters are a popular attraction.

_____[his, A]_____ 2. Have you read *Roy Nickerson's* book on otters?

_____[Its, A]_____ 3. *California's* laws now ban the use of gill nets.

_____[their, A]_____ 4. The laws protect otters from being caught in *fishermen's* nets.

_____[Its, A]_____ 5. *A gill net's* victim might include a harbor porpoise.

_____[theirs, P]_____ 6. These laws were one of *Friends of the Sea Otters* accomplishments.

_____[Their, A]_____ 7. *Oil tankers'* spilled oil also endangers otters.

_____[her, P]_____ 8. The otter relocation idea was *a woman's* idea.

_____[its, A]_____ 9. Being playful and fun to watch is *an otter's* attraction.

_____[ours, P]_____ 10. An otter's need for clean and safe water is like *our need.*

30. Identifying Reflexive Pronouns

A **reflexive pronoun** ends in *–self* or *–selves*. A reflexive pronoun is often the object or indirect object of a verb or the object of a preposition. It refers to the same person, place, or thing as the subject of the sentence.

She informed herself about the rent rules.

A reflexive pronoun can also be used to show emphasis.

She herself signed the lease.

A. Underline the reflexive pronoun in each sentence. If it is used to show emphasis, write **E** on the line at the left.

___[E]___ 1. Bev and Wes themselves chose to do a report on Thomas Edison.

_____ 2. They familiarized themselves with his many achievements.

___[E]___ 3. Bev herself wondered how one person could have patented as many as 1,093 inventions.

_____ 4. Wes said that it was possible because Edison never allowed himself to rest.

___[E]___ 5. He added, "Edison himself defined genius as 1 percent inspiration and 99 percent perspiration."

_____ 6. The two decided to re-enact Edison's light bulb experiment for themselves.

___[E]___ 7. They followed the same steps that the inventor himself had followed many years earlier.

___[E]___ 8. They also found that the filament itself was not the only important factor.

_____ 9. After countless attempts and two successful lightings, both students were proud of themselves.

_____ 10. They concluded that Edison's genius spoke for itself.

B. Complete each sentence with a reflexive pronoun. Write **E** on the line at left if the pronoun is used to show emphasis.

_____ 1. My brother bought a new jigsaw puzzle for ____[himself]____.

___[E]___ 2. The puzzle's instruction sheet ____[itself]____ was hard to figure out.

___[E]___ 3. You ____[yourself]____ are responsible for this puzzle, I told him.

_____ 4. I told ____[myself]____ I wouldn't put one piece in.

___[E]___ 5. The puzzle image ____[itself]____ turned out to be a person putting together a puzzle.

Name _____

31. Identifying Correct Agreement of Reflexive Pronouns

A reflexive pronoun must agree with its antecedent in person, number, and gender.

A. Circle the reflexive pronoun in each sentence. Write on the line at the left the person, number, and gender of its antecedent.

____[2nd, sing., m/f]____ 1. Did you hurt (yourself) when you fell?

____[1st, plural, m/f]____ 2. We made (ourselves) comfortable in the boat.

____[1st, sing., m/f]____ 3. I (myself) find little that is new in the navigation course.

____[3rd, sing., masc.]____ 4. He has no confidence in (himself.)

____[3rd, sing., fem.]____ 5. Jean (herself) completed the work on her small sailboat.

____[3rd, sing., fem.]____ 6. My sister (herself) cooked lunch in the boat's microwave.

____[2nd, sing., m/f]____ 7. You should prepare (yourself) for a storm on Monday.

____[3rd, sing., fem.]____ 8. She (herself) lost courage after that last outing.

____[3rd, sing., fem.]____ 9. She blamed nobody but (herself) for the tragedy.

____[1st, plural, m/f]____ 10. Suddenly we found (ourselves) in a beautiful harbor.

B. Rewrite each sentence, adding a reflexive pronoun. **[Sample answers are shown.]**

1. Martin Luther King, Jr., and other African American civil rights leaders found a place in history.
[Martin Luther King, Jr., and other African American civil rights leaders found a place in history for themselves.]

2. I recently read King's "I Have a Dream" speech.

[I recently read King's "I Have a Dream" speech for myself.]

C. Rewrite each sentence, using a reflexive pronoun for emphasis.

3. Martin Luther King, Jr., was jailed for his nonviolent protests.

[Martin Luther King, Jr., himself was jailed for his nonviolent protests.]

4. King's supporters were often the targets of violence.

[King's supporters themselves were often the targets of violence.]

5. The work for civil rights is carried on by Coretta Scott King.

[The work for civil rights is carried on by Coretta Scott King herself.]

Name _____

32. Identifying Interrogative Pronouns

An **interrogative pronoun** is used in asking a question.
Who, whom, and *whose* are used when asking about persons. *Who* is used when the pronoun is the subject of the question. *Whom* is used when the pronoun is the object of the verb or of a preposition. *Whose* is used when asking about a possession. *Which* is used when asking about one of a class or group of persons, places, or things. *What* is used when asking about things.

Pronouns

A. Underline the interrogative pronouns. Write on the line whether the pronoun seeks information about a person, place, or thing.

[person] 1. Who has driven along the coast of California?

[thing] 2. What are some of the sights we can see?

[thing] 3. What should you take for the climate changes?

[place] 4. Which is the best park to visit in Big Sur?

[person] 5. My mother wants to know which was the author that lived on Cannery Row.

[person] 6. Who wants to go to the aquarium?

[place] 7. Which of the state parks has the elephant seals?

[person] 8. For whom was Hearst Castle named?

[person] 9. Who is worried about driving on Highway 1?

[place] 10. Which attraction has been written about most often?

B. Circle the interrogative pronoun in each sentence. Write on the line whether it is used as the subject **(S)**, the subject complement **(SC)**, the direct object **(DO)**, the indirect object **(IO)**, or the object of a preposition **(OP)**.

_[S]_ 1. Which of Edison's inventions is most important?

_[S/SC]_ 2. Who was Jan Matzeliger?

_[S]_ 3. Who invented the traffic light?

_[OP]_ 4. To whom is industry indebted for the automatic lubricator?

_[DO]_ 5. Which of the problems faced by farmers in the West did Glidden solve?

_[IO]_ 6. Mrs. Swenson gave whom the report on Baekland's important new material?

_[S]_ 7. Who discovered electricity?

_[DO]_ 8. What do you wish to invent, Natalie?

_[OP]_ 9. In which of the references did you find information on Margaret Knight?

_[DO]_ 10. Whom do you admire?

33. Identifying the Correct Use of the Interrogative Pronouns <u>Who</u> and <u>Whom</u>

> *Who* is used when the pronoun is the subject of the question. *Whom* is used when the pronoun is the direct or indirect object of the verb or the object of a preposition.

A. Circle the interrogative pronoun in each sentence. Write whether it is the subject (**S**), the subject complement (**SC**), the direct object (**DO**), the indirect object (**IO**), or the object of a preposition (**OP**).

__[S]__ 1. (Who) directed the 1981 Academy Award–winning *Chariots of Fire?*

__[OP]__ 2. To (whom) did Dorothy turn for help in *The Wizard of Oz?*

__[S]__ 3. (Who) wrote the poems for the movie *Il Postino?*

__[S/SC]__ 4. (Who) is the lead actor in *Gladiator?*

__[OP]__ 5. By (whom) was the Ark of the Covenant stolen in the first Indiana Jones movie?

__[IO]__ 6. Shostakovich gave (whom) permission to use his musical score?

__[DO]__ 7. (Whom) did you meet at the Oscar party?

__[S]__ 8. (Who) owned the small bookshop in *You've Got Mail?*

__[S/SC]__ 9. (Who) was the oldest person to have won an Oscar?

__[OP]__ 10. To (whom) was the Oscar for best picture in 2000 given?

__[S]__ 11. (Who) acted in *Gone with the Wind?*

__[DO]__ 12. (Whom) did you see at the movies last night?

B. Complete each sentence with *who* or *whom*.

13. ____[Who]____ was chained to a cliff for a monster to devour but was rescued by Perseus?

14. ____[Who]____ slew the Minotaur and married Ariadne?

15. With ____[whom]____ did the nymph Echo fall in love?

16. ____[Whom]____ did Zeus kill for driving the sun chariot too close to the earth?

17. ____[Whom]____ did Paris carry to Troy and thus cause the Trojan War?

18. ____[Who]____ was the Queen of Heaven and the wife of Zeus?

19. ____[Who]____ unwittingly murdered his father and married his mother?

20. By ____[whom]____ was Medusa, the gorgon, slain?

Name _____

34. Identifying Relative Pronouns

A relative clause is a dependent clause that describes or gives information about a noun. Every relative clause has a **relative pronoun.** The relative pronouns are *who, whom, whose, which,* and *that. Who, whom,* and *whose* refer to persons. *Which* refers to places or things. *That* refers to persons, places or things.

Hal (*antecedent*), who (*relative pronoun*) grew up in Indonesia, lives in Chicago.

A. Underline the relative pronoun in each sentence. Circle its antecedent.

1. Mountains are (landforms) that are higher than their surroundings.

2. The (mountain) that you hike up may be a hill to someone else.

3. The (Alps) which are a younger mountain range, are a mere fifteen million years old.

4. Sir Edmund Hillary was the first (person) who climbed Mount Everest, in 1953.

5. Tenzing Norgay was the Sherpa (guide) who accompanied Hillary.

6. Other (climbers) whom you may have read about have also accomplished the feat.

7. (Mount Whitney) which is in the Sierra Nevada range, is the highest mountain in California.

8. (Ararat) which is in Turkey, is where Noah's Ark is supposed to have rested.

9. (Mountain climbers) whose journals are often published, can have interesting tales to tell.

10. (Into Thin Air) which chronicled one climb, was widely read.

B. Underline the relative pronoun in each sentence. Write on the line whether it is a subject or object and how it is used in the sentence.

EXAMPLE:
subject of is outstanding   **The Newberry Library has a collection of maps that is outstanding.**

[subj. of **are used**]   1. Maps are tools that are used by travelers and students.

[subj. of **shows**]   2. A map that shows the surface of the earth is called a physical map.

[obj. of **upon**]   3. Road maps, upon which I depend for my job, are designed for travelers.

[obj. of **from**]   4. Scale, from which a user can determine real distance, is an important map feature.

[subj. of **is mounted**]   5. A globe is a map that is mounted on a ball.

37

Name _____

35. Identifying the Correct Use of Relative Pronouns Who and Whom

> The relative pronoun *who* is used when the pronoun is the subject of the relative clause.
> **The girl <u>who</u> entered the room was Carrie.**
> The relative pronoun *whom* is used when the pronoun is an object in the relative clause.
> **The first person <u>whom</u> we will visit is Uncle Dan.**

A. Circle the correct relative pronoun in parentheses. Write on the line whether it is a subject or an object and how it is used in the sentence.

___[obj. of *met*]___ 1. The young woman (who (whom)) you met is Augusta Reed Thomas, composer-in-residence.

___[subj. of *has received*]___ 2. Bach was a composer ((who) whom) has received much study.

___[obj. of *favor*]___ 3. Mozart is the composer (who (whom)) I favor.

___[subj. of *wrote*]___ 4. He is the one ((who) whom) wrote *The Magic Flute.*

___[subj. of *composed*]___ 5. Was it Beethoven ((who) whom) composed *Fidelio?*

B. Complete each sentence with a dependent clause that contains the relative pronoun *who.* [Sample answers are given.]

1. The singer, ____[who lives in Vienna]____, performs once each year.

2. Her accompanist, ____[who is her sister]____, plays in a jazz group.

3. Another artist, ____[who plays the trumpet]____, lives in our building.

4. At a New York hotel, I saw Stevie Wonder, ____[who is my favorite]____.

5. I work for the conductor, ____[who works half the year in Brazil]____.

C. Complete each sentence with a dependent clause that contains the relative pronoun *whom.* [Sample answers are given.]

1. Have you seen the oboist, ____[about whom we read]____?

2. Hugh, ____[for whom I baby-sit]____, wanted to see an opera.

3. Dr. Yurkanin, ____[with whom I study violin]____, telephoned for tickets.

4. I wrote a thank-you note to Francesca, ____[through whom I met the cellist]____.

5. The diva, ____[about whom I had heard so much]____, was a joy to hear.

38

Pronouns

36. Identifying Indefinite Relative Pronouns

An indefinite relative pronoun is formed by adding –ever to *who, whom, what,* or *which.* An indefinite relative pronoun functions like a relative pronoun. An indefinite relative pronoun refers to an unknown or uncertain antecedent.

A. The relative clause in each sentence is *italicized.* Circle the indefinite relative pronoun.

1. You may give the book to (whoever) *is going to the library.*

2. Take (whichever) *you prefer.*

3. The librarian helped (whomever) *he met.*

4. Send the tutor to (whoever) *needs him most.*

5. (Whoever) *comes to our computer lab* will be surprised.

6. The floodlight shines directly at (whoever) *enters the room.*

7. (Whoever) *installed that* has an eye for security.

8. The principal handed detention slips to (whoever) *kept materials too long.*

9. Pay strict attention to (whatever) *she tells you.*

10. Caroline gives great advice *about* (whatever) *you are researching.*

B. Complete each sentence with a relative clause. The indefinite relative pronoun is given. **[Sample answers are given.]**

1. Whichever _____ [has more mass] _____ will sink to the bottom.

2. We should be grateful to whoever _____ [does the job] _____ .

3. Whoever _____ [studies hard] _____ is wise.

4. Ted can make friends with whomever _____ [he chooses] _____ .

5. I will buy you whatever _____ [fits the occasion] _____ .

6. I studied whatever _____ [my teacher assigned] _____ .

7. Have you seen whoever _____ [is at the door] _____ ?

8. The writer told her to write whatever _____ [she thought of] _____ .

9. Sherlock Holmes investigated whoever _____ [behaved criminally] _____ .

10. Whichever _____ [is selected] _____ is fine with me.

Name _____

37. Identifying Demonstrative Pronouns

> A **demonstrative pronoun** points out a definite person, place, or thing. *This* and *these* are used for objects that are near. *That* and *those* are used for objects that are distant.

A. Circle the demonstrative pronoun in each sentence. Write whether it indicates near or distant objects.

___[near]___ 1. (This) is the painting you wanted to see.

___[near]___ 2. Look at the brush strokes and notice how (these) are close together.

___[near]___ 3. (This) is a painting far superior to the one in the brochure.

___[distant]___ 4. (Those) are among the paintings in the gallery on the second floor.

___[near]___ 5. The curator is happy that you brought (these) in today.

___[near]___ 6. Do you like (this?)

___[distant]___ 7. (Those) are similar to woodcuts we saw last year in Europe.

___[distant]___ 8. Unfortunately, (that) was the trip we had to cut short.

___[near]___ 9. (This) was painted by Rembrandt in his early years.

___[near]___ 10. (These) are unique frames.

B. Complete each sentence with the correct demonstrative pronoun.

1. The softest pillows are ___[these]___ on this couch.

2. Is ___[that]___ your car at the end of the driveway?

3. ___[This]___ is the first time I have seen the recipe.

4. ___[These]___ are the only pieces left in this box.

5. ___[Those]___ in the next room are from the Ming dynasty.

6. Was ___[that]___ your brother on the bus?

7. The only change I could find is ___[this]___ in my pocket.

8. Mother's flowers are ___[these]___ at our feet.

9. ___[Those]___ are my friends standing on the next corner.

10. What is ___[that]___ rising over the mountain?

Pronouns

Name _____

38. Identifying Indefinite Pronouns

An **indefinite pronoun** refers to any or all members of a group of persons, places, or things. The indefinite pronouns are *all, another, both, each, either, few, many, neither, nothing, several, some,* and pronouns that begin with *"any"* or *"every."*

Each must pass the physical.

Anyone who is qualified can join.

A. Underline the indefinite pronouns in each sentence.

1. One of the officials blew a whistle, and each of the windsurfers paddled out to sea.

2. Today was the windsurfing race, and everybody was on the beach.

3. The brisk wind quickly filled all of the sails.

4. After about ten seconds several of the surfers stood up on their boards.

5. A few headed to the south, and many went to the southeast.

6. An official said that either of the routes would be fast because of the strong wind.

7. After an hour someone caught sight of two sails on the horizon.

8. Neither was close enough, and as a result it was impossible for anyone to tell who was in the lead.

9. As they neared, both seemed to be the same distance from shore.

10. Somebody said that it would be a photo finish!

B. Underline the indefinite pronouns. Write on the line whether each pronoun is used as a subject **(S)**, a subject complement **(SC)**, a direct object **(DO)**, an indirect object **(IO)**, or the object of a preposition **(OP)**.

___[S]___ 1. Has anybody ever been to a focus test?

___[IO]___ 2. The company sent each of us an invitation.

___[S]___ 3. After the introduction, everybody tasted the cheese spreads.

___[DO]___ 4. One woman found neither of them satisfactory.

___[DO]___ 5. After the cheese test, the moderator introduced another.

___[DO]___ 6. Did the moderator give you both of the yogurts to try?

___[IO]___ 7. After the tasting, the moderator gave each of us a rating sheet to complete.

___[OP]___ 8. I received curious looks from a few of the reviewers.

___[S]___ 9. Neither of the reviewers next to me wanted to fill out the form.

___[DO]___ 10. We wrote anything to get out of there.

39. Identifying Correct Agreement with Indefinite Pronouns

Indefinite pronouns do not refer to a specific person or thing. Some indefinite pronouns are always singular; others are always plural.

SINGULAR: **anyone, anybody, anything, each, either, neither, everyone, everybody, everything, one, no one, nobody, nothing**

PLURAL: **all, both, few, many, several, some**

A. Circle the correct word in parentheses. Underline its antecedent.

1. <u>Each</u> of the women was satisfied with
   (her) their) booth at the bazaar.

2. <u>Neither</u> of the food booths
   had (its) their) food ready in time.

3. <u>Many</u> of the guests did not
   park (her (their) cars in the lot.

4. <u>All</u> of the people showed up for (his (their) free movie passes.

5. <u>Everyone</u> showed much interest in (his) their) own project.

B. Complete each sentence with an appropriate pronoun or possessive adjective. The pronouns and adjectives must agree in person, number, and gender with the *italicized* word.

1. If *anybody* wishes to study earthquakes, ___[he/she]___ can start now.

2. *Both* of my sisters liked ___[their]___ earth science classes.

3. *Everyone* is expected to do ___[his/her]___ own lab assignments.

4. *Many* of the students have read ___[their]___ assignments already.

5. A *few* of the students dropped ___[their]___ science courses this semester.

6. *Each* had ___[his/her]___ volcano model evaluated by an expert.

7. Has anyone completed ___[his/her]___ seismograph project?

8. Last year *neither* of the seismologists admitted that ___[he/she]___ had missed the warning signs.

9. *Several* of the new students wondered if ___[they]___ had the right teachers.

10. Generally, *all* of the students are satisfied with ___[their]___ courses.

40. Reviewing Pronouns

A. Circle the correct pronoun in parentheses. Write on the line whether the pronoun is the subject (**S**), the subject complement (**SC**), the direct object (**DO**), the indirect object (**IO**), or the object of a preposition (**OP**).

_[SC]_ 1. It was ((they) them) who invited us to the party.

_[OP]_ 2. Charlie made a celebratory lunch for ((her) she).

_[IO]_ 3. He plans to send Maria and (she (her)) the leftovers.

_[S]_ 4. Charlie and (me (I)) planned the surprise months ago.

_[S]_ 5. Could (us (we)) keep it a secret?

_[OP]_ 6. Charlie kept the plans with (he (him)) in his journal.

_[DO]_ 7. Sunday we finally told ((her) she).

B. Underline the reflexive pronoun in each sentence. Write **E** on the line if it is used for emphasis.

_[E]_ 8. I <u>myself</u> knew his voice when I heard it.

_____ 9. She looked at <u>herself</u> in the mirror.

_____ 10. The twins made the iced tea for <u>themselves</u>.

_[E]_ 11. He <u>himself</u> told me the story.

C. Underline the pronoun in each sentence. Write whether the pronoun is demonstrative, indefinite, possessive, or interrogative.

[demonstrative] 12. <u>That</u> was the movie I saw last week.

[indefinite] 13. Sam noted that <u>each</u> of the actors wore black.

[indefinite] 14. The movie gave <u>neither</u> a fair portrayal.

[interrogative] 15. <u>What</u> is the kind of story that makes the best screenplay?

[indefinite] 16. <u>Someone</u> once said real-life dramas make the best movies.

[possessive] 17. That opinion isn't <u>mine</u>.

CONTINUED

Pronouns

D. Complete each sentence with *who* or *whom.*

18. _____[Who]_____ wrote *The Maltese Falcon?*

19. To _____[whom]_____ was the starring role given?

20. _____[Whom]_____ did Sidney Greenstreet play
    in the movie?

21. Do you know _____[who]_____ played opposite
    Humphrey Bogart?

E. Circle the correct pronoun following *than* and *as.*

22. Jim is as excited about the car trip as (she) her).

23. George has planned his vacation more carefully than (they) them).

24. My dad liked the Yellowstone campsite better than (he) him).

25. Bridget enjoyed hiking on the trails as much as (we) us).

26. Fran complained more than (me (I)).

F. Circle the correct possessive adjective in parentheses.

27. Either of my brothers will give you (his) their) baseball glove.

28. Neither of my sisters remembered (her) their) workout clothes.

29. Each of the girls on the track team wore (her) their) own sweat pants.

30. Several of the girls' parents offered (his (their)) help to buy uniforms.

Try It Yourself
On a separate sheet of paper, write four sentences about something you treasure. Be sure to use pronouns correctly.

Check Your Own Work
Choose a selection from your writing portfolio, your journal, a work in progress, an assignment from another class, or a letter. Revise it, applying the skills you have learned in this chapter. The checklist will help you.

✔ Have you remembered to make pronouns and their antecedents agree?

✔ Have you used subject and object pronouns correctly?

41. Distinguishing Common and Proper Adjectives

> An **adjective** describes or limits a noun. A proper adjective is formed from a proper noun. It is capitalized.
>
> **Elizabethan, Japanese**
>
> All other adjectives are common adjectives.
>
> **pretty, talented**

A. Identify the *italicized* adjectives by writing **C** above the common adjectives and **P** above the proper adjectives.

1. The Renaissance was a period of *artistic* [C] and *cultural* [C] advancement.
2. It took place following the *medieval* [C] period and affected *many* [C] *European* [P] countries.
3. Artists were influenced by *Greek* [P] and *Roman* [P] art of the *classical* [C] period.
4. Michelangelo was an *Italian* [P] artist of the Renaissance.
5. He was a *talented* [C] artist who achieved fame as a painter, an architect, and a sculptor.
6. Did you know that *Renaissance* [P] artists often painted *religious* [C] themes?
7. Michelangelo's most *famous* [C] painting is probably the ceiling of the Sistine Chapel.
8. A work of *enormous* [C] size, it took him years to complete.
9. To paint the ceiling of this *Catholic* [P] church, he had to lie on top of a *large* [C] platform.
10. Each year thousands of tourists visit this *Vatican* [P] destination just to see this *visionary* [C] work.

B. Underline the descriptive adjectives. Write **C** above the common adjectives and **P** above the proper adjectives.

1. William Henry Seward was an <u>American</u> [P] statesman.
2. He had a <u>long</u> [C] and <u>distinguished</u> [C] career.
3. Seward began as a member of the <u>Whig</u> [P] party.
4. This <u>political</u> [C] party later split over the <u>slavery</u> [C] issue.
5. As a senator, Seward established an <u>antislavery</u> [C] policy.
6. He helped organize the <u>Republican</u> [P] Party.
7. During the Civil War he was a <u>valuable</u> [C] member of Lincoln's cabinet.
8. As Secretary of State, he needed to prevent <u>European</u> [P] intervention.
9. After the war, he obtained <u>congressional</u> [C] approval for the purchase of Alaska.
10. Alaska had previously been a <u>Russian</u> [P] territory.

42. Placing Adjectives Correctly

An adjective may come before a noun or after a linking verb. An adjective that follows a linking verb is a subject complement.

My teacher is <u>young</u>.

An adjective that follows the direct object and completes the thought expressed by the transitive verb is an object complement.

Pretzels make me <u>thirsty</u>.

Adjectives

A. Above each *italicized* adjective, write **U** for usual position, **SC** for subject complement, or **OC** for object complement.

1. Perhaps you have seen a *small, birdlike* animal at night.
   [U] [U]

2. It was probably a bat, one of the most *unusual* and *mysterious* creatures.
   [U] [U]

3. This *small, swift* creature is actually a *flying* mammal.
   [U] [U] [U]

4. It sleeps during the day and becomes *active* at night.
   [SC]

5. Contrary to *popular* belief, bats are not *blind*.
   [U] [SC]

6. Most possess *keen* eyesight as well as a *sonar* system.
   [U] [U]

7. Their ears, which are somewhat *oversized*, pick up echoes
   [SC]
   of the bat's *own* sounds.
   [U]

8. Despite some *bad* habits, these *birdlike* creatures are *useful*.
   [U] [U] [SC]

9. They make *outdoor* life *bearable* by consuming *great* numbers of insects.
   [U] [OC] [U]

10. Scientists find bats *intriguing* and continue to learn more about them.
    [OC]

B. Underline the adjectives in each sentence. On the line write **U** for usual position, **SC** for subject complement, or **OC** for object complement.

[U]	1. Valley Forge is a <u>historical</u> park.
[SC, SC]	2. Louis thought the park was <u>fun</u> and <u>informative</u>.
[SC]	3. It was <u>important</u> during the Revolutionary War.
[SC]	4. The location was <u>strategic</u>.
[U]	5. George Washington kept his <u>winter</u> quarters there.
[OC]	6. Some of his soldiers found it <u>intolerable</u>.
[SC]	7. The weather was <u>severe</u>.
[U, SC, SC, SC]	8. <u>Many</u> soldiers were <u>cold</u>, <u>hungry</u>, and <u>unfit</u> for service.
[U]	9. It was, however, a <u>turning</u> point for the army.
[U]	10. Valley Forge is in <u>southeastern</u> Pennsylvania.

Name _____

43. Identifying Words Used as Nouns and Adjectives

> Some words can be used as nouns or as adjectives. A noun is a name word.
> An adjective describes a noun.

Write whether the word in *italics* is used as a noun or as an adjective.

__[A]__ 1. Anne Sullivan was an *American* educator.

__[N]__ 2. She specialized in teaching the *blind.*

__[A]__ 3. Anne went to a school for *blind* students.

__[A]__ 4. Her sight had been weakened
by a *childhood* infection.

__[A]__ 5. Though she never went blind, she learned
the *manual* alphabet.

__[A]__ 6. This is an alphabet in which the letters are
represented by *finger* positions.

__[N]__ 7. After graduation Anne dedicated her life to *teaching.*

__[N]__ 8. Her most famous *student* was Helen Keller.

__[A]__ 9. She instructed Helen through a system of *touch* teaching.

__[A]__ 10. This system was a *key* factor in Helen Keller's rapid advancement.

__[N]__ 11. Anne would spell into Helen's hand with her *finger.*

__[N]__ 12. In this manner Helen learned to read in a short *period* of time.

__[N]__ 13. Anne later taught her to speak after only one month of *study.*

__[A]__ 14. Their lives were later the basis of a play and a *motion* picture.

__[A]__ 15. Anne never stopped campaigning for *education* rights for the blind.

__[A]__ 16. Helen became celebrated for overcoming her *physical* handicaps.

__[A]__ 17. Together they traveled the world on *lecture* tours.

__[A]__ 18. They brought *public* support to the American Foundation for the Blind.

__[A]__ 19. They would remain *constant* companions until Anne's death in 1936.

__[A]__ 20. Their extraordinary story remains an inspiration to *future* educators.

Anne Sullivan persevered in teaching young Helen Keller because she believed in
what she was doing. Give an example of something you believe strongly. How are
you working to make that belief a reality? Write about it.

Adjectives

44. Identifying Types of Adjectives

Demonstrative adjectives point out definite persons, places, or things. The demonstrative adjectives are *this, that, these,* and *those.*

Possessive adjectives show possession or ownership. The possessive adjectives are *my, your, his, her, its, our,* and *their.*

Indefinite adjectives refer to any or all of a group of persons, places, or things. The indefinite adjectives include *both, few, every, several, all, some, many, each, either,* and *neither.*

Interrogative adjectives ask a question. The interrogative adjectives are *what, which,* and *whose.*

Numeral adjectives indicate an exact number.

The indefinite articles *a* and *an* refer to any of a class of things. The definite article *the* refers to one or more specific things.

Adjectives

A. Write whether the *italicized* adjective in each sentence is indefinite, interrogative, demonstrative, or possessive.

___[indefinite]___ 1. *All* jazz fans are familiar with the music of Duke Ellington.

___[possessive]___ 2. Ellington did not use the term "jazz"; he referred to "the music of *my* people."

___[possessive]___ 3. Known primarily for *his* jazz compositions, Ellington also wrote orchestral pieces.

___[indefinite]___ 4. *Some* Ellington compositions combine jazz and classical styles.

___[indefinite]___ 5. He was comfortable in *either* style.

___[interrogative]___ 6. *What* other musicians experimented with different musical styles?

___[indefinite]___ 7. George Gershwin wrote *some* music for piano.

___[indefinite]___ 8. In 1924 he wrote *Rhapsody in Blue,* using elements of *both* classical and jazz.

___[demonstrative]___ 9. Today, symphony orchestras often play *that* composition.

___[demonstrative]___ 10. Many years later, *these* musicians remain popular.

B. Complete each sentence with an adjective of the correct type. [**Sample answers are given.**]

possessive 1. Mr. Bloom took ___[his]___ vacation last week.

demonstrative 2. It was his first vacation ___[this]___ year.

indefinite 3. ___[Each, Every]___ year he goes to the same park.

interrogative 4. To ___[which, what]___ park does he go?

indefinite 5. It is in ___[either]___ California or Oregon.

indefinite   6. His trip is short, so he lives ____[each]____ day to its fullest.

possessive   7. Does his wife bring ____[her]____ dogs?

demonstrative   8. ____[That]____ park does not allow animals.

interrogative   9. On [what, which] day will he return?

indefinite   10. He returns ____[either]____ Saturday or Sunday.

C. Circle each article. Underline each numeral adjective.

1. <u>Two</u> brothers, Wilbur and Orville Wright, are recognized as (the) inventors of (the) airplane.

2. They built (the) <u>first</u> effective airplane in 1903.

3. Powered by (a) small engine, (the) plane flew <u>one hundred and twenty</u> feet before landing.

4. Less than <u>twenty-five</u> years later, air travel had come (a) long way.

5. In (the) year 1927 Charles Lindbergh flew by himself from New York City to Paris.

6. This was (the) <u>first</u> solo transcontinental flight ever attempted.

7. He had to stay awake for <u>thirty-three</u> straight hours.

8. <u>Five</u> years later, this feat was accomplished for (the) <u>first</u> time by (a) female pilot.

9. That pilot, Amelia Earhart, later attempted to be (the) <u>first</u> pilot to fly around (the) world.

10. Tragically, <u>six</u> weeks after she set out, her plane disappeared in (the) South Pacific.

D. Underline the articles in each sentence. Write **D** if the article is definite or **I** if it is indefinite.

___[I]___   1. Louisa May Alcott is <u>an</u> author whose books appeal to children.

___[I, D]___   2. *Little Women* is <u>an</u> autobiographical novel about <u>the</u> four Alcott sisters.

___[D, I]___   3. <u>The</u> novel was made into <u>a</u> movie in 1994.

___[I, I]___   4. <u>A</u> thriller she wrote under <u>an</u> assumed name was published recently.

___[I, D]___   5. These events have sparked <u>a</u> new interest in <u>the</u> author.

45. Using Articles and Demonstrative Adjectives

When two or more nouns or adjectives joined by *and* refer to different persons, places, or things, use an article before each noun.

When two or more nouns or adjectives joined by *and* refer to the same person, place, or thing, use an article before only the first noun.

The demonstrative adjectives *this, that, these,* and *those* agree in number with the nouns they modify.

Adjectives

A. Circle the article in parentheses if it is needed. Put an X through it if it is not.

1. We found a tan and (a) white purse. (one purse)

2. We organized an athletic club and (a) book club.

3. The secretary and (the) treasurer's office is on the tenth floor.

4. Both the doctor and (the) nurse were present for the hearing.

5. They have sold the black and (the) white spaniel. (one spaniel)

6. The director's and (the) producer's rooms are behind the auditorium.

7. My brother is the captain and (the) quarterback of the LaSalle team.

8. The janitor moved the desk and (the) chair.

9. The letter was addressed to Mr. Roy Day, the president and (the) manager.

10. The participle and (the) gerund are verb forms.

B. Complete each sentence with the correct demonstrative adjective.

1. _____[This]_____ *(near)* river flows past the Temple of Karnak.

2. _____[That]_____ *(distant)* disease causes the fingers and toes to move uncontrollably.

3. Please look up the addresses for

   _____[these]_____ *(near)* names.

4. _____[This]_____ *(near)* mountain is the highest in the continental United States.

5. _____[Those]_____ *(distant)* birds are on the endangered species list.

6. _____[That]_____ *(distant)* country's flag flies over the island of Ibiza.

7. _____[These]_____ *(near)* states border Nebraska.

8. *The Return of the King* is a sequel to _____[this]_____ *(near)* book.

9. Put your mail with _____[those]_____ *(distant)* letters over there.

10. Can you see _____[those]_____ *(distant)* ships on the horizon?

46. Identifying Comparative and Superlative Adjectives

> The positive degree of an adjective shows a quality of a noun.
> The comparative degree shows a quality of two nouns in greater or lesser degree.
> The superlative degree shows a quality of a noun in the greatest or least degree.
>
> | POSITIVE DEGREE | COMPARATIVE DEGREE | SUPERLATIVE DEGREE |
> |---|---|---|
> | intelligent | more intelligent | most intelligent |
> | smart | smarter | smartest |

A. Above each *italicized* adjective, write the degree of comparison. Use **P** for positive degree, **C** for comparative degree, and **S** for superlative degree.

1. Birds have *many* **[P]** specialized traits that allow them to fly.

2. Their *hollow* **[P]** bones make them *lighter* **[C]** than most animals.

3. Taking flight is *more difficult* **[C]** for *large* **[P]** birds than it is for *smaller* **[C]** ones.

4. The *heaviest* **[S]** flying bird is the bustard.

5. The ostrich is the *largest* **[S]** bird, and it cannot fly at all.

6. It is the *fastest* **[S]** two-legged animal on Earth.

7. Birds breathe *faster* **[C]** than any other animal.

8. The hummingbird is the *smallest* **[S]** of all birds.

9. A *small* **[P]** bird's heart beats up to 1,000 times per minute.

10. Birds that live at *high* **[P]** altitudes have *larger* **[C]** hearts.

B. Write the comparative and superlative forms of each adjective.

	COMPARATIVE	SUPERLATIVE
1. small	[smaller]	[smallest]
2. high	[higher]	[highest]
3. beautiful	[more beautiful]	[most beautiful]
4. cloudy	[cloudier]	[cloudiest]
5. many	[more]	[most]
6. dark	[darker]	[darkest]
7. rich	[richer]	[richest]
8. bad	[worse]	[worst]
9. large	[larger]	[largest]
10. good	[better]	[best]

Adjectives

Name _____

47. Using Comparative and Superlative Adjectives

Use the comparative form of the adjective to compare two things.
> **Carmen is smaller than her sister.**

Use the superlative form to compare two or more things.
> **Carmen is the smallest student in the class.**

Use *fewer* and *less* to compare quantities. Use *fewer* to compare things that can be counted. Use *less* to compare things that cannot be counted.

A. Cross out the incorrect word in parentheses.

1. California is the (~~more~~ most) populous state in the United States.

2. Of Florida and New York, Florida has the (faster ~~fastest~~) growing population.

3. Death Valley is the (~~lower~~ lowest) point in the western hemisphere.

4. Of all fifty states, Hawaii is the (~~younger~~ youngest).

5. Which is the (taller ~~tallest~~) peak, Mount McKinley or Mount Rainier?

6. Mount McKinley is the (~~higher~~ highest) mountain peak in North America.

7. Alaska has the (~~greater~~ greatest) land mass of any state.

8. Is Texas (larger ~~largest~~) than Florida?

9. Texas is the (~~bigger~~ biggest) of the forty-eight contiguous states.

10. Of the Ohio, Mississippi, and Missouri Rivers, the Mississippi is the (~~longer~~ longest).

B. Complete each sentence with *fewer* or *less*.

1. ____[Less]____ rainfall occurs in Utah than in Oregon.

2. Connecticut has ____[less]____ national park land than Nebraska.

3. Connecticut also has ____[fewer]____ parks.

4. Alabama produces ____[less]____ cotton than Texas.

5. There are ____[fewer]____ farmable acres in Alabama.

6. Sally has been to ____[fewer]____ states than Juanita.

7. Rhode Island has ____[less]____ landmass than any other state.

8. Wyoming, however, has ____[fewer]____ citizens.

9. Lake Erie has ____[fewer]____ miles of coastline than Lake Superior.

10. It also has ____[less]____ volume.

Name _____

48. Reviewing Adjectives

A. Underline the descriptive adjectives. Write **C** above the common adjectives and **P** above the proper adjectives.

1. Mary Cassatt was an **[P]** American painter.

2. A **[C]** talented artist, she was closely associated with the **[P]** French impressionists.

3. She often painted **[C]** domestic scenes.

4. Her **[C]** later paintings show the influence of **[P]** Japanese woodcuts.

5. **[C]** Official recognition came in the form of an award from the **[P]** French government.

B. Write on the line whether each *italicized* adjective is in the usual position (**U**), a subject complement (**SC**), or an object complement (**OC**).

_____[U, U]_____ 6. The *hot, dry* desert has many unusual animals.

_____[SC]_____ 7. Most desert animals are *nocturnal.*

_____[U]_____ 8. They remain in *underground* burrows during the day.

_____[OC]_____ 9. The animals find the daytime heat *intolerable.*

_____[SC]_____ 10. During the night the temperature is *cooler.*

C. Write whether each *italicized* adjective is demonstrative (**D**), possessive (**P**), indefinite (**Ind**), interrogative (**Int**), or numeral (**N**).

__[N]__ 11. John Adams was the *second* president of the United States.

[P, Ind] 12. Before *his* presidency, he held *many* political positions.

[Int] 13. In *which* city was he inaugurated?

__[D]__ 14. Philadelphia was the nation's capital at *that* time.

__[P]__ 15. During *his* term, the capital was moved to Washington, D.C.

__[N]__ 16. He was the *first* president to live in the White House.

[Ind] 17. *Each* year brought new challenges to the young country.

[P, Ind] 18. *His* son was elected president *several* years later.

__[D]__ 19. *That* circumstance has only happened twice.

__[N]__ 20. John Quincy Adams was the *sixth* president.

D. Write the comparative and the superlative forms of each adjective.

21. green   ___[greener]___   ___[greenest]___

22. slow   ___[slower]___   ___[slowest]___

23. beautiful   ___[more beautiful]___   ___[most beautiful]___

24. original   ___[more original]___   ___[most original]___

25. full   ___[fuller]___   ___[fullest]___

E. Circle the correct adjective in parentheses.

26. The blue whale is the (larger (largest)) animal that ever lived.

27. Its body is ((bigger) biggest) than that of any known dinosaur.

28. The blue whale also makes the (louder (loudest)) sound of any animal.

29. The female of the species is ((more talkative) most talkative) than the male.

30. Once threatened with extinction, blue whales now exist in ((greater) greatest) numbers.

F. Complete each sentence with *fewer* or *less.*

31. If you eat poorly, you will have ___[less]___ energy.

32. Vegetables have ___[fewer]___ calories than junk food.

33. But junk food provides ___[fewer]___ vitamins.

34. The ___[less]___ you exercise, the ___[fewer]___ calories you will burn.

35. The ___[less]___ junk food you eat, the better you will feel.

Try It Yourself

On a separate sheet of paper, write five sentences that describe an exciting event in your life. Use adjectives correctly.

Check Your Own Work

Choose a piece of writing from your portfolio or journal, a work in progress, an assignment from another class, or a letter. Revise it, applying the skills you have learned in this chapter. The checklist will help you.

✔ Have you included appropriate adjectives?

✔ Have you used the comparative forms of adjectives correctly?

✔ Have you chosen adjectives that create a clear picture for your reader?

✔ Have you used your thesaurus?

Name _____

49. Identifying Regular and Irregular Verbs

A **verb** expresses action or being. The past and past participle of a regular verb are formed by adding –d or –ed to the present form.

> **sharpen, sharpened, has sharpened**

The past and past participle of an irregular verb are not formed by adding –d or –ed to the present form.

> **eat, ate, have eaten**
> **leave, left, has left**
> **go, went, have gone**

A. Write the past and past participle of each verb. Then write whether it is regular or irregular.

	PAST	PAST PARTICIPLE	
1. wait	[waited]	[(has) waited]	[regular]
2. catch	[caught]	[(has) caught]	[irregular]
3. choose	[chose]	[(has) chosen]	[irregular]
4. return	[returned]	[(has) returned]	[regular]
5. miss	[missed]	[(has) missed]	[regular]
6. steal	[stole]	[(has) stolen]	[irregular]
7. leave	[left]	[(has) left]	[irregular]
8. haunt	[haunted]	[(has) haunted]	[regular]
9. eat	[ate]	[(has) eaten]	[irregular]
10. forget	[forgot]	[(has) forgotten]	[irregular]

B. Complete each sentence with the past or the past participle of the verb.

read   1. Have you ever _____[read]_____ any of Aesop's fables?

tell   2. Fables were _____[told]_____ to teach a useful lesson.

feel   3. Aesop _____[felt]_____ that his humorous writings would help people.

hide   4. Lessons in some fables are _____[hidden]_____.

write   5. Aesop had _____[written]_____ a story about a lion.

represent   6. In the story the lion _____[represented]_____ the king.

grow   7. He _____[grew]_____ old and could not hunt for his food.

come   8. When visitors _____[came]_____ to see him, he ate them up.

choose   9. The fox had _____[chosen]_____ not to visit the lion.

come   10. The fox believed the other animals had not _____[come]_____ out of the lion's den.

Name _____

50. Identifying Troublesome Verbs

The following pairs of verbs are easy to confuse. Learning the meaning
of each word is the best way to avoid mistakes.

teach (taught, taught) means "to give knowledge"
learn (learned, learned) means "to receive knowledge"

take (took, taken) means "to carry from a near place to a more distant place"
bring (brought, brought) means "to carry from a distant place to a near place"

lend (lent, lent) means "to let someone use something of yours"
borrow (borrowed, borrowed) means "to use something that belongs to someone else"

lie (lay, lain) means "to recline"   *sit (sat, sat)* means "to take a seat"
lay (laid, laid) means "to place"   *set (set, set)* means "to put down"

rise (rose, risen) means "to get up"   *let (let, let)* means "to allow"
raise (raised, raised) means "to lift up"   *leave (left, left)* means "to go away"

A. Circle the correct verb in each sentence.

1. Dorothy (rises, raises) before sunrise every morning.

2. I would never (let, leave) my dog eat chocolate.

3. Would you (bring, take) my book over here when you come?

4. Every experience (learns, teaches) you a lesson.

5. Charlene (borrowed, lent) me her tent when I went camping.

6. Lamont (sat, set) the pie on the counter after he baked it.

7. The hot air balloon (rose, raised) above the treetops.

8. It is too crowded to (sit, set) in the cafeteria.

9. Lou (raised, rose) the flag as the parade passed by.

10. Karen (lies, lays) on the sofa for half an hour every afternoon to watch TV.

B. Complete each sentence with the correct form of the verb.

set   1. The older students _____[set]_____ a good example for the younger ones.

lay   2. Maz _____[laid]_____ his books on the table after he got home from school.

lie   3. They have _____[lain]_____ there ever since.

leave   4. The bird had _____[left]_____ the nest after it matured.

take   5. The teacher asked, "Who has _____[taken]_____ Lenny's pencil?"

lend   6. I know you _____[lent]_____ me a dollar last week, but I am still broke.

teach   7. Regina has _____[taught]_____ her sister to play chess.

raise   8. Camille _____[raised]_____ her hand because she knew the answer.

rise   9. Johann _____[rose]_____ slowly after the bruising tackle.

bring 10. When Isabelle went to the bakery, she _____[brought]_____ me back a Danish.

51. Identifying Transitive and Intransitive Verbs

> A transitive verb expresses an action that goes from a doer to a receiver.
> It has a direct object.
>
> **Frost killed the flowers.**
>
> An intransitive verb has no receiver of the action. It does not have a direct object.
>
> **The flowers died.**

A. Underline the verbs in each sentence. If the verb is transitive, write **T** on the line. If it is intransitive, write **I**. If the verb is transitive, circle the receiver of the action.

__[I]__ 1. In the early 1800s passenger pigeons <u>numbered</u> in the billions.

__[T]__ 2. Their flocks once <u>darkened</u> the (skies)

__[I]__ 3. Less than 100 years later, they <u>became</u> extinct in the wild.

__[T]__ 4. Many factors <u>caused</u> the bird's (extinction)

__[T]__ 5. Hunting, trapping, and loss of habitat each <u>played</u> a (role)

__[I]__ 6. They <u>lived</u> in the eastern United States and Canada.

__[T]__ 7. Settlers <u>found</u> the (pigeons) an endless source of meat.

__[I]__ 8. Their feathers <u>were</u> useful in pillows and mattresses.

__[I]__ 9. Passenger pigeon populations <u>dwindled</u>.

__[I]__ 10. By 1880, the decline in numbers <u>had become</u> irreversible.

__[T]__ 11. Scientists <u>bred</u> the (birds) unsuccessfully in captivity.

__[T]__ 12. Nothing <u>could save</u> the (bird)

__[I]__ 13. The last passenger pigeon <u>died</u> in captivity in 1914.

__[I]__ 14. Today, many other species <u>are threatened</u> with extinction.

__[T]__ 15. The passenger pigeon <u>teaches</u> a valuable (lesson)

B. Some verbs can be either transitive or intransitive. Write **T** if the *italicized* verb is transitive and **I** if it is intransitive.

__[I]__ 1. Sandy sat on the porch and *read* all afternoon.

__[T]__ 2. Ken *read* "Jack and the Beanstalk" to the twins.

__[I]__ 3. Today the Cooking Club *baked,* roasted, and broiled.

__[T]__ 4. I *baked* Tom's birthday cake myself.

__[I]__ 5. We *rode* along the lakefront bike path.

52. Using Linking Verbs

A linking verb couples or links the subject with a subject complement (a noun, a pronoun, or an adjective).

It <u>is</u> she. I <u>became</u> hungry. Washington <u>was</u> president.

A. The linking verb in each sentence is *italicized.* Underline its complement. Write above the complement whether it is a noun **(N)** or an adjective **(A)**.

1. Most folk songs *are* <u>ballads</u> [N] that tell simple stories.

2. Many of these songs *are* an <u>expression</u> [N] of political or religious beliefs.

3. The composers of these songs often *remain* <u>anonymous</u> [A].

4. As the songs are passed to new generations, the melodies often *become* <u>simpler</u> [A].

5. In many songs the verses *are* a <u>story</u> [N], and a chorus is sung between them.

6. The guitar *is* the most popular <u>instrument</u> [N] used by folksingers today.

7. Many folk songs *were* work <u>songs</u> [N].

8. Other folk songs *became* simple <u>entertainment</u> [N].

9. Singers today *feel* <u>sympathetic</u> [A] toward social concerns.

10. As a source of enjoyment in many countries, folk music *remains* very <u>popular</u> [A].

B. Complete each sentence with an appropriate linking verb. **[Sample answers are given.]**

1. An opera ____[is]____ a drama set to music.

2. The texts of operas ____[are]____ sung.

3. Martin ____[became, was]____ an opera singer last year.

4. He ____[is, was]____ a lyric soprano.

5. As he ____[grows, becomes]____ older, his voice may get deeper.

6. Right now his voice ____[sounds, is]____ very high and clear.

7. He gets excited when he ____[is]____ the star of the show.

8. With his costume on, he ____[appears, looks]____ much older.

9. Martin's favorite composer ____[is]____ Mozart.

10. Mozart ____[became]____ a composer at the age of six.

Name _____

53. Using the Active and Passive Voices

Any sentence that uses a transitive verb can be written in either active or passive voice. When the subject of a verb initiates the action, the verb is in the active voice.

John Hancock <u>signed</u> the Constitution.

When the subject of the verb receives the action, the verb is in the passive voice.

The Constitution <u>was signed</u> by John Hancock.

Underline the verb in each sentence. Write **A** on the line if it is in the active voice and **P** if it is in the passive voice.

_[P]_ 1. A million tons of chocolate <u>will be consumed</u> in America this year.

_[P]_ 2. Much of this chocolate <u>is produced</u> by the Hershey Corporation.

_[A]_ 3. In 1872, at age 15, Milton Hershey <u>started</u> a candy-making apprenticeship.

_[A]_ 4. By 1886 he <u>had founded</u> a successful caramel company.

_[P]_ 5. A second company <u>was</u> soon <u>created.</u>

_[A]_ 6. This company <u>produced</u> only chocolate.

_[P]_ 7. The business <u>was located</u> in Derry Church, Pennsylvania.

_[P]_ 8. Milton Hershey <u>had been born</u> there.

_[P]_ 9. The factory <u>was completed</u> in 1905.

_[A]_ 10. An affluent community quickly <u>grew</u> around the factory.

_[P]_ 11. A year later the town <u>was renamed</u> Hershey.

_[A]_ 12. Milton Hershey <u>believed</u> advertising to be unethical.

_[P]_ 13. Instead, the factory <u>was opened</u> to the public.

_[P]_ 14. The company <u>was promoted</u> through word of mouth.

_[A]_ 15. Hershey <u>donated</u> much of his time and money to the town.

_[A]_ 16. In 1909 Hershey <u>established</u> a school for orphans.

_[P]_ 17. The school <u>was endowed</u> with stock from his company.

_[A]_ 18. The school now <u>owns</u> more than a third of the company's stock.

_[A]_ 19. Hershey <u>employs</u> many of the school's graduates.

_[A]_ 20. Today Hershey <u>produces</u> more chocolate than any other company.

54. Identifying Simple Tenses

The simple present tense tells about a simple or habitual action or condition. The simple past tense tells about an action or condition that happened in the past. The future tense tells about an action or condition that will happen in the future.

PRESENT   PAST   FUTURE
I <u>eat</u> hot dogs.   I <u>ate</u> a hot dog last night.   I <u>will eat</u> a hot dog for lunch tomorrow.

A. Underline the verb in each sentence. Write its tense on the line.

___[present]___ 1. The human body <u>contains</u> more than six hundred muscles.

___[past]___ 2. Scientists <u>discovered</u> three kinds of muscles in the body.

___[present]___ 3. These <u>are</u> the skeletal, the smooth, and the cardiac muscles.

___[present]___ 4. The cardiac muscles <u>are located</u> only in the heart.

___[present]___ 5. The skeletal muscles <u>hold</u> the skeleton together.

___[present]___ 6. Smooth muscles <u>are found</u> in the organs of the body.

___[present]___ 7. The body processes <u>are controlled</u> by these muscles.

___[future]___ 8. Muscle functions <u>will stop</u> under certain conditions.

___[past]___ 9. Sudden muscular contractions <u>caused</u> severe muscle cramps in many athletes.

___[future]___ 10. After repeated exercise and work, your muscles <u>will be</u> capable of strenuous work.

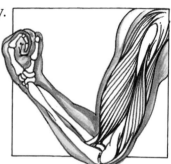

B. Complete each sentence with the correct form of the verb.

grow–*past*   1. Last summer Serena ___[grew]___ a vegetable garden.

eat–*past*   2. She ___[ate]___ fresh vegetables every day.

be–*present*   3. Vegetables ___[are]___ the edible products of herbaceous plants.

has–*present*   4. Unlike fruit, vegetables ___[have]___ a soft stem.

water–*past*   5. Serena ___[watered]___ the plants each morning.

hope–*present*   6. She ___[hopes]___ to have a garden again next year.

plant–*past*   7. Last year she ___[planted]___ carrots, potatoes, and squash.

add–*future*   8. Next summer she ___[will add]___ tomatoes and peppers.

be–*present*   9. Tomatoes ___[are]___ actually a fruit.

help–*future*   10. Her grandfather ___[will help]___ her plant the seeds.

Verbs

55. Using Progressive Verb Forms

> The progressive tenses are formed with the present participle and a form of *be*. Progressive tenses express continuing action. The present progressive tense tells about something that is happening right now.
>
> **The Tower of Pisa <u>is leaning</u>.**
>
> The past progressive tense tells about something that was happening in the past.
>
> **It <u>was leaning</u> many years ago.**
>
> The future progressive tense tells about something that will be happening in the future.
>
> **Engineers <u>will be trying</u> to stop it from leaning farther.**
>
> The perfect progressive tense tells about something that has been happening for some time.
>
> **I <u>have been working</u> in the garden all day.**
>
> **She <u>had been working</u> there for years when she heard the news.**
>
> The progressive tenses can be active or passive.

A. Complete each sentence with the progressive form of the verb.

study–*present perfect, active* 1. Scientists __[have been studying]__ the Galapagos Islands for many years.

observe–*past, active* 2. Charles Darwin __[was observing]__ the islands in 1835.

work–*past perfect, active* 3. He __[had been working]__ as a naturalist on the HMS *Beagle*.

take–*past, passive* 4. Notes __[were being taken]__ about everything Darwin saw.

find–*past, active* 5. He __[was finding]__ many unique species on the islands.

B. Underline the progressive verb phrase in each sentence. Write its tense and voice on the line.

__[present, active]__ 1. Today humans <u>are causing</u> many problems for the Galapagos.

__[past perfect, active]__ 2. The Galapagos tortoises <u>had been living</u> without natural predators.

__[past, passive]__ 3. But by the 16th century the islands <u>were being visited</u> by humans.

__[past, active]__ 4. Pirates and whalers <u>were butchering</u> the tortoises for food.

__[past, active]__ 5. Settlers <u>were</u> also <u>introducing</u> foreign species to the ecosystem.

__[present, passive]__ 6. The tortoises <u>are being endangered</u> by these new species.

__[present, active]__ 7. Dogs brought by settlers <u>are attacking</u> the defenseless animals.

__[present, active]__ 8. Goats <u>are eating</u> the plants that tortoises once fed upon.

__[future, active]__ 9. Until they are removed, goats <u>will be stripping</u> away the vegetation.

__[present, active]__ 10. Environmentalists <u>are trying</u> to preserve the Galapagos tortoise.

56. Identifying Compound Tenses

The perfect tenses are formed with the past participle and a form of *have*. The present perfect tense tells about an action that took place at an indefinite time in the past.

I have eaten breakfast.

The past perfect tense tells about a past action that happened before another past action.

I had eaten breakfast before I left for school.

The future perfect tells about an action that will be completed before a specific time in the future.

I will have eaten breakfast by that time.

A. Underline the verb in each sentence. Write its tense on the line.

[present perfect] 1. It has been a century since Teddy Roosevelt's inauguration.

[past perfect] 2. He had served as William McKinley's vice president.

[past perfect] 3. After only months into his term, McKinley had been assassinated.

[past perfect] 4. At 42, Roosevelt had become the youngest president ever.

[present perfect] 5. He has remained the youngest president in U.S. history.

[past perfect] 6. In 1905 he had negotiated a treaty for the Russo-Japanese War.

[past perfect] 7. The Grand Canyon had been named a National Monument by him.

[present perfect] 8. This park has been preserved since 1893.

[future perfect] 9. By December millions of tourists will have visited the park.

[present perfect] 10. Roosevelt's conservation policies have continued to be influential.

B. Complete each sentence with the correct form of the verb.

remain–*present perfect* 1. Charlie Chaplin ___[has remained]___ popular for nearly a century.

study–*present perfect* 2. We ___[have studied]___ his films in our history class.

move–*past perfect* 3. A native of England, Chaplin ___[had moved]___ to Hollywood by 1910.

star–*past perfect* 4. By 1957 he ___[had starred]___ in more than seventy films.

see–*present perfect* 5. Our teacher ___[has seen]___ every one.

watch–*future perfect* 6. We ___[will have watched]___ *City Lights* by tomorrow.

knight–*past perfect* 7. By 1975 the British government ___[had knighted]___ him.

become–*past perfect* 8. After many years Chaplin ___[had become]___ an icon.

begin–*past perfect* 9. Knighthood is a significant achievement for a performer who ___[had begun]___ as a mime.

continue–*present perfect* 10. Chaplin ___[has continued]___ to enthrall audiences ever since.

Verbs

57. Understanding the Indicative Mood

> The indicative mood is used to state a fact or ask about a fact.
>
> **Our family vacationed in New England.**
>
> **Have you ever been to the ocean?**

Underline the verb in each sentence. Write on the line whether the verb makes a statement or asks a question.

_____[question]_____ 1. Has your class studied the Constitution?

_____[statement]_____ 2. We learned about it today in social studies.

_____[statement]_____ 3. The U.S. Constitution is the world's oldest constitution still in force.

_____[question]_____ 4. How old is the U.S. Constitution?

_____[statement]_____ 5. It was adopted officially on March 4, 1789.

_____[question]_____ 6. Has the Constitution ever been revised?

_____[statement]_____ 7. It has been amended 27 times since 1789.

_____[statement]_____ 8. In the first two years alone, it was amended ten times.

_____[statement]_____ 9. The first ten amendments are known as the Bill of Rights.

_____[question]_____ 10. Are these amendments still enforced?

_____[statement]_____ 11. The Bill of Rights remains intact today.

_____[statement]_____ 12. These amendments protect many of our most basic rights.

_____[question]_____ 13. How do the amendments protect us?

_____[statement]_____ 14. The first amendment guarantees the freedom of speech.

_____[statement]_____ 15. The seventh assures trial by jury in civil cases.

_____[question]_____ 16. When was the last amendment added to the Constitution?

_____[statement]_____ 17. The 27th amendment was passed in 1992.

_____[statement]_____ 18. It will likely be revised further in the future.

_____[question]_____ 19. Why does the Constitution allow for such changes?

_____[statement]_____ 20. Much of the Constitution's strength is derived from its flexibility.

Verbs

58. Using Emphatic Verb Forms and Modal Auxiliaries

> The emphatic form is used to give emphasis to the verb. The emphatic simple present is formed by adding *do* before the base form of the verb.
>
> > **I do want to go to the prom.**
>
> The emphatic simple past is formed by adding *did* before the base form of the verb.
>
> > **You did hear we have a test today.**
>
> The modal auxiliaries *may, might, can, could, must, should,* and *would* are used to express permission, possibility, ability, necessity, or obligation.
>
> > **You should have studied for the test.**

A. Underline the emphatic verb form. Write the tense on the line; use **A** for present tense; **B** for past tense.

__[B]__ 1. I did study the material before the test.

__[A]__ 2. Football players do injure themselves occasionally.

__[B]__ 3. Sandor did work all summer for the bicycle.

__[B]__ 4. After his heart attack, he did try to eat more healthfully.

__[B]__ 5. My sister did teach kindergarten for several years.

__[A]__ 6. When she reads, she does wear glasses.

__[A]__ 7. Since they lost the game, the team does try harder.

__[A]__ 8. All the students do appreciate the work of their teacher.

__[B]__ 9. Luigi did get nauseated after he ate the clams.

__[A]__ 10. I do wonder why he always wears that long jacket.

B. Underline the modal auxiliary. Write on the line whether it expresses permission, possibility, ability, necessity, or obligation.

__[permission]__ 1. In a democracy voters may decide who their leader will be.

__[obligation]__ 2. In Australia every eligible citizen must vote.

__[permission]__ 3. Americans, however, may choose whether they wish to vote.

__[obligation]__ 4. Every citizen should vote on election day.

__[possibility]__ 5. Ignatius might be out of the country on that day.

__[ability]__ 6. He could cast an absentee ballot.

__[permission]__ 7. Any U.S. citizen above 18 may participate in an election.

__[ability]__ 8. At one time only white males could vote.

__[ability]__ 9. Now citizens of all colors and genders can vote.

__[necessity]__ 10. For a democracy to work, every vote must be counted.

Name _____

59. Identifying the Imperative and the Subjunctive Moods

> The imperative mood is used to give commands. To form a command in the second person, use the simple present tense of the verb. To form a command in the first person plural, use *let's* or *let me*. To form a command in the third person, use *let*.
>
> **Tell him your name.**
> **Let's tell him what we did.**
> **Don't let anyone think he or she can fool the teacher.**
>
> The subjunctive mood is used to express a wish or desire, an uncertainty, or a condition contrary to fact, or a command after *that*. The modal auxiliaries and the subordinate conjunctions *if, as if, provided, though, whether,* and *unless* sometimes introduce a verb in the subjunctive.
>
> **I wish that the prize were [not *was*] ours already.**
> **Whether he be [not *is*] guilty or not, he deserves a fair trial.**
> **If Jackson were [not *was*] single, I would move to California.**

Verbs

A. Write on the line whether the *italicized* verb is in the subjunctive or the imperative mood.

[sub.] 1. If I *were* to go with you, I couldn't work tonight.

[sub.] 2. Chan has a car and has proposed that Sam *use* it for errands.

[sub.] 3. If his arms *were* not so short, he would be a great swimmer.

[imp.] 4. If you go out, *wear* your snow pants.

[sub.] 5. If we *lived* here, we would be home by now.

[imp.] 6. *Stay* out of my room, Curtis.

[sub.] 7. I wish we *had* dessert with every meal.

[imp.] 9. *Read* the directions carefully.

[imp.] 8. *Pick* up your toys, Christina.

[sub.] 10. Dale insisted that he *be allowed* to go home early.

B. Circle each verb in the imperative mood. Underline each verb in the subjunctive mood. Write on the line what each sentence expresses.

[contrary to fact] 1. If I were Brenda, I would not miss any more school.

[wish] 2. May you have good luck on the test today.

[command] 3. Always (walk) in the hallway.

[wish] 4. I wish I could play the piano like Glenn.

[contrary to fact] 5. Every time we have a test, he acts as if he were sick.

[uncertainty] 6. "If this be treason, make the most of it!" cried Patrick Henry.

[command] 7. (Rise) quietly in the morning.

[wish] 8. I preferred that Owen invite me to the dance.

[command] 9. Please (keep) your voices down.

[contrary to fact] 10. If it were possible, I would have visited Valley Forge.

60. Making Subjects and Verbs Agree

A verb always agrees with its subject. Except for the verb *be*, the only time a change is needed is in the present tense of a third person singular subject.

The man <u>rides</u> a bicycle.

The men <u>ride</u> bicycles.

Sometimes a phrase comes between the subject and the verb. However, the verb must agree with the subject, not the phrase.

The dog, like many other pets, <u>gets</u> fleas.

A meal of potatoes and hot dogs <u>is</u> filling.

A. Complete each sentence with the correct form of the present tense of the verb.

bring   1. Olympic events ____[bring]____ together the world's finest athletes.

bear   2. Couriers ____[bear]____ a lighted torch from the valley of Olympia, Greece.

carry   3. The final runner ____[carries]____ the torch into the stadium.

light   4. Here the runner ____[lights]____ the Olympic Flame to open the games.

burn   5. This flame ____[burns]____ until the end of the games.

B. Circle the correct form of the verb in parentheses.

1. The 1936 Olympic competition, held in Berlin, (was) were) emotionally tense.

2. Imagine the year is 1936 and Adolf Hitler (lead (leads)) Germany.

3. Hitler, the leader of the Nazis, (want (wants)) his athletes to win.

4. It is Jesse Owens, however, who (is) are) the star of the Olympics.

5. Owens, among the first African-American U.S. Olympians, (win (wins)) three solo gold medals.

6. He and his other team members also (triumph) triumphs) in the 100 meter relay.

7. Owens and the other Americans (shatter) shatters) the Nazi leader's hopes.

8. The image of Owens decorated with four gold medals (was) were) an inspiration to persecuted people everywhere.

9. After the Olympics, Owens (was) were) active in youth athletic programs.

10. Owens, one of the world's great athletes, (remains) remain) a source of inspiration.

Jesse Owens inspired people everywhere with his courage and determination. What inspires you? Write about how another person has inspired you.

61. Using Doesn't and Don't Correctly

The correct use of *doesn't* and *don't* can be confusing. If the subject of the sentence is in the third person singular, use *doesn't.*

Lucy doesn't care.

Use *don't* if the subject is third person plural.

Lucy's friends don't care.

If the subject of the sentence is the first or second person, the correct form is *don't,* whether the subject is singular or plural:

I don't care. We don't care. You don't care.

A. Circle the correct form of the verb in parentheses.

1. I (doesn't (don't)) remember who she is.

2. Most Americans (doesn't (don't)) work on Labor Day.

3. Why ((doesn't) don't) Anita drink her tea while it's hot?

4. My mother ((doesn't) don't) want me to stay up late.

5. We (doesn't (don't)) have a blender.

6. Nina ((doesn't) don't) have to practice on Saturday.

7. You (doesn't (don't)) need to read chapter seven.

8. Mr. Esposito ((doesn't) don't) have any children.

9. ((Doesn't) Don't) Jerry know he shouldn't wear his hat inside the house?

10. Those three dogs (doesn't (don't)) belong to Randy.

B. Complete each sentence with *doesn't* or *don't.*

1. A rainbow ____[doesn't]____ always appear after it rains.

2. Carmen ____[doesn't]____ have enough time to see a movie.

3. We ____[don't]____ want to spend our vacation in Antarctica.

4. Sid realized he ____[doesn't]____ look like Abraham Lincoln.

5. The security guard ____[doesn't]____ allow anyone in after six.

6. We ____[don't]____ care if she has ever played baseball before.

7. ____[Don't]____ you have any homework tonight?

8. Tina and Harriet ____[don't]____ want to miss the concert.

9. The dress ____[doesn't]____ have to be blue.

10. I ____[don't]____ want to hear any more about your stamp collection.

62. Making Compound Subjects and Verbs Agree

Compound subjects connected by *and* usually require a plural verb. However, if the subjects connected by *and* refer to the same person, place, or thing, or express a single idea, the subject is considered singular.

Chickens and ducks <u>are</u> both poultry.

Ham and eggs <u>is</u> my favorite breakfast.

A. **Circle the correct form of the verb in parentheses.**

1. Rock and roll (is are) a style of music that originated in America in the 1950s.

2. Many adults and children (was were) shocked by this new form of music.

3. Jazz and country music (was were) incorporated into rock and roll.

4. But rhythm and blues (is are) considered its main influence.

5. Bill Haley and the Comets (was were) one of the first successful acts.

6. "Shake, Rattle, and Roll" (was were) probably their biggest hit.

7. Chuck Berry and Fats Domino (was were) also popular singers.

8. The most famous singer and performer (was were) Elvis Presley.

9. This musician and actor (remain remains) popular today.

10. *Frankie and Johnny* (is are) but one of the movies Elvis starred in.

B. **Complete each sentence with *is* or *are*.**

1. Macaroni and cheese ____[is]____ a popular side dish.

2. Macaroni and cheese ____[are]____ the two main ingredients in the casserole.

3. "To serve and protect" ____[is]____ the motto of our police department.

4. Serving and protecting ____[are]____ worthy goals of any police officer.

5. Fox and Geese ____[is]____ an old children's game.

6. The fox and the geese ____[are]____ making a ruckus in the barnyard.

7. *Bob and Ray* ____[is]____ an old radio program.

8. Bob and Ray ____[are]____ the names of two radio personalities.

9. Stars and stripes ____[are]____ painted all over Jessica's toy chest.

10. ____[Is]____ "Stars and Stripes" going to be played at the veterans' ceremony?

Name _____

63. Making Verbs and Subjects Preceded by Each, Every, Many a, or No Agree

> When two or more singular subjects connected by *and* are preceded by *each, every, many a,* or *no,* the verb is singular.
>
> **Each cat and dog is checked for ticks.**
>
> If two or more singular subjects are <u>followed</u> by the word *each,* the verb is plural.
>
> **The dog and cat each have ticks.**

A. Circle the correct form of the verb in parentheses.

1. Every man, woman, and child (has̲ have) heard of Bigfoot.

2. Each report and piece of evidence (feed feeds̲) the public's imagination.

3. The Himalayan Yeti and the Canadian Sasquatch each (fit̲ fits) the description.

4. No culture or society (is̲ are) without some form of this legend.

5. Russian folklore, Greek mythology, and Anglo-Saxon fables each (has have̲) a similar figure.

6. Many a scientist and investigator (doubt doubts̲) the existence of Bigfoot.

7. Each photograph and sighting (is̲ are) examined.

8. Every bird and mammal (leave leaves̲) some trace behind.

9. A family says every story and report (was̲ were) false.

10. They say each footprint and sound attributed to Bigfoot (was̲ were) created by a family member.

B. Complete each sentence with the correct form of the present tense of the verb.

has   1. Many a clam and oyster __[has]__ been found in that bay.

is   2. Every mother and father __[is]__ coming to the play.

walk   3. Each student and teacher __[walks]__ outside when the alarm bell rings.

show   4. Every boy and girl here __[shows]__ signs of improvement.

is   5. At the airport every bag and box __[is]__ inspected.

has   6. The football team and the soccer team each __[have]__ pep rallies.

bring   7. Every friend and relative __[brings]__ a present.

has   8. No child or adult __[has]__ received a ticket to the fair.

need   9. The lion and the tiger each __[need]__ a separate cage.

read   10. Many a teacher and student __[reads]__ the school paper.

Name _____

64. Making Verbs and Compound Subjects Connected by <u>Or</u> and <u>Nor</u> Agree

> When a compound subject is joined by *or* or *nor,* the verb agrees with the subject nearest to it.
>
> **Neither the dog nor the cats are inside.**
> **Neither the cats nor the dog is inside.**

A. Circle the correct form of the verb in parentheses.

1. Neither the lunch nor the dinner (come (comes)) with dessert.

2. ((Was) Were) either Muriel or Pedro at the wedding?

3. Neither he nor I ((work) works) on Sunday.

4. Either Mr. Anderson or you (is (are)) responsible.

5. Neither the gas bill nor the electric bill ((was) were) mailed on time.

6. Either my grandparents or my father (pick (picks)) me up from school.

7. Neither the horse's feet nor its legs (was (were)) injured when it fell.

8. Neither the pillows nor the mattress (arrive (arrives)) today.

9. Either Logan or I (has (have)) to baby-sit Veronica.

10. Neither the teacher nor the students ((know) knows) who will be selected.

B. Complete each sentence with the correct form of the present tense of the verb.

is   1. Either the tuna or the mayonnaise _____[is]_____ rancid.

watch   2. Neither he nor I ___[watch]___ television on weeknights.

is   3. Neither Madeline nor her friends ___[are]___ going to the meeting.

feed   4. Either Walter or his daughters ___[feed]___ the fish when I am away.

read   5. Neither the man nor his wife ___[reads]___ the newspaper.

like   6. Neither I nor my brother ___[likes]___ taking tests.

walk   7. Either Homer or I ___[walk]___ the dog before school.

know   8. Neither the players nor their coach ___[knows]___ how to get to the stadium.

match   9. Either the hat or the gloves ___[match]___ her coat.

smell   10. Neither the trainer nor his animals ___[smell]___ bad.

Name _____

65. Making Collective Nouns and Verbs Agree

A collective noun names a *group: audience, team, family.* A collective noun that is thought of as a unit requires a singular verb.

The orchestra is practicing.

Use a plural verb if the collective noun denotes separate individuals not operating as one unit.

The orchestra are tuning their instruments.

A. Circle the correct form of the verb in parentheses.

1. The choir (is) are) not back from its concert tour to New England and Canada.

2. The faculty (was (were)) debating all sides of the issue.

3 The faculty ((was) were) unanimous in its decision.

4. The French club (meet (meets)) in the library after school on Wednesday.

5. The jury ((has) have) been selected by the attorneys.

6. His family (is (are)) currently living in Florida and Georgia.

7. Congress ((was) were) in session all week.

8. The flock of birds ((flies) fly) north after the summer ends.

9. The team ((was) were) operating as smoothly as a Swiss watch.

10. The audience ((have) has) taken their seats, and now the concert is about to begin.

B. Write sentences using the collective noun as subject.
[Answers will vary. Sample answers are given.]

club 1. [The gaming club is less popular with the older kids.]

team 2. [The team have milkshakes or root beer floats after practice.]

herd 3. [The herd of cattle grazes on the prairie.]

band 4. [Paul's band was quite famous.]

group 5. [A group of teachers meets in the library every week.]

Name _____

66. Making Indefinite Pronouns and Verbs Agree

An **indefinite pronoun** points out no particular person, place, or thing. The pronouns *each, either, neither, one, anyone, no one, anybody, nobody, someone, somebody, every,* and compounds with *every* are always singular and require a singular verb:

Each person <u>lives</u> in an apartment. **Nobody** <u>lives</u> in a house.

A. Underline the subject in each sentence. Circle the correct form of the verb in parentheses.

1. <u>Everyone</u> in Basil and Manuel's class (ⓘs are) going on a field trip.

2. <u>Neither</u> of them (ⓗas have) turned in his permission slip.

3. <u>Everyone</u> in their class (get ⓖets) to see the Guggenheim Museum.

4. <u>Anyone</u> who forgets his or her permission slip (ⓘs are) not allowed to go.

5. <u>Each</u> of the students who (remember ⓡemembers) gets to go.

6. <u>No one</u> (want ⓦants) to miss this trip.

7. <u>Everyone</u> in the class (know ⓚnows) that Frank Lloyd Wright designed the museum.

8. <u>One</u> of the 20th century's greatest architects (ⓘs are) Frank Lloyd Wright.

9. <u>Each</u> of his buildings (remain ⓡemains) influential.

10. <u>Anyone</u> who goes to the museum (know ⓚnows) it is a work of art in itself.

B. Underline the subject in each sentence. Complete each sentence with the correct form of the present tense of the verb at left.

play
1. <u>Nobody</u> _____[plays]_____ as well as Diego.

bring
2. <u>Someone</u> _____[brings]_____ Maria the newspaper every day.

be
3. <u>Neither</u> of the dogs _____[is]_____ tired of playing.

ride
4. In Europe <u>everyone</u> _____[rides]_____ a bicycle.

prepare
5. <u>Someone</u> different _____[prepares]_____ dinner each night.

goes
6. The night before a test, <u>everybody</u> _____[goes]_____ to bed early.

have
7. <u>Anyone</u> who _____[has]_____ more than one serving will be in trouble.

need
8. <u>One</u> of these cakes _____[needs]_____ icing.

appear
9. <u>Nobody</u> _____[appears]_____ to have watered the vegetables.

want
10. <u>No one</u> _____[wants]_____ to drink water from that pond.

67. Solving Special Agreement Problems

> Some nouns are plural in form but singular in meaning. Some of these nouns are *measles, mathematics, mumps, news, ethics, physics, molasses,* and *economics.* In a sentence these nouns require a singular verb.
>
> **The <u>news</u> <u>is</u> terrible.**
>
> Other nouns are used only in the plural, for example, *ashes, clothes, eaves, goods, pincers, pliers, proceeds, scissors, shears, suspenders, glasses, scales, thanks, tongs, trousers,* and *tweezers.* These nouns require a plural verb.
>
> **<u>Thanks</u> <u>are</u> in order.**

A. **Underline the subject in each sentence. Circle the correct verb in parentheses.**

1. The <u>tweezers</u> (go) goes) in the medicine cabinet.

2. <u>Molasses</u> (taste (tastes)) good on pancakes and waffles.

3. The <u>ashes</u> from the fireplace (have) has) not been removed.

4. The garden <u>shears</u> (make) makes) the job a lot easier.

5. The <u>eaves</u> on the guest house (was (were)) painted last summer.

6. Bernadette's <u>clothes</u> (give) gives) her a formal appearance.

7. Diego's <u>suspenders</u> (keep) keeps) his pants from falling down.

8. <u>News</u> (spread (spreads)) quickly in this modern electronic age.

9. The <u>proceeds</u> from the bake sale (was (were)) used to buy new uniforms.

10. Abby's <u>glasses</u> (need) needs) to be fixed.

B. **Complete each sentence with *is* or *are.***

1. The pliers _____[are]_____ in the toolbox.

2. Safety scissors _____[are]_____ better for young children.

3. Civics _____[is]_____ an interesting and important subject for children to study.

4. Rupert's slacks _____[are]_____ made out of linen.

5. Mumps _____[is]_____ an infectious disease.

6. Thanks _____[are]_____ due to our parents for their kindness and support.

7. Those rusty tongs _____[are]_____ of no use to anyone.

8. Mathematics _____[is]_____ Dejuan's favorite subject.

9. Emma's clothes _____[are]_____ in need of ironing.

10. The news _____[is]_____ coming on at six.

68. Reviewing Subject-Verb Agreement

A. Complete each sentence with the correct form of the present tense of the verb.

consist   1. The U.S. government _____[consists]_____ of three branches.

be   2. These branches _____[are]_____ the legislative, the executive, and the judicial.

be   3. Each of the three branches _____[is]_____ accountable to the others.

call   4. We _____[call]_____ this a system of checks and balances.

help   5. This system _____[helps]_____ to maintain the balance of power.

include   6. The judicial branch _____[includes]_____ the federal courts.

hear   7. These courts _____[hear]_____ cases that challenge our laws.

be   8. The Supreme Court _____[is]_____ the highest federal court.

nominate   9. The president _____[nominates]_____ Supreme Court justices.

serve   10. A Supreme Court justice _____[serves]_____ for life.

B. Circle the correct form of the verb in parentheses.

1. Congress, which has two chambers, (make (makes)) up the legislative branch.

2. These (is (are)) the Senate and the House of Representatives.

3. Voters (elect) elects) the members of Congress who will represent their state.

4. The House, which has 435 seats, (hold (holds)) elections every two years.

5. Senators (serve) serves) six-year terms.

6. Each state (has) have) two senators.

7. State population (determine (determines)) membership in the House.

8. The president (head (heads)) the executive branch.

9. Voters (decide) decides) who the president will be.

10. A president's term (last (lasts)) four years.

Verbs

Name _____

69. Reviewing Verbs

A. Underline the verb in each sentence. On the first line write **T** if the verb is transitive or **I** if it is intransitive. On the second line write **A** if the verb is active or **P** if it is passive.

[I]   [A]   1. Some animals <u>migrate</u> every year.

[T]   [A]   2. Pacific salmon <u>take</u> a lifetime to complete their migration.

[I]   [P]   3. These fish <u>are born</u> in freshwater streams.

[I]   [A]   4. They then <u>travel</u> to the ocean.

[I]   [A]   5. Each fish then <u>returns</u> to the stream
        it was born in to mate before dying.

B. Underline the linking verb in each sentence. Circle the subject complement.

6. There <u>are</u> different (reasons) why animals migrate.

7. Irruption <u>is</u> an unpredictable (form) of migration.

8. Lemmings <u>are</u> an (example) of an animal
   that migrates in this manner.

9. Many scientists <u>are</u> (intent) on studying irruption.

10. Animal migration <u>is</u> (hard) for scientists to track.

C. Complete each sentence with the correct form of the verb.

study–*present progressive, active*   11. June's class ___[is studying]___ animal migration.

taught–*present perfect, passive*   12. They ___[have been taught]___ many interesting facts.

visit–*future, active*   13. They ___[will visit]___ the Columbia River
        next semester.

migrate–*future progressive, active*   14. The Chinook salmon ___[will be migrating]___
        by that time.

travels–*present, active*   15. This salmon ___[travels]___ more than
        2,000 miles to spawn.

D. Write whether the *italicized* verb is in the progressive or the emphatic form.

___[emphatic]___   16. He *does understand* the assignment.

___[progressive]___   17. Dabney *has been playing* soccer for three seasons.

___[progressive]___   18. The students *are working* on their homework.

___[emphatic]___   19. Delphine *did take* the bus to school today.

___[progressive]___   20. The zookeeper *is feeding* the elephants.

Verbs

CONTINUED

75

E. Write on the line the mood of the *italicized* verb. Use **A** for indicative, **B** for imperative, and **C** for subjunctive.

__[B]__ 21. *Return* these books to the library.

__[C]__ 22. Lamont wishes he *were* already on vacation.

__[A]__ 23. My sister *is reading* a scary book.

__[C]__ 24. If Emily *were* here, she would know what to do.

__[A]__ 25. Nathan *can walk* to school if he chooses.

F. Circle the correct verb in parentheses.

26. The team (is) are) meeting before the game.

27. The team (has) have) to win to advance in the tournament.

28. Each of the players (want (wants)) to do well.

29. Neither of the captains (know (knows)) whom the team is playing yet.

30. After the game was over, everyone (raised (rose)) to leave.

Try It Yourself

On a separate sheet of paper write five sentences about something you and your friends do. Be sure to use verbs correctly.

Check Your Own Work

Choose a selection from your writing portfolio, your journal, a work in progress, an assignment from school, or a letter. Revise it, applying the skills you have learned in this chapter. The checklist will help you.

✔ Have you conveyed the meaning clearly and accurately by using the correct form of the verb?

✔ Have you written the correct form of the troublesome verbs?

✔ Have you used verb tense correctly?

Name _____

70. Identifying Participles

> A present or past **participle** can be used to modify a noun.
>
> **The cat <u>chasing</u> the mouse grew tired.**
>
> **The cat, <u>having chased</u> the mouse, was tired.**

Underline the participle in each sentence. Circle the word it modifies.

1. <u>Walking</u> at night, (Kay) often sees shooting stars.

2. <u>Streaking</u> across the sky, (shooting stars) are a magnificent sight.

3. A small (body) <u>entering</u> a planet's atmosphere from outer space is called a meteor.

4. Brilliant (meteors,) <u>known</u> as fireballs, are quite dramatic.

5. They are often followed by a (trail) of light <u>lasting</u> minutes.

6. (Some) <u>called</u> bolides, have even been observed to explode like thunder.

7. <u>Dissipating</u> in flight, most (meteors) fall to earth as dust.

8. A (meteor) <u>reaching</u> a planet in one piece is called a meteorite.

9. (Kay,) <u>listening</u> in class, learned that comets break up and form meteors.

10. Asteroids and comets are small solid (objects) <u>orbiting</u> the sun.

11. The three largest known (asteroids,) <u>called</u> Ceres, Pallas, and Vesta, are found in a single asteroid belt.

12. <u>Located</u> between Mars and Jupiter, (they) do not pose a threat to Earth.

13. (Some) however, <u>intersecting</u> Earth's orbit, could be dangerous.

14. A giant (asteroid) may once have hit the earth, <u>striking</u> the Yucatan Peninsula.

15. The (Yucatan,) <u>located</u> in Mexico, is marked by a giant crater.

16. (Scientists,) <u>dating</u> the crater, say it struck some 65 million years ago.

17. <u>Coinciding</u> with the end of the dinosaurs, (it) is believed by some to have killed them off.

18. Another (comet) that size <u>hitting</u> Earth could be catastrophic.

19. (Earth) <u>colliding</u> with an asteroid has become a common movie plot.

20. But the odds of an (asteroid) <u>striking</u> the planet are actually quite miniscule.

71. Identifying Participial Adjectives

> A participle used as an adjective can come before a noun or after a linking verb.
> **Do not cry over spilled milk.**

A. Underline the participial adjective in each sentence.
Circle the word it modifies.

1. The melting (icicle) fell from the gutter.

2. It is dangerous to drive fast on the winding (road).

3. The dentist pulled my aching (tooth).

4. It is important to watch for falling (rocks) while climbing.

5. The battle of Gettysburg was a turning (point) in the Civil War.

6. The growling (dog) scared off the hoodlums.

7. Simon had only one misspelled (word) in his paper.

8. We must repair that broken (window).

9. A disturbing (figure) appeared at Mabel's door.

10. Chan threw out the chipped (plate).

11. The baby chick emerged from the cracked (egg).

12. The branches of the weeping (willow)
    swayed gracefully in the breeze.

13. The sound of running (water) attracted the deer to the water's edge.

14. We listened to the exciting (story).

15. The written (word) is an important link to the past.

B. Use each phrase in a sentence. Underline each participial adjective.
Circle the noun it modifies. **[Sample answers are given.]**

raging storm   1. **[The boat got caught in the raging (storm).]** _____

retired athlete   2. **[The retired (athlete) became a used-car salesman.]** _____

purring cat   3. **[It is nice to come home to a purring (cat).]** _____

freezing rain   4. **[School was cancelled because of the freezing (rain).]** _____

known facts   5. **[The detective evaluates all the known (facts) before arriving at conclusions.]** _____

72. Identifying and Correcting Dangling Participles

A participle is used as an adjective and therefore modifies a noun or a pronoun. A participle that does not modify another word in the sentence is called a **dangling participle.**

> **Working for days, the paper was completed.**

Specifying the noun the participle modifies helps in correcting a dangling participle.

> **Working for days, the student completed the paper.**

A. Write **C** to the left of those sentences in which the participle is correctly used. Underline the participle and circle the word it modifies.

__[C]__   1. Sitting at the table, (we) were served pancakes and milk.

_____   Sitting at the table, pancakes and milk were served.

_____   2. Walking along the beach, there was a beautiful sunset.

__[C]__   Walking along the beach, (I) saw a beautiful sunset.

_____   3. Nursing an injury, the performance was terrible.

__[C]__   Nursing an injury, the (dancer) performed terribly.

__[C]__   4. Lacking the money, (John) did not buy the bicycle.

_____   Lacking the money, the bicycle remained unpurchased.

_____   5. Having eaten ice cream already, the lunch remained untouched.

__[C]__   Having eaten ice cream already, (Eve) left her lunch untouched.

B. Rewrite the following sentences to avoid the dangling participle. **[Sample answers are given.]**

1. Climbing out of the pool, the beach chair came into view.
   [Climbing out of the pool, we saw the beach chair.]

2. Reaching into the refrigerator, the milk was taken out.
   [Reaching into the refrigerator, she took the milk out.]

3. Reading all night, the book was finished.
   [Reading all night, Leonard finished the book.]

4. Jogging early in the morning, the cool breeze is refreshing.
   [Jogging early in the morning, she found the cool breeze refreshing.]

5. Standing at the chalkboard, the lesson was presented by the teacher.
   [Standing at the chalkboard, the teacher presented the lesson.]

Participles, Gerunds, Infinitives

73. Using Gerunds as Subjects

> A **gerund** is a verb form ending in *–ing* that is used as a noun. A gerund may be used as the subject of a sentence.
>
> **Exercising is good for your health.**
>
> Like a verb, a gerund may have a direct object and may be modified by an adverb. A gerund phrase may be used as the subject of a sentence.
>
> **Running marathons is hard work.**

A. Circle the gerund(s) in each sentence. Underline the gerund phrase.

1. (Catching) fish is fun.
2. (Baiting) the hook is not as much fun.
3. (Threading) a worm on a hook requires patience.
4. (Selecting) a flashy lure is cleaner.
5. (Making) lures with exotic feathers is a popular hobby.
6. For some, (rowing) the boat is the best part of fishing.
7. (Being) outside is enough for others.
8. For my father (chasing) the big one is the goal.
9. (Cooking) and (eating) the fish are my mother's favorite part.
10. (Identifying) the names of fish is as close as I want to get.

B. Write sentences using the gerund or gerund phrase as a subject. **[Sentences will vary.]**

walking around the track	1.	[Walking around the track is good exercise.]
exercising	2.	
drinking milk	3.	
listening	4.	
eating balanced meals	5.	
competing in organized sports	6.	
warming up	7.	
cooling down	8.	
sleeping	9.	
enjoying games	10.	

74. Using Gerunds as Direct Objects

A gerund may be used as the direct object in a sentence.

Sara dislikes painting.

A gerund may also take a direct object.

Shawn enjoys reviewing movies.

A. Underline the gerund phrase in each sentence. Draw an additional line under the gerund if it is used as the direct object. Write **DO** over any word that is the direct object of a gerund.

EXAMPLE: **The workers began laying the foundation.**
                                                    DO

1. The master carver has started carving the limestone columns **[DO]** with a chisel and mallet.

2. Carvers and workers began building the Cathedral of Saint **[DO]** John the Divine in New York more than one hundred years ago.

3. Have the quarriers finished cutting all the limestone needed? **[DO]**

4. World War II prevented their working.

5. In the 1970s the Very Reverend James Parks Morton suggested starting construction again. **[DO]**

6. Masonry draftsmen like studying the original plans. **[DO]**

7. The plans suggest making templates for each block of stone. **[DO]**

8. A special arrangement specifies hiring young people as apprentices. **[DO]**

9. Laws forbid working without protective gear.

10. I have enjoyed watching the cathedral take shape over the years. **[DO]**

B. Use a gerund phrase from the list to complete each sentence. Your gerund phrase will be the direct object in each sentence. **[Sentences will vary.]**

running three times around the track
selling tickets for the tournament
reading about the sport you like first

comparing our scores and the pros'
going to away games by car or bus

1. The team has started _____.

2. Do you prefer _____?

3. Try _____.

4. The bowling coach enjoys _____.

5. My coach's workout includes _____.

Participles, Gerunds, Infinitives

81

Name _____

75. Using Gerunds as Subject Complements

A gerund may be used as a subject complement.

Mom's hobby is sewing. Dad's is gardening indoors. *(gerund phrase)*

Remember that a subject complement completes the meaning of a linking verb.
Common linking verbs include *seem, be, appear,* and *feel.*

A. Underline the gerund phrase in each sentence. Draw an additional line under the gerund if it is used as the subjective complement. Write **DO** over any word that is the direct object of a gerund.

EXAMPLE: **My job at home is washing the dishes.** [DO]

1. Every Sunday my favorite treat is reading the newspaper. [DO]

2. My first activity is scanning the headlines. [DO]

3. A good clue to his chief interest would be his poring over the sports pages.

4. My favorite thing could never be scouring the want ads. [DO]

5. A favorite pastime did become checking the entertainment scene. [DO]

6. My mother's response to the editorial this week was writing her own letter. [DO]

7. Entertainment for me is laughing over the antics in my favorite comic strip.

8. Sadness for me is realizing there will be no new Peanuts cartoons.

9. The biggest challenge now is earning enough money for home delivery. [DO]

10. Our neighbor's favorite joke is hiding the newspaper somewhere near the house. [DO]

B. Complete each sentence with a phrase that contains a gerund.
Your gerund will be the subject complement of your sentence. **[Answers will vary.]**

1. Her favorite kind of cooking is _____.

2. Her least favorite kind of cooking is _____.

3. One of her best techniques is _____.

4. Her most famous method for cooking meat is _____.

5. One source of relaxation for her is _____.

6. What upset her was _____.

7. What I don't understand is _____.

8. Her greatest joy as a chef is _____.

9. The hardest part of being a chef is _____.

10. The main job of a restaurant chef is _____.

76. Using Gerunds as Objects of Prepositions

> A gerund may be used as the object of a preposition.
> **Our job starts with cleaning the gym.**

A. Underline the gerund phrase(s) in each sentence. Draw an additional line under the gerund if it is used as the object of a preposition. Circle the preposition that introduces the gerund phrase.

EXAMPLE: **Have you read (about) his winning the boat race?**

1. Being kind is one way (of) helping others.

2. The art (of) caring deeply is not acquired all at once.

3. Nothing great was ever accomplished (without) working hard.

4. We can improve our world (by) working for peace.

5. I'm angry at Al (for) buying violent toys.

6. Conflict resolution is a way (of) solving differences peacefully.

7. Have you read (about) her negotiating the peace treaty?

8. She was exhausted (from) talking.

9. We are indebted to the group (for) supporting her efforts.

10. She impressed the president (by) describing the difficult situation in a simple way.

B. Use a gerund phrase from the list to complete each sentence. Your sentence will have a gerund as the object of a preposition. Add other words to fill out the sentence if you wish. **[Sentences will vary.]**

through writing	**in answering**	**for singing**
from eating	**by studying**	

1. He was slow _____.

2. She was known _____.

3. You can learn _____.

4. We can improve _____.

5. He was sick _____.

77. Using Gerunds as Appositives

A gerund may be used as an appositive.

Justin's role, playing the part of an up-and-coming writer, was very believable.

Remember that an appositive is a word or group of words that gives more information about a noun or pronoun.

A. Underline the gerund phrase in each sentence. Draw an additional line under the gerund if it is used as an appositive.

1. The work of Lister, <u>introducing antiseptics into surgery</u>, was a medical breakthrough.

2. The achievement of Cyrus Field, <u>laying the Atlantic cable</u>, brought him fame.

3. Bell's accomplishment, <u>transmitting the human voice over the telephone</u>, took years of work.

4. Leo Hirshfield's legacy, <u>developing a sweet treat named after his daughter Tootsie</u>, is what I remember.

5. <u>Creating laborsaving devices</u> doesn't always work out.

6. Garrett A. Morgan's idea, <u>using a signal to direct traffic at intersections</u>, has been improved on over the years.

7. <u>Mass-producing goods and using interchangeable parts</u> helped the automobile industry on its way.

8. Strauss and Davis's idea, <u>sewing pants with rivets on the seams</u>, did work out.

9. The class assignment, <u>writing a report on a favorite inventor</u>, is due tomorrow.

10. Our teacher accomplished her goal, <u>finishing the chapter</u>.

B. Complete each sentence with one of the following gerund phrases. **[Answers will vary.]**

cleaning out the attic
writing e-mails to friends
reading romance novels

spending time with young children
becoming an astronaut

1. Juan's task, _____, was not easy.

2. That is Grandmother's latest accomplishment,

_____.

3. Melanie's experience, _____,
helped her get a job.

4. Donald's dream, _____, motivated
him to study hard.

5. Cindy has a favorite pastime, _____.

Name _____

78. Reviewing Gerunds

Underline the gerund(s) in each sentence. Write on the line whether it is used as a subject (S), a direct object (DO), the object of a preposition (OP), a subject complement (SC), or an appositive (A).

__[OP]__ 1. The task of saving wildlife is crucial after an oil spill.

__[S]__ 2. Cleaning up oil on sea birds is no small job.

__[A]__ 3. In 1989 the mission of the *Exxon Valdez*, hauling oil off the coast of Alaska, led to disaster.

__[S]__ 4. The spilling of eleven million gallons of crude oil occurred when the tanker hit a reef.

__[SC]__ 5. One of the first tasks was locating oil-containment equipment.

__[DO]__ 6. Snow did not permit their getting the equipment quickly.

__[OP]__ 7. The job of containing the oil spill was hampered by good weather.

__[DO]__ 8. Calm winds did not permit using dispersants to break up the oil.

__[S]__ 9. Using buckets to scoop up oil produced little result.

__[A, OP]__ 10. Crews worked at containment, keeping the oil from spreading, but their efforts weren't effective.

__[A]__ 11. The greatest fear, picking up dead sea animals, began to be a reality.

__[S]__ 12. Seeing thousands of dead birds on the beaches was heartbreaking.

__[DO, OP]__ 13. Rescue workers took the dying to centers for cleaning.

__[A]__ 14. A terrible consequence, freezing from fur too oil-soaked to insulate them from the cold, caused the death of many otters.

__[SC, OP]__ 15. Our job should be preventing such disasters from happening.

B. Follow the instructions and write sentences using the following gerund phrase: *swimming in the lake.* [Sample answers are given.]

16. *(Use as a subject.)* __[Swimming in the lake is great fun.]__

17. *(Use as a direct object.)* __[I dislike swimming in the lake.]__

18. *(Use as a subject complement.)* __[One thing I do enjoy is swimming in the lake.]__

19. *(Use as the object of a preposition.)* __[We cooled off by swimming in the lake.]__

20. *(Use as an appositive.)* __[My favorite pastime, swimming in the lake, is impossible in winter.]__

79. Working with Gerunds, Participles, Nouns, and Verbs

> Use a possessive noun or pronoun to modify a gerund.
>
> **Jared's running away was a shock.** (*Jared's* modifies the gerund *running.*)
> **Our camping in the woods was fun.** (*Our* modifies the gerund *camping.*)

A. Circle the correct modifier.

1. (We **Our**) camping in the woods proved to be an endurance test.

2. Mother agreed to (**their** them) staying in tents.

3. My scout leader was shocked at (me **my**) wanting to go on the hike.

4. (**Joe's** Joe) cooking the pioneer stew was the topic of the school paper.

5. (Him **His**) receiving the award pleased everyone.

6. The (dog **dog's**) barking awakened the family in the next tent.

7. Everyone was surprised at (Martha **Martha's**) sleeping in the tent.

8. The (**owl's** owl) hooting alarmed Greg.

9. (Cynthia **Cynthia's**) refusing to speak was troubling to Maggie.

10. The ranger was dismayed by (Ruth **Ruth's**) complaining.

B. Underline the words that end in *–ing.* Write whether each is a progressive verb form, a participle, a participial adjective, or a gerund.

_____[gerund]_____ 1. Harold experiences <u>ringing</u> in his ears.

__[progressive verb form]__ 2. Those bells have been <u>ringing</u> all day.

__[participial adjective]__ 3. We heard the <u>ringing</u> bells early this morning.

_____[participle]_____ 4. The woman <u>ringing</u> the bell is the principal.

_____[gerund]_____ 5. <u>Playing</u> chess is an art.

__[progressive verb form]__ 6. Erin and Lois are <u>playing</u> a table game.

__[participial adjective]__ 7. That new game uses <u>playing</u> cards.

_____[participle]_____ 8. The children <u>playing</u> that game live nearby.

_____[participle]_____ 9. <u>Wishing</u> for gold, Jasper continued his search.

__[progressive verb form]__ 10. Jim is always <u>wishing</u> for new clothes.

80. Using Infinitives as Subjects

> An **infinitive** is a verb form, usually preceded by *to*, that can be used as a verb, a noun, an adjective, or an adverb. Like a verb, an infinitive can have a direct object and may be modified by an adverb. An infinitive or an infinitive phrase may be used as the subject of a sentence.
>
> **To interpret the law is the chief duty of the Supreme Court.**

A. Underline the infinitive phrase in each sentence. Write **DO** over any word that is the direct object of an infinitive.

                    DO   **DO**
EXAMPLE: **To save lives and property is the work of a firefighter.**

               [DO]
1. To solve the puzzle takes some time.

                      [DO]
2. To hear the watchdog's bark is often frightening.

3. To have been chosen was a great honor.

              [DO]
4. To learn embroidery requires patient effort.

5. To drive carelessly endangers the lives of others.

             [DO]
6. To serve the country is the job of any person in the armed forces.

7. To persevere to the end demands constant effort.

                 [DO]
8. To rescue the lost fishermen required a life raft and two sailors.

            [DO]
9. To join the club was the best thing Steve did.

10. To exercise daily is an excellent habit.

B. Use an infinitive phrase from the list to complete each sentence. Your infinitive phrase will be the subject of the sentence. **[Sentences will vary.]**

To save money for college	To build a model ship	To exercise daily
To do well in school	To hear the dog bark	

1. _____ requires great skill.

2. _____ is the goal of many people.

3. _____ is very rewarding.

4. _____ can be annoying.

5. _____ is worthwhile.

81. Using Infinitives as Direct Objects

> An infinitive may be used as the direct object in a sentence.
> **My aunt plans to visit Greece.**

A. Underline the infinitive phrase in each sentence. Draw an additional line under the infinitive if it is used as the direct object. Write **DO** over any word(s) that is the direct object of an infinitive.

> EXAMPLE: My dog never wants <u><u>to take</u></u> a **DO** walk during a storm.

1. A lobbyist is a person who tries <u><u>to influence</u> the</u> **[DO]** proceedings of Congress.

2. Young people should try <u><u>to think</u> for themselves about politics.</u>

3. Have you begun <u><u>to learn</u> the</u> **[DO]** names of the new cabinet members?

4. The new president resolved <u><u>to make</u> changes</u> **[DO]** immediately.

5. The president hopes <u><u>to travel</u> to Europe.</u>

6. The vice president promised <u><u>to serve</u> the</u> **[DO]** president.

7. Republicans attempted <u><u>to pass</u> tax laws</u> **[DO]** quickly.

8. Democrats wanted <u><u>to slow</u> their actions.</u> **[DO]**

9. We must learn <u><u>to cooperate</u> with others on important issues.</u>

10. The work of the men and women in Congress deserves <u><u>to be praised.</u></u>

B. Use an infinitive phrase from the list to complete each sentence. Your infinitive phrase will be the direct object of each sentence. **[Sentences will vary.]**

to drive a racecar	to wrestle	to write a novel
to learn all the dance steps	to prepare for tomorrow	

1. Jonathan would like _____.

2. Have the children been taught _____?

3. Several teammates tried _____.

4. Before we retire, we must try _____.

5. Does she want _____?

Participles, Gerunds, Infinitives

Name _____

82. Using Infinitives as Subject Complements

> An infinitive may be used as a subject complement.
>
> **A physicist's goal is <u>to understand the universe</u>.**
>
> Remember that a subject complement completes the meaning of a linking verb, such as *seem, be, appear,* or *feel.*

A. Underline each infinitive phrase. Draw an additional line under the infinitive if it is used as the subject complement. Write **DO** over any word that is the direct object of the infinitive.

1. Marie Curie's life's work was to study radioactive substances. **[DO]**

2. An early goal was to learn about radioactivity in uranium ore.

3. The ore seemed to contain more radioactivity **[DO]** than the uranium in the ore.

4. She and her husband were to become a team.

5. The result of their work was to discover radium **[DO]** and polonium, highly radioactive elements. **[DO]**

6. Another result would be to win a Nobel Prize **[DO]** in physics.

7. After her husband's death, Marie Curie's work was to earn another Nobel Prize, **[DO]** this time in chemistry.

8. Her work was to isolate radium **[DO]** and to study its properties. **[DO]**

9. Another accomplishment was to start the Radium Institute **[DO]** in Paris.

10. Curie's idea was to take X-ray machines **[DO]** to the battlefields.

11. Her hope was to use X rays **[DO]** for locating bullets in soldier's wounds.

12. Today one goal of the Institute remains to train female scientists. **[DO]**

B. Complete each sentence with a phrase that contains an infinitive used as the subject complement. **[Sentences will vary.]**

13. A scientist's main job is _____.

14. The object of higher education has always been _____.

15. One purpose of the American Society of Physicists is _____.

 Marie Curie worked in the fields of physics and chemistry, making discoveries that continue to be of great benefit to people today. Write about a way you might work to improve the lives of others.

83. Using Infinitives as Objects of Prepositions

> An infinitive may be used as the object of a preposition.
> **The visitors are about to go now.**

A. Underline the infinitive phrase in each sentence. Draw an additional line under the infinitive if it is used as the object of a preposition. Circle the preposition that introduces the infinitive phrase.

1. The flag is (about) to be raised.

2. There was nothing left to do (except) to stand at attention.

3. The principal-for-the-day is (about) to lead us in the Pledge of Allegiance.

4. We will do nothing (except) to listen carefully.

5. Is the parade (about) to start?

6. This float has no purpose (except) to carry the football players.

7. Who is the person (about) to board the drama float?

8. The pep band is (about) to play.

9. The onlookers have no aim (but) to watch the show.

10. I want nothing (except) to enjoy the day.

B. Use an infinitive phrase from the list to complete each sentence. Your sentence will have an infinitive as the object of a preposition. Add other words to fill out the sentence if you wish. [**Sentences will vary.**]

> **to stay overnight**   **to write a short story**
> **to forgive them**   **to learn algebra**
> **to leave for Africa**

1. You have no choice but _____.

2. Is he about _____?

3. I had no other ambition but _____.

4. There seems to be nothing to do except _____.

5. The winner has no request but _____.

84. Using Infinitives as Appositives

An infinitive may be used as an appositive.

Martin's wish, <u>to become a poet</u>, finally came true.

Remember that an appositive is a group of words that names or gives more information about a noun or pronoun it follows.

A. Underline the infinitive phrase in each sentence. Draw an additional line under the infinitive if it is used as an appositive.

1. John Adams fulfilled his responsibility, <u>to serve his country loyally</u>, by taking on many government posts.

2. One huge task, <u>to develop Washington, D.C., into the nation's capital</u>, was undertaken during his presidency.

3. John Adams's duty <u>to serve as president</u> came first.

4. After the election the Federalist plan, <u>to unseat Adams</u>, began early.

5. The goal of the Federalists, <u>to organize a strong government</u>, was espoused by Hamilton.

6. The Republicans' goal, <u>to respond to the needs of ordinary citizens</u>, was espoused by Jefferson.

7. One aim of Adams, <u>to move into the president's house in Washington</u>, was accomplished.

8. The country's potential dilemma, <u>to have a tie vote in the electoral college</u>, became a reality in 1800.

9. The vote in the House of Representatives, <u>to break the tie between Jefferson and Burr</u>, took days.

10. The final vote <u>to elect Jefferson</u> came after thirty-six ballots.

B. Complete each sentence with one of the following infinitive phrases. **[Sentences will vary.]**

to study politics　　　　　　　**to help make education a priority**
to run for office　　　　　　　**to vote**
to elect more women and minorities

1. Their hope, _____, will require time and effort.

2. The proposal, _____, was raised at the town hall meeting.

3. My plan, _____, was applauded.

4. Mrs. Hughes's decision, _____, was difficult.

5. He had one ambition, _____.

Name _____

85. Reviewing Infinitives Used as Nouns

A. Underline the infinitive in each sentence. Write on the line whether it is used as a subject (**S**), direct object (**DO**), object of a preposition (**OP**), subject complement (**SC**), or appositive (**A**).

__[S]__   1. To eat nourishing food keeps one in good health.

__[S]__   2. To wash vegetables before eating or cooking them is a good idea.

__[DO]__   3. Scientists have begun to experiment with new vegetables.

__[SC]__   4. The goal of this research is to provide more and better foods.

__[SC]__   5. My greatest wish is to create a bigger strawberry.

__[A]__   6. The latest research, to grow a grain called golden rice, is controversial.

__[S]__   7. To increase the harvest of healthful grains should be everyone's concern.

__[DO]__   8. Try to understand this concept.

__[DO]__   9. Will the wealthier nations plan to increase food production?

__[SC]__   10. The only thing we can do is to try our best.

__[S]__   11. To help people with new technologies seems right.

__[DO]__   12. Do you wish to learn more?

__[A]__   13. The college's aim, to educate people about plant research, is a good one.

__[OP]__   14. I want nothing except to provide food for others.

__[DO]__   15. I intend to register for the class tomorrow.

B. Follow the instructions and write sentences using the following infinitive phrase: *to graduate with honors.* [**Sample answers are given.**]

16. *(Use as a subject.)* __[To graduate with honors is a worthy goal.]_____

17. *(Use as a direct object.)* __[I've wanted to graduate with honors since my freshman year.]__

18. *(Use as a subject complement.)* __[My goal is to graduate with honors.]_____

19. *(Use as the object of a preposition.)* __[I've desired nothing except to graduate with honors.]__

20. *(Use as an appositive.)* __[My goal, to graduate with honors, will be difficult to achieve.]__

Participles, Gerunds, Infinitives

92

86. Using Infinitives as Adjectives and Adverbs

An infinitive can be used as an adjective and modify a noun or a pronoun.

We have no time <u>to waste</u>.

An infinitive can be used as an adverb and may modify a verb, an adjective, or another adverb. Remember that an adverb tells when, where, how much, and in what manner.

The politicians came <u>to express</u> their views.

You should be ashamed <u>to be idle</u>.

These evergreens are large enough <u>to transplant</u>.

A. Underline each infinitive used as an adjective. Circle the word it modifies.

1. Steam has the (power) <u>to run</u> machinery.

2. The *Clermont* was one of the first (boats) <u>to run</u> on steam.

3. Robert Fulton was the first American (inventor) <u>to make</u> steam travel a financial success.

4. As a child, it was Fulton's (hobby) <u>to invent</u> things.

5. He made a (device) <u>to cut</u> marble.

6. He invented a (machine) <u>to dig</u> canal channels.

7. He labored on an (invention) <u>to travel</u> underwater.

8. Was this a good (idea) <u>to pursue</u>?

9. The (invention) <u>to be perfected</u> was the submarine.

10. Fulton did not have a (chance) <u>to finish</u> it.

B. Underline the infinitive used as an adverb in each sentence. Circle the word(s) it modifies. On the line write whether the word the infinitive modifies is a verb, an adjective, or an adverb.

<u>[adjective]</u> 1. Big dogs are (expensive) <u>to feed</u>.

<u>[adverb]</u> 2. These puppies are old (enough) <u>to go</u> to new homes.

<u>[verb]</u> 3. The fencing (is intended) <u>to corral</u> the dogs.

<u>[verb]</u> 4. Dog sleds (were developed) <u>to transport</u> people.

<u>[adjective]</u> 5. Are you (ready) <u>to select</u> a puppy?

<u>[adjective]</u> 6. Be (sure) <u>to read</u> the pet care book.

<u>[adjective]</u> 7. We are (eager) <u>to bring</u> her home.

<u>[verb]</u> 8. Dad (wanted) us <u>to keep</u> the puppy on the porch.

<u>[adjective]</u> 9. The cage was too (small) <u>to accommodate</u> Lady.

<u>[verb]</u> 10. The kids all (came) <u>to admire</u> our pet.

Participles, Gerunds, Infinitives

93

87. Identifying Hidden and Split Infinitives

After certain verbs, such as *hear, see, know, feel, let, make,* and *help,* the preposition *but,* and the conjunction *than,* the infinitive is used without *to.*

I heard the bird sing.

Her stories always make me laugh.

A hidden infinitive may be used after the preposition *but* and the conjunction *than:*

I do nothing but study all day.

An adverb placed between *to* and the verb is said to split the infinitive. Good writers try to avoid split infinitives.

A. Underline the hidden infinitive in each sentence.

1. Will you let me hold the baby?

2. My mother does nothing but work all day.

3. All night I heard the rain pound on the roof.

4. "I thought I felt something move!" she whispered.

5. The patient did nothing but sleep after the surgery.

6. I have never seen him run so fast.

7. I heard the child cry.

8. The teacher helped the students study the new assignment.

9. Your performances always make me laugh.

10. Let not your hearts be troubled.

B. Each sentence contains a split infinitive. Rewrite the sentence, placing the adverb in a correct position. **[Sample answers are given.]**

1. The teacher asked us to completely erase the boards.

   [The teacher asked us to erase the boards completely.]

2. Be sure to correctly answer the essay question.

   [Be sure to answer the essay question correctly.]

3. The doctor was unwilling to indefinitely postpone the surgery

   [The doctor was unwilling to postpone the surgery indefinitely.]

4. We like to slowly stroll along the beach.

   [We like to stroll along the beach slowly.]

5. Our family is planning to immediately leave on vacation.

   [Our family is planning to leave on vacation immediately.]

Name _____

88. Reviewing Infinitives

A. Underline the infinitive in each sentence. Write on the line whether it is used as a subject **(S)**, direct object **(DO)**, object of a preposition **(OP)**, subject complement **(SC)**, or appositive **(A)**.

[DO]   1. My sister has never learned to skate.

[OP]   2. You have no choice but to travel by bus.

[DO]   3. We would prefer to go with you.

[S]   4. To write well requires practice.

[SC]   5. The purpose of the game is to learn math facts.

[DO]   6. Try to finish the work before noon.

[SC]   7. The reason she is coming is to baby-sit.

[A]   8. Ms. Henry's motion, to adjourn the meeting, passed quickly.

[S]   9. To be happy is an important goal in my life.

[A]   10. My worst fear, to fail in school, motivates me.

B. Write on the line whether the *italicized* infinitive is used as an adjective or an adverb.

[adverb]   11. Quarantine is sometimes necessary *to protect* others.

[adverb]   12. My cousin is coming *to visit* us.

[adjective]   13. Youth is the time *to sow* the seeds of character.

[adverb]   14. Philip lunged *to tackle* the quarterback.

[adverb]   15. They were afraid *to undertake* the journey.

[adverb]   16. Quotation marks are used *to enclose* the words of a speaker.

[adjective]   17. Efforts *to eliminate* the use of pesticides are gratifying.

[adjective]   18. How did our school raise the money *to build* the gym?

[adjective]   19. The power *to run* the mill comes from water.

[adjective]   20. Her efforts *to improve* are visible.

C. Underline the hidden infinitive in each sentence.

21. Did you hear the dog <u>bark</u>?

22. She would rather learn to swim than <u>skate</u>.

23. Darlene does nothing but <u>giggle</u> when she is corrected.

24. All through the storm, we heard the wind <u>howl</u>.

25. Watch me <u>dive</u> into the pool.

D. Rewrite each sentence. Place the adverb in a better position. **[Sample answers are given.]**

26. I expect you to wholeheartedly support me.

    [I expect you to support me wholeheartedly.]

27. The janitor does not expect to constantly pick up after us.

    [The janitor does not expect to pick up after us constantly.]

28. To quickly eat your lunch may give you indigestion.

    [To eat your lunch quickly may give you indigestion.]

29. To suddenly end our support would be disastrous for them.

    [To end our support suddenly would be disastrous for them.]

30. To positively respond to the questionnaire would aid the cause.

    [To respond positively to the questionnaire would aid the cause.]

E. Follow the instructions and write sentences using the following infinitive phrase: *to visit a foreign country.* **[Sample answers are given.]**

31. *(Use as a subject.)* [To visit a foreign country is an exciting adventure.]

32. *(Use as a direct object.)* [I would like to visit a foreign country.]

33. *(Use as a subject complement.)* [One goal is to visit a foreign country.]

34. *(Use as the object of a preposition.)* [There is nothing I'm afraid to do, except to visit a foreign country.]

35. *(Use as an appositive.)* [My desire, to visit a foreign country, pleases my grandmother.]

Participles, Gerunds, Infinitives

Name _____

89. Reviewing Participles, Gerunds, and Infinitives

A. Underline the participle in each sentence. Circle the word it modifies.

1. The audience applauded the (couple) skating in the competition.

2. The (trophy) won by the ice hockey team will be on display in the school hall.

3. Having eaten their lunch, the (students) went out onto the ice.

4. Spectators gathered to watch the (skaters) flying around the rink.

5. (Ellen,) having trained for years, prepared to perform.

6. The school trophy case contains the (names) of the winners engraved in brass.

7. Having given his promise to return, our (coach) left his college job.

8. (Skaters) trained in northern states are comfortable on the ice.

B. Write sentences using each participial phrase. **[Sentences will vary.]**

standing on the corner   9. _____

_____

blown by the wind   10. _____

_____

having delivered the speech   11. _____

_____

C. Underline the gerund in each sentence. Write on the line whether it is used as a subject **(S)**, direct object **(DO)**, object of a preposition **(OP)**, subject complement **(SC)**, or appositive **(A)**.

__[A]__ 12. My job, working in the retirement home, gives me great satisfaction.

__[SC]__ 13. My brother's chief service is reading books for the visually impaired.

__[OP]__ 14. We show that we care by helping others.

__[DO]__ 15. I enjoy planning activities for senior citizens.

__[S]__ 16. Working with older adults might be a career choice.

D. Follow the instructions and write sentences using the following infinitive phrase: *to attend college.* [**Sample answers are given.**]

17. *(Use as a subject.)* _____ [To attend college is an important goal for many people.] _____

18. *(Use as a direct object.)* _____ [I chose to attend college; no one influenced my decision.] _____

19. *(Use as an appositive.)* _____ [My goal, to attend college, will require many sacrifices.] _____

E. Underline the infinitive in each sentence. Write on the line whether it is used as a subject (**S**), direct object (**DO**), object of a preposition (**OP**), subject complement (**SC**), or appositive (**A**).

_[DO]_ 20. My class wants to attend a good high school.

_[A]_ 21. My goal, to win a scholarship, may not be realistic.

_[S]_ 22. To afford room and board is one reason for wanting a scholarship.

_[DO]_ 23. Most teachers try to prepare students for the future.

_[OP]_ 24. I was about to take the examination for entrance into high school.

_[SC]_ 25. My hope is to achieve a high score.

Try It Yourself

On a separate sheet of paper, write five or six sentences about something you'd like to do in the future. Be sure to use participles, gerunds, and infinitives correctly.

Check Your Own Work

Choose a piece of writing from your portfolio or journal, a work in progress, an assignment from another class, or a letter. Revise it, applying the skills you have learned. The checklist will help you.

✔ Have you used participles, gerunds, and infinitives correctly?

✔ Have you avoided dangling participles?

✔ Have you avoided splitting the infinitives you used?

90. Classifying Adverbs

Adverbs modify verbs (*he ran quickly*), adjectives (*very serious illness*), and other adverbs (*she sang quite enthusiastically*). Adverbs do not modify nouns or pronouns; only adjectives do that.

Adverbs are classified into categories of time, place, degree, manner, affirmation, and negation.

TIME: **She ate later in the day.**   MANNER: **He easily lifted the weight.**
PLACE: **She looked back.**   AFFIRMATION: **The music was quite loud.**
DEGREE: **The pie was very sweet.**   NEGATION: **He was not angry.**

A. Write whether the *italicized* modifier is an adverb or an adjective.

[adverb]   1. Have you *ever* wondered what causes the tides to change?

[adjective]   2. Tides are caused by the *gravitational* pull of the sun and the moon.

[adverb]   3. The moon, *much* nearer Earth, is the principal determinant.

[adverb]   4. The moon pulls *strongly* on the side of Earth facing the moon.

[adjective]   5. This *strong* pull makes water flow toward it.

[adverb]   6. A dome of water rises *directly* below the moon.

[adverb]   7. This dome of water is *commonly* called high tide.

[adverb]   8. The moon's pull is weaker on the side facing *away* from the moon.

[adjective]   9. But even here the moon causes a *smaller* tide to rise.

[adverb]   10. Two high and two low tides occur daily at *nearly* every shore on Earth.

B. Underline the adverb in each sentence. Write on the line whether it is an adverb of time (**T**), place (**P**), degree (**D**), manner (**M**), affirmation (**A**), or negation (**N**).

[T]   1. Yesterday Astrud's class went on a field trip.

[D]   2. They went to the most northerly ocean shore in Maine.

[M]   3. Astrud's class closely watched the tides on their field trip.

[D]   4. They found the moon's effect was much stronger than the sun's.

[M]   5. Unfortunately it rained for part of their trip.

[A]   6. Doubtless they could have accomplished more.

[N]   7. With the rain they could not find
time to measure the sun's pull.

[D]   8. Her teacher said the sun's pull was only
about 46 percent that of the moon's.

[D]   9. During full moons the tides are much larger.

[M or P] 10. This is because the sun, moon, and Earth are directly in line.

91. Identifying Simple and Interrogative Adverbs

> An adverb modifies a verb, an adjective, or another adverb.
>
> **She _carefully_ prepared the meal.**
>
> Interrogative adverbs are used in asking questions.
>
> **_When_ will she finish?**

Underline each simple adverb once and each interrogative adverb twice.
Circle the word(s) that the adverb modifies.

1. <u><u>When</u></u> (did) the first man (walk) on the moon?

2. Neil Armstrong <u>first</u> (walked) on the moon in 1969.

3. Armstrong was one of the <u>first</u> (civilian) astronauts.

4. He (had) <u>earlier</u> (flown) in a Gemini mission in 1966.

5. <u>Later</u>, in 1968, he (was made) commander of the _Apollo 11_ mission.

6. _Apollo 11_'s mission was (to take) men to the moon and (return) safely.

7. The space shuttle (was) <u>officially</u> (named) _Columbia_.

8. <u><u>Why</u></u> (was) it (named) _Columbia_?

9. America (was) <u>once</u> (called) _Columbia_ after Christopher Columbus.

10. The lunar module, which <u>actually</u> (landed) on the moon, was called the _Eagle_.

11. <u><u>When</u></u> (did) the _Apollo 11_ mission (occur)?

12. It launched July 16, 1969, and (arrived) in the moon's orbit four days <u>later</u>.

13. After fourteen orbits of the moon, the _Eagle_ <u>successfully</u> (undocked) from the _Columbia_.

14. Neil Armstrong (began) <u>actively</u> (piloting) 5,000 feet from the moon.

15. After three hours the _Eagle_ (touched) <u>down</u>.

16. Armstrong <u>gently</u> (landed) the _Eagle_.

17. At 10:56 he <u>carefully</u> (stepped) onto the moon's surface.

18. Buzz Aldrin, another _Apollo 11_ astronaut, (emerged) from the _Eagle_ <u>later</u>.

19. Michael Collins, who flew the _Columbia_, (stayed) <u>inside</u>.

20. The _Apollo 11_ remains the <u>most</u> (famous) space mission of all time.

Adverbs

92. Identifying a Special Use of Nouns

An adverbial noun is a noun that performs the function of an adverb by modifying a verb. An adverbial noun expresses time, distance, measure, weight, value, or direction.

The cake should bake forty-five <u>minutes</u>.

TO EXPRESS USE WORDS LIKE	time hours	distance miles	measure pint	weight pound	value dollars	direction north

A. Underline each noun used as a modifier. Write on the line whether it expresses time, distance, measure, weight, value, or direction.

_____[time]_____ 1. Gold has been cherished for more than 3,000 <u>years</u>.

_____[measure]_____ 2. It can be hammered 0.000005 <u>inches</u> thick.

_____[distance]_____ 3. One ounce can be stretched 62 <u>miles</u>.

_____[measure]_____ 4. It will not melt until it reaches 1,947 <u>degrees</u> Fahrenheit.

_____[weight]_____ 5. The largest gold nugget ever found weighed 150 <u>pounds</u>.

_____[time]_____ 6. It turned up accidentally 130 <u>years</u> ago in Australia.

_____[direction]_____ 7. The American gold rush caused fortune hunters to head <u>west</u>.

_____[time]_____ 8. Americans waited forty-one <u>years</u>, until 1974, for the ban on private ownership of gold to be lifted.

_____[measure]_____ 9. The amount of American gold now used for dental work approaches nine <u>percent</u>.

_____[value]_____ 10. Gold is now worth 400 <u>dollars</u> an ounce.

B. Complete each sentence with an adverbial noun that expresses the quality in parentheses. [Sample answers are given.]

time   1. The opera will last three _____[hours]_____.

distance   2. The theater is seven _____[miles]_____ away.

direction   3. Tell the cab driver to turn _____[left]_____ after the light.

time   4. We have only fifteen _____[minutes]_____ till the curtain rises.

measure   5. Last time there was a line three _____[blocks]_____ long.

value   6. The tickets cost fifty _____[dollars]_____ apiece.

distance   7. But the singers traveled many _____[miles]_____ to be here.

time   8. The star tenor arrived just this _____[evening]_____.

value   9. His vocal cords are worth at least a million _____[dollars]_____.

time   10. His last performance in America was _____[years]_____ ago.

Adverbs

Name _____

93. Comparing with Adverbs

> The comparative and superlative of most adverbs that end in –ly are formed by adding *more/most* or *less/least* before the positive.
>
> **more sadly, most sadly; less sadly, least sadly**
>
> The comparative and superlative of adverbs that don't end in –ly are formed by adding –er or –est.
>
> **farther, farthest**

A. Complete the chart with degrees of comparison.

POSITIVE	COMPARATIVE	SUPERLATIVE
1. slowly	more/less slowly	[most/least slowly]
2. far	[farther]	[farthest]
3. [badly]	[worse]	worst
4. [noisily]	more noisily	[most noisily]
5. soon	[sooner]	[soonest]
6. [playfully]	[more playfully]	most playfully
7. quickly	[more quickly]	[most quickly]
8. [cheaply]	more/less cheaply	[most/least cheaply]
9. [highly]	more highly	[most highly]
10. well	[better]	[best]

B. Underline the adverb in each sentence. Write its degree of comparison on the line.

_____[comparative]_____ 1. Two people can often travel <u>more cheaply</u> than one.

_____[positive]_____ 2. Maggie <u>quickly</u> realized this in Europe last summer.

_____[comparative]_____ 3. Money stretches <u>further</u> when you can share travel accommodations.

_____[positive]_____ 4. Much of her money was <u>rapidly</u> spent on hotels.

_____[superlative]_____ 5. Deals on plane tickets can be made <u>most easily</u> when a person buys two or more.

_____[comparative]_____ 6. You can also travel <u>more safely</u> as a pair.

_____[superlative]_____ 7. Criminals <u>most often</u> target people who are by themselves.

_____[superlative]_____ 8. All tourists should travel <u>most cautiously</u> at night.

_____[positive]_____ 9. <u>Fortunately</u>, Maggie was not the victim of a pickpocket.

_____[positive]_____ 10. Planning a trip <u>carefully</u> will pay off in the long run.

Adverbs

94. Distinguishing Between Adjectives and Adverbs

> Adjectives modify nouns and pronouns. Adverbs modify verbs, adjectives, adverbs, participles, gerunds, and infinitives. Some words may be used as adjectives or as adverbs. Their use in a sentence is determined by the part of speech they modify.

A. Circle the correct modifier in parentheses. Underline the word(s) it modifies. Write on the line whether the modifier is an adjective or an adverb.

__[adverb]__ 1. Winston Churchill is remembered for having (brave (bravely)) led Great Britain through World War II.

__[adjective]__ 2. He held ((numerous) numerously) political offices in his lifetime.

__[adverb]__ 3. But he is remembered (chief (chiefly)) as a prime minister.

__[adverb]__ 4. Germany was (aggressive (aggressively)) invading Europe.

__[adjective]__ 5. Churchill enlisted the aid of then ((neutral) neutrally) America.

__[adjective]__ 6. A ((powerful) powerfully) alliance was formed with America and Russia.

__[adjective]__ 7. Germany was defeated, and the ((terrible) terribly) war ended in 1945.

__[adverb]__ 8. Churchill (increasing (increasingly)) had to accept America's postwar plans.

__[adverb]__ 9. (Sad (Sadly)), Roosevelt ignored Churchill's warnings about the Soviet empire.

__[adverb]__ 10. Churchill (vain (vainly)) sought a summit between the Eastern and Western powers.

B. Write whether the *italicized* word is used as an adjective or an adverb. Underline the word(s) it modifies.

__[adjective]__ 1. After the war Churchill encouraged solidarity against the *rapidly* growing threat of communism.

__[adverb]__ 2. The term "iron curtain" was *first* used in a speech given by Churchill.

__[adjective]__ 3. In 1953 he was among the *first* persons knighted by Queen Elizabeth II.

__[adjective]__ 4. As if that were not *enough* recognition, he was awarded the Nobel Prize for literature that same year.

__[adverb]__ 5. Winston Churchill is *still* regarded as one of Britain's greatest leaders.

Winston Churchill acted with courage and compassion in a difficult time. Not everyone will lead a country. But everyone can act with courage and compassion. Tell how you have acted bravely and compassionately.

Adverbs

103

95. Using Farther and Further, As . . . As, So . . . As, and Equally Correctly

Farther refers to distance. *Further* means "in addition to."

> **The further into the game it got, the farther Jack was hitting the ball.**

When comparing persons, places, or things use *as...as* in positive statements.

> **It is as windy here as it is in Chicago.**

When comparing persons, places, or things use *so...as* in negative statements.

> **His new book is not so long as his previous one.**

Equally means "as" when it modifies an adjective. Never use *as* between *equally* and the word it modifies.

> **She was equally skilled.**

A. Complete each sentence with *farther* or *further*.

1. The _____[farther]_____ he ran, the more his knee bothered him.

2. The suspect refused to discuss the matter any _____[further]_____ without his lawyer.

3. The _____[further]_____ he examined the necklace, the more certain he was that the rubies were artificial.

4. Helen was _____[further]_____ convinced she should have stayed home when it began raining.

5. The _____[farther]_____ she went into the woods, the thicker the underbrush became.

B. Circle the correct word(s) in parentheses.

1. The Ohio River is not (so) as) long as the Mississippi.

2. I wonder if it is (so (as)) deep as the Mississippi.

3. My new shirt does not fit (so) as) well as my old one.

4. The apple pie is not (so) as) sweet as the chocolate cake.

5. The new library was just (so (as)) large as the previous one.

6. Before he went to Germany he was (so (as)) thin as a rail.

7. Her poetry is not (so) as) deep as a well.

8. All the players who tried out were ((equally qualified) equally as qualified).

9. Both of the actors were ((equally deserving) equally as deserving) of the award.

10. Every morsel of food was (equally as delicious (equally delicious)).

Name _____

96. Reviewing Adverbs

A. Underline each adverb. Write its classification on the line (time, place, degree, manner, affirmation, negation).

____[place]____   1. Christopher Columbus sailed <u>westward</u> from Spain in 1492.

____[manner]____   2. He was <u>actually</u> looking for Asia when he landed in America.

____[time]____   3. Christopher Columbus is <u>often</u> credited with America's discovery.

____[time]____   4. But civilizations were <u>already</u> here when he arrived.

____[manner]____   5. Many of these were <u>highly</u> developed cultures.

B. Complete each question with an appropriate interrogative adverb.

6. ____[Where]____ did the first people to reach America come from?

7. __[When, Where]__ did they first arrive?

8. ____[Why]____ did they come to America?

9. ____[How]____ did they manage to get to a continent surrounded by water?

10. ____[Where]____ did they go after they got here?

C. Underline the adverb in each sentence. Write its degree of comparison on the line: positive, comparative, or superlative.

____[superlative]____   11. The first Americans <u>most likely</u> came by way of the Bering Strait.

____[positive]____   12. The Bering Strait is <u>widely</u> believed to have frozen long ago.

____[positive]____   13. This occurred <u>roughly</u> 30,000 years ago.

____[superlative]____   14. These first Americans were <u>most probably</u> nomadic tribes.

____[comparative]____   15. Scarcity caused them each day to search <u>farther</u> for their food.

CONTINUED

Adverbs

D. Write on the line whether the *italicized* words are adjectives or adverbs.

___[adjective]___ 16. *Most* Native American cultures had developed agriculture by 2000 B.C.

___[adverb]___ 17. Maize was the *most commonly* grown grain.

___[adverb]___ 18. Livestock was *less* important to Native American cultures.

___[adverb]___ 19. Protein was obtained *primarily* through plants.

___[adjective]___ 20. *Additional* protein was obtained through hunting and fishing.

E. Circle the correct word(s) in parentheses.

21. Jude had to hike (further (farther)) than he expected to reach the ocean.

22. The band did not play any ((further) farther) after the police came.

23. The (further (farther)) you hike up the mountain the thinner the air.

24. Recklessly spending money, he went ((further) farther) into debt.

25. The waves are not ((so) as) rough as they were this morning.

26. Alyssa's boat is (so (as)) big as a house.

27. The chips are not ((so) as) salty as the pretzels.

28. But the chips are (so (as)) fattening as the cake.

29. The dogs were ((equally dirty) equally as dirty) after their swim.

30. The dresses were ((equally expensive) equally as expensive)).

Try It Yourself
On a separate sheet of paper, write five or six sentences about something you have learned to do recently. Be sure to use adverbs correctly.

Check Your Own Work
Choose a selection from your writing portfolio, journal, work in progress, an assignment from class, or a letter. Revise it, applying the skills you have learned in this chapter. The checklist will help you.

✔ Have you included appropriate adverbs?

✔ Have you distinguished between adjectives and adverbs?

✔ Have you used the comparison of adverbs correctly?

Adverbs

97. Identifying Prepositions

A **preposition** is a word that relates a noun, a pronoun, or a phrase to some other word in the sentence.

The cow jumped <u>over</u> the moon.

The object of a preposition is a noun, a pronoun, or a group of words used as a noun. A preposition usually precedes its object.

A. Circle the preposition(s) in each sentence. Underline the object of each preposition.

1. Pumas, or mountain lions, are (among) the rarest <u>animals</u> (in) the <u>world</u>.

2. (Without) <u>protection</u>, they stand little chance (of) <u>survival</u>.

3. Pumas are found (from) <u>British Columbia</u> (to) <u>Patagonia</u>.

4. Their coats range (from) a reddish-brown <u>color</u> (to) a bluish-gray <u>hue</u>.

5. A puma's body can be six feet long, (without) its long <u>tail</u>.

6. Its head is small and has black spots (above) the <u>eyes</u>.

7. Females bear (from) two to four <u>young</u> (in) a <u>litter</u>.

8. Pumas sometimes attack cattle (on) <u>ranches</u>.

9. (As) a <u>result</u>, the pumas have been exterminated (from) many <u>areas</u>.

10. Development has also encroached (onto) their <u>territory</u>.

B. Complete each sentence with a prepositional phrase. **[Sample answers are given.]**

1. After you are finished, put the milk _____[in the refrigerator]_____ .

2. Bernard's family has a cottage _____[on the lake]_____ .

3. We picked all these apples _____[at the orchard]_____ .

4. Kara planted a vegetable garden _____[in her backyard]_____ .

5. Unfortunately, no pets are allowed _____[on the beach]_____ .

6. The bird has a nest _____[in the tallest tree]_____ .

7. There is an old phonograph _____[in the attic]_____ .

8. The dog followed me home _____[from the store]_____ .

9. The athlete could never have won the contest _____[without training]_____ .

10. The bank has many branches _____[around the city]_____ .

98. Using Prepositions Correctly

You need to be careful to use certain prepositions correctly.

Beside means "at the side of or next to"; *besides* means "in addition to."

Between is used when speaking of two persons, places, or things; *among* is used in speaking of more than two.

In denotes position within; *into* denotes motion or change of position.

Differ with denotes disagreement; *differ from* denotes that two things or people are not the same.

One is *angry with* a person but *angry at* a thing.

From means "coming from the possession of someone"; *off* means "away from."

Behind indicates location outside and at the rear of.

A. Circle the correct preposition in parentheses.

1. There is a pond (beside) besides) Eva's house.

2. Many frogs lay their eggs (in) into) this water.

3. Tadpoles will hatch (from) off) these eggs.

4. Tadpole is a stage (among (between)) egg and frog.

5. A tadpole will later turn (in (into)) a frog.

6. Bullfrogs have special receptors for hearing (behind) at the back of) their eyes.

7. These receptors allow them to hear calls (from) off) other bullfrogs.

8. Eva gets mad (with (at)) these noisy frogs when she is in bed.

9. Toads differ (from) with) frogs in that they spend most of their lives on land.

10. (Beside (Besides)) this contrast, frogs have teeth, and toads do not.

B. Complete each sentence with a correct preposition. **[Sample answers are given.]**

1. A caterpillar will eventually turn _____[into]_____ a butterfly.

2. Did you study the debate _____[between]_____ Lincoln and Douglas?

3. The candy was equally distributed _____[among]_____ the triplets.

4. _____[Besides]_____ Stuart Little, E. B. White also wrote *Charlotte's Web.*

5. Mr. Blair was angry _____[with]_____ his son for breaking the window.

6. Devita got a soda _____[from]_____ the vending machine at lunch.

7. The picture fell_____[off]_____ the desk when the ball hit it.

8. The trees differ _____[from]_____ each other in more ways than one.

9. He does not look so tall when he stands _____[beside]_____ the basketball player.

10. The broom belongs _____[in]_____ the closet when it's not being used.

99. Distinguishing Between Words Used as Adverbs and Words Used as Prepositions

A preposition shows the relation between its object and some other word in the sentence.
> **Jack fell down the hill.**

An adverb tells *how, when,* or *where.*
> **Jack fell down.**

A. Write on the line whether the *italicized* word is an adverb **(A)** or a preposition **(P)**.

[P]   1. The Eiffel Tower is one of the seven wonders *of* the modern world.

[P]   2. It is located *in* Paris, France.

[A]   3. It went *up* before the World's Fair in 1889.

[P]   4. The Eiffel Tower is *on* the bank of the Seine.

[P]   5. The tower was built *by* the engineer Alexandre-Gustave Eiffel.

[A]   6. One may walk *up* or take an elevator.

[A]   7. Every day thousands of people go to the top to look *around.*

[P]   8. From the very top you can see clear *across* Paris.

[A]   9. If I were at the top, I would be afraid to look *down.*

[P] 10. The uppermost platform is almost 1,000 feet *from* the ground.

B. Write sentences using each word as an adverb. **[Sentences will vary; sample answers are given.]**

away   1. [Lucy was sad when her dog ran away.] _____

in   2. [Mr. Hale can still wear his tuxedo if he sucks his stomach in.] _____

over   3. [I skinned my knee when the bike fell over.] _____

before   4. [The man had been arrested before.] _____

around   5. [The pirate climbed the mast and looked around.] _____

C. Write sentences using each word as a preposition. **[Sentences will vary; sample answers are given.]**

near   1. [The horse likes to run near the water.] _____

beyond   2. [There are some alligators sunning beyond the rocks.] _____

down   3. [Her engagement ring was accidentally washed down the drain.] __

between   4. [I would not want to sit between those loud gentlemen.] _____

off   5. [He broke his leg when he fell off the roof.] _____

Prepositions, Conjunctions, Interjections

Name _____

100. Classifying Conjunctions

A **conjunction** is a word that connects other words or groups of words. Coordinate conjunctions connect words, phrases, or clauses that have the same function or use in a sentence: *and, but, for, nor, or, so,* and *yet.*

> **London and Liverpool are in England.**

Correlative conjunctions are conjunctions that are always used in pairs: *both/and, neither/nor, not only/but also, whether/or,* and *either/or.*

> **Both London and Liverpool are in England.**

The conjunctive adverbs *however, moreover, nevertheless, also, therefore,* and *consequently* can be used to link independent clauses. Use a semicolon before a conjunctive adverb.

> **I am tired; nevertheless, I will read one more chapter in my history book.**

Underline the conjunctions or conjunctive adverbs in each sentence. Identify each one, using **A** for coordinate conjunction, **B** for correlative conjunction, and **C** for conjunctive adverb.

__[B]__ 1. Elizabeth I was the queen of <u>both</u> England <u>and</u> Ireland.

__[C]__ 2. She ruled from 1558 to 1603; <u>consequently,</u> this period is called the Elizabethan age.

__[A]__ 3. She was the daughter of King Henry VIII <u>and</u> his wife Anne Boleyn.

__[B]__ 4. Her siblings included <u>not only</u> King Edward VI <u>but also</u> Queen Mary.

__[C]__ 5. Edward was only nine when Henry VIII died; <u>nevertheless,</u> he was made king.

__[A]__ 6. He soon died of tuberculosis, <u>so</u> Mary ascended to the throne.

__[A]__ 7. Elizabeth had supported Mary's accession, <u>yet</u> Mary had her imprisoned.

__[C]__ 8. She was locked in the tower of London; <u>also,</u> she was threatened with execution.

__[B]__ 9. But <u>neither</u> Edward <u>nor</u> Mary was to last long.

__[A]__ 10. Mary reigned for five years, <u>and</u> Elizabeth succeeded her.

__[C]__ 11. Elizabeth was young when she became queen; <u>however,</u> she ruled with great skill.

__[C]__ 12. Her navy defeated the Spanish armada in 1588; <u>therefore,</u> invasion was prevented.

__[A]__ 13. Her reign is also noted for the poetry <u>and</u> drama of the English Renaissance.

__[B]__ 14. Elizabethan dramatists include <u>both</u> Shakespeare <u>and</u> Christopher Marlowe.

__[A]__ 15. The Elizabethan age was a time of great prosperity <u>and</u> achievement.

Queen Elizabeth I was a supporter of poets, artists, and musicians. Describe a way you can encourage the creativity of others.

Prepositions, Conjunctions, Interjections

Name _____

101. Using Subordinate Conjunctions

A subordinate conjunction connects an independent and a dependent clause. Common subordinate conjunctions include *although, because, even though, in order that, so that, if, since, before, after, when,* and *while.*

CLAUSE	SUBORDINATE CONJUNCTION	CLAUSE
Ludwig went to practice	**even though**	**it was almost over.**

A. Circle each subordinate conjunction. Underline the dependent clauses.

1. (Although) she is fictitious, Rosie the Riveter played an important role in World War II.

2. (Before) the war started, most American women did not work outside the house.

3. But many jobs were left vacant (when) men began enlisting in the army.

4. (Because) a war was being fought, American production also increased.

5. Something had to be done (so that) America's productivity did not flag during the war.

6. (Since) women were needed, an ad campaign was designed to recruit them.

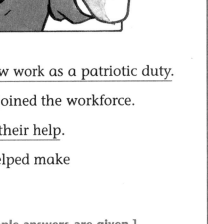

7. Rosie the Riveter was created (in order that) women would view work as a patriotic duty.

8. (Before) the war was over, more than six million women had joined the workforce.

9. America would have fallen far behind (if) it had not been for their help.

10. (Although) many lost their jobs after the war, these women helped make working outside the home acceptable.

B. Write sentences using the following dependent clauses. [**Sample answers are given.**]

because it was cold inside   1. [Sara wore a jacket because it was cold inside.]

if we are going   2. [If we are going to the concert, we need to leave now.]

unless we hear otherwise   3. [The dance is in the auditorium unless we hear otherwise.]

although it was raining   4. [Although it was raining, we stood in line for tickets.]

so that everyone gets a turn   5. [Make a single-file line so that everyone gets a turn.]

102. Using <u>Without</u>, <u>Unless</u>, <u>Like</u>, <u>As</u>, and <u>As if</u> Correctly

The correct use of prepositions and conjunctions may be confusing.
Without is a preposition and introduces a word or a phrase.

> **They will be lost <u>without</u> a map.**

Unless is a conjunction and introduces a clause.

> **They will get lost <u>unless</u> you go with them.**

Like is a preposition and introduces a word or a phrase.

> **She runs <u>like</u> a cheetah.**

As can be used as a preposition to introduce a word or phrase or as a conjunction to introduce a clause. *As if* is a conjunction and introduces a clause.

> **She runs <u>as if</u> she has been training.**

A. Circle the correct word in parentheses.

1. You won't see a camel in America ((unless) without) you go to a zoo.

2. They have been introduced to America but (unless (without)) success.

3. They can bear severe heat (like (as if)) it were nothing.

4. Camels can go ((without) unless) water for several days.

5. They can also drink salt water ((without) unless) getting sick.

6. Many people think a camel's hump acts ((like) as if) a water thermos.

7. The humps actually contain fat that gets absorbed (like (as)) the camel becomes hungry.

8. During sandstorms, a camel's nostrils can close (like (as)) shutters do.

9. Just (like (as)) their nostrils are protected, their eyes are shielded by long lashes.

10. I would not want to cross a desert (without (unless)) I had a camel.

B. Complete each sentence with the correct word: *without, unless, as,* or *like.*

1. _____[As]_____ a fire moves across land, it usually kills the vegetation in its path.

2. But the protea flower cannot survive ___[without]___ fire.

3. After a protea is fertilized, bracts encase the flower head ____[like]____ a shell.

4. ___[Unless]___ the plant is scorched by fire, it will not release its seeds.

5. ___[As]___ the fire passes, the bracts open and the seeds are released.

6. The plant will hold the seeds until it dies ___[unless]___ there is a fire.

7. Fire provides sunlight for smaller plants ___[as]___ it burns down large shade trees.

8. The ashes also act ___[as]___ fertilizer for the soil.

9. ___[Without]___ these advantages, the protea would have a hard time surviving.

10. So the fire is ___[like]___ a sign that tells the plant it is okay to release its seeds.

Prepositions, Conjunctions, Interjections

Name _____

103. Reviewing Conjunctions and Conjunctive Adverbs

A. Write on the line whether the *italicized* words are **A** coordinate conjunctions, **B** correlative conjunctions, **C** subordinate conjunctions, or **D** conjunctive adverbs.

[B] 1. *Neither* jellyfish *nor* Portuguese men-of-war possess spines.

[D] 2. They are invertebrates; *therefore,* they are without backbones.

[D] 3. The man-of-war is similar to a jellyfish; *nevertheless,* it is a separate species.

[B] 4. A man-of-war is actually *not* one animal *but* many acting as a unit.

[A] 5. It has many dangling tentacles *and* a saillike crest.

[A] 6. Each reaches a length of about six inches *and* trails tentacles more than 100 feet long.

[C] 7. They are very dangerous *because* their poison is similar to a cobra's.

[A] 8. The poison can cause severe pain, a drop in blood pressure, *or* even death.

[D] 9. There is no antidote; *however,* vinegar neutralizes some of the poison's effects.

[C] 10. Even *after* a man-of-war dies, its poison remains active and should be avoided.

B. Underline the conjunctions or conjunctive adverbs in each sentence. Write on the line what kind each is, using the letters from exercise A.

[B] 1. The Dead Sea is <u>neither</u> dead <u>nor</u> a sea.

[C] 2. <u>Although</u> its name implies otherwise, it is actually a lake.

[D] 3. It does sustain life forms; <u>therefore,</u> it is not dead.

[D] 4. Fish cannot live in the salty water; <u>however,</u> some micro-organisms thrive there.

[C] 5. The Dead Sea contains seven times more salt <u>than</u> sea water contains.

[A] 6. Nearly a third of the lake consists of salt <u>and</u> other solid minerals.

[C] 7. <u>Because</u> of the water's density, the human body floats easily on the surface.

[A] 8. The Dead Sea is fed by the Jordan River <u>and</u> several smaller streams.

[D] 9. The lake has no outlet; <u>consequently,</u> water is carried off solely by evaporation.

[B] 10. The ruins of <u>both</u> Sodom <u>and</u> Gomorrah are thought to lie beneath the lake.

104. Identifying Interjections

An **interjection** expresses a strong or sudden emotion. An interjection may not be part of a sentence grammatically. It is either punctuated with an exclamation point or attached to a sentence with a comma.

> **Ouch!** The sand is hot.
> **Wow,** the view from here is incredible.

Interjections may convey many different emotions: delight, anger, surprise, anticipation, warning, impatience, pain, wonder, and so on.

A. Underline the interjection. Write on the line what emotion it expresses. [Sample answers are given.]

_____[wonder]_____ 1. Listen! You can hear the waves crashing on the beach.

_____[anticipation]_____ 2. Hello, is anyone at home?

_____[warning]_____ 3. Careful! The lifeguard said there was an undertow.

_____[anger]_____ 4. Goodness! This mattress must be filled with broken crockery.

_____[impatience]_____ 5. Quiet! The baby is sleeping.

_____[impatience]_____ 6. See, that is what happens when you leave milk out overnight.

_____[wonder]_____ 7. Look! There are dolphins out in the water.

_____[surprise]_____ 8. Oh! I did not know anyone was in here.

_____[impatience]_____ 9. Well, I see that the lawn has not been mowed in a few months.

_____[anger]_____ 10. Hey! No pets are allowed in the museum.

B. Write sentences using interjections to express each emotion below. [Sample answers given.]

pain   1. [Ouch! The water is hot.]

joy   2. [Yes! We are getting out of class early today.]

assent   3. [Okay, I admit you were right about not playing with fireworks.]

disgust   4. [Gross! That dog has ticks all over its back.]

wonder   5. [Wow! It's amazing the way the sun sets over the sea.]

impatience 6. [Quiet! I can't hear myself think.]

surprise   7. [What! You still haven't finished your homework?]

sorrow   8. [Alas, our basketball team won only two games this year.]

warning   9. [Beware! That ice is really slippery.]

delight   10. [Oh my! German chocolate is my favorite.]

Prepositions, Conjunctions, Interjections

Name _____

105. Reviewing Prepositions, Conjunctions, and Interjections

A. Underline each preposition. Circle its object.

1. Sperm whales have the heaviest brain of any (animal).
2. The brain of a sperm (whale) can exceed twenty pounds.
3. The human brain, in (comparison,) has a weight of three (pounds).
4. The whales' heads make up one-third of their (bodies).
5. Sperm whales are found from the (Tropics) to the (Arctic).

B. Circle the correct preposition in parentheses.

1. There are many differences (among (between)) whales and fish.
2. Most importantly, whales differ ((from) with) fish in being mammals.
3. (Beside (Besides)) this distinction, whales move their fins up and down.
4. Whales are found ((in) into) all the world's oceans and even a few rivers.
5. Most whales gather (in (into)) groups when they migrate.

C. Write on the line whether each *italicized* word is an adverb (**A**) or a preposition (**P**).

[P] 1. Recent fossil discoveries have shed new light *on* whale evolution.

[A] 2. They raise interesting questions about where whales came *from*.

[P] 3. Many scientists now believe their ancestors lived *on* land.

[P] 4. These creatures foraged for food *along* the ocean shore.

[A] 5. Eighty million years passed before they became the whales they evolved *into*.

[A] 6. An amphibious, seal-like stage was first passed *through*.

[P] 7. The *Pakicetus*, which lived *in* Pakistan, was one such creature.

[P] 8. It lived *in* swampy areas around fifty million years ago.

[A] 9. It had nostrils instead of a blow hole to breathe *through*.

[P] 10. Fossils of modern whales did not appear *until* millions of years later.

D. Circle the subordinate conjunctions. Underline the dependent clauses.

1. Whales are born tail-first (so that) they do not drown during birth.

2. This form of delivery is necessary (because) whales breathe air.

3. (After) the calf is born, the mother helps it to the surface.

4. This is no easy task (since) a newborn whale can weigh two tons.

5. Another female will often help the mother raise the calf to the surface (when) it is born.

E. Underline the conjunctions or conjunctive adverbs in each sentence. Write on the line whether they are **A** coordinate conjunctions, **B** correlative conjunctions, or **C** conjunctive adverbs.

___[A]___ 1. Whales are hunted for food and oil.

___[C]___ 2. They were once widely hunted; consequently, many species are now scarce.

___[B]___ 3. Both humpbacks and blue whales are endangered species.

___[A]___ 4. They are protected in many countries, yet some people still condone whale hunting.

___[C]___ 5. This hunting threatens the whale populations; moreover, pollution adds a new threat.

F. Write sentences using each interjection. **[Sentences will vary. Sample answers are given.]**

Good 1. ___[Good! We get to go on a field trip.]___

Look out 2. ___[Look out! You are driving off the road.]___

Pay attention 3. ___[Pay attention! This material will be on the test tomorrow.]___

Careful 4. ___[Careful! If that snake bites you, it's all over.]___

Wow 5. ___[Wow! Time seems to move so slowly.]___

Try It

On a separate sheet of paper, write several sentences about an exciting event in your life. Use prepositional phrases, conjunctions, and interjections in your sentences.

Check Your Own Work

Choose a selection from your writing portfolio, journal, work in progress, an assignment from another class, or a letter. Revise it, applying the skills you have learned in this chapter. The checklist will help you.

✔ Have you used interjections as words expressing strong or sudden emotion?

✔ Have you used conjunctions to combine sentences?

✔ When beginning a sentence with a dependent clause, have you inserted a comma after the clause?

Name _____

106. Identifying Phrases

> A **phrase** is a group of words without a subject and verb that is used as a single part of speech. Phrases take several forms.
>
> PARTICIPIAL: **The inventor, <u>thinking creatively</u>, solved the problem.**
> INFINITIVE: **<u>To win</u>, Ellen needed a solution.**
> GERUND: **The whole class enjoys <u>solving problems</u>.**
> PREPOSITIONAL: **Ms. Guerra divided them <u>into teams</u>.** (A prepositional phrase consists of a preposition and a noun or pronoun.)
> A prepositional phrase is used as an adjective or an adverb.
>
> ADJECTIVAL PHRASE: **The original plan <u>for the game</u> was too complicated.**
> ADVERBIAL PHRASE: **<u>On Monday</u> we found the answer.**

Write the form of each *italicized* phrase. If it is a prepositional phrase, indicate how the phrase is used; write **Adj** for adjective or **Adv** for adverb.

[prepositional]	[Adv]	1. Basketball was invented *in 1891*.
[prepositional]	[Adv]	2. At that time no major sport was played *during the winter months*.
[infinitive]	_____	3. James A. Naismith's ambition was *to provide an interesting sport*.
[participial]	_____	4. Naismith, *having little money,* nailed up peach baskets.
[prepositional]	[Adj]	5. Another piece of equipment *for the new game* was a tall ladder.
[prepositional]	[Adv]	6. The players were divided *into two teams*.
[participial]	_____	7. *Using an old soccer ball,* the teams began to play.
[infinitive]	_____	8. *To score,* a player would throw the ball into the opposite basket.
[prepositional]	[Adj]	9. There was not a standard number of players *on a team*.
[participial]	_____	10. Naismith, *having watched the first game,* drafted the original 13 rules of play.
[prepositional]	[Adj]	11. Changes *to the game* were soon adopted.
[prepositional]	[Adj]	12. Metal hoops *with net bags* replaced the baskets.
[gerund]	_____	13. *Pulling a cord* on the net released the ball.
[prepositional]	[Adv]	14. Baskets with bottomless nets came into use *about 1913*.
[prepositional]	[Adv]	15. Playing basketball has spread *throughout the world*.

James Naismith used little money but a lot of imagination to invent a new sport. How can you use your imagination to teach or entertain people?

117

107. Identifying Clauses

A **clause** is a part of a sentence that has a subject and a predicate. An independent clause expresses a complete thought and can stand on its own as a sentence.

The Seven Wonders of the Ancient World were identified in about 120 B.C.

A dependent clause does not express a complete thought and cannot stand alone.

Although only one structure stands today, the list of wonders has survived.

A dependent clause can be used as an adjective or an adverb.

A. Identify each clause as independent or dependent.

[independent] 1. the Pharos of Alexandria was an ancient lighthouse

[dependent] 2. because the bonfire burned continuously

[independent] 3. the bonfire served as a beacon

[dependent] 4. when sailors saw the light

[dependent] 5. as the ships approached the rocks

B. Underline the adjectival clause in each sentence. Circle the word(s) it modifies.

1. People travel to Egypt to see the (pyramids) that were built over four thousand years ago.

2. The pyramids are the only ancient (Wonder) that is still in existence.

3. The Great Pyramid was built as a tomb for (Khufu) who was known to the Greeks as Cheops.

4. The (pyramids) which are made of millions of stone blocks, are an engineering marvel.

5. (Archaeologists) who have studied the pyramids think it may have taken 100,000 men more than twenty years to build the Great Pyramid.

6. The (blocks) of stone that were hauled into place each weighed about 2.5 tons.

7. The (Great Pyramid) which rose to a finished height of 482 feet, was built in layers of stone blocks.

8. Each (layer) that fit atop the previous one covered a smaller area.

9. The stones were dragged up a (ramp) which was made higher for each layer.

10. The finished (structure) which looked like a set of stairs, was then filled in with white limestone.

108. Writing Sentences with Adjectival Clauses

An adjectival clause is a dependent clause used as an adjective. An adjectival clause usually begins with a relative pronoun *(who, whom, whose, which, that)* or a relative adverb *(when, where, why)*. It modifies a noun or a pronoun by telling what kind or which one.

In the year **that has just gone by**, I have opened a pizza parlor. *(That has just gone by modifies year.)*

The business, **which is located in the mall**, is beginning to grow. *(Which is located in the mall modifies business.)*

A. Rewrite each sentence, adding an adjectival clause to modify the *italicized* word.
[Answers will vary. Sample answers are given.]

1. My *neighbor* has a pizza business.
   [My neighbor who lives next door has a pizza business.]

2. The *business* intrigued me.
   [The business, which makes a lot of money, intrigued me.]

3. Each weekend I talked to *Mr. Hawkins* about the business.
   [Each weekend I talked to Mr. Hawkins, who is the owner, about the business.]

4. He offered me a part-time *position*.
   [He offered me a part-time position, which I accepted.]

5. Every weekend I worked the late *shift*.
   [Every weekend I worked the late shift, which no one likes.]

6. During that time, I learned all the aspects of *pizza making*.
   [During that time, I learned all the aspects of pizza making, which involves many steps.]

7. *Working* with the customers was quite a challenge.
   [Working with the customers when they became demanding was quite a challenge.]

8. My *boss* taught me that the customer is always right.
   [My boss, whose opinion I value, taught me that the customer is always right.]

9. His *patience* is amazing.
   [His patience, which seems endless, is amazing.]

10. Now we are working toward opening a pizza parlor at a second *location*. [Now we are working toward opening a pizza parlor at a second location, which is across from the high school.]

B. Write sentences, using an adjectival clause to modify each noun. [Sample answers are given.]

homework 1. [The homework, which is assigned daily, matches the class discussions.]

television 2. [Television is an invention that changed society.]

amusement park 3. [The amusement park that was built last year just opened.]

gift 4. [The gift that I liked best came from Mom.]

holiday 5. [Christmas, a holiday that many people celebrate, comes on Tuesday this year.]

Phrases, Clauses, Sentences

119

109. Identifying Adverbial Clauses

An adverbial clause is a dependent clause used as an adverb. An adverbial clause modifies a verb, an adjective, or an adverb. It tells where, when, in what way, to what extent, under what condition, or why. An adverbial clause may also modify a participle, gerund, or infinitive.

At Yellowstone, the mud pots—bubbling pools of mud—were formed when steam and gas rose from the ground and changed the rock into clay.

A. Underline the adverbial clause in each sentence. Circle the word(s) it modifies.

1. If you visit the West, you should make a trip to Yellowstone National Park.

2. Because there is so much to do, plan to stay several days.

3. Yellowstone National Park is older than any other national park.

4. Because Yellowstone sits on magma, it has geysers and thousands of hot springs.

5. When the major geysers erupt, tourists are usually there to see the boiling water shoot into the air.

6. Geysers have been compared to volcanoes because they are similar.

7. Geysers shoot boiling water, while volcanoes shoot out melted rock.

8. After a geyser has erupted, the water seeps back into the earth.

9. When the minerals in the water dry, you can see beautiful formations.

10. At Yellowstone, bears, elk, and bison roam wherever they want.

11. The balance of nature is maintained even though it sometimes seems cruel.

12. If the park's elk population becomes too large, many animals starve in winter.

13. Feeding animals is prohibited because it alters their natural feeding habits.

14. Even though the black bears seem friendly, people should be cautious.

15. Before you camp in the wilderness, you need a permit.

B. Use each adverbial clause in a sentence. [Sample answers are given.]

1. If you stop to think about it, [you will realize that having friends is important] .

2. Until the rain stops, [we can't go home] .

3. After I finish my homework, [I will go skating] .

4. Although I am good in math, [I am better in reading] .

5. Since the computer was invented, [shopping has never been easier] .

110. Writing Sentences with Adverbial Clauses

An adverbial clause always begins with a subordinate conjunction that serves to connect two ideas by making one idea subordinate, or less important, to the other.

We serve fruits and vegetables because they are important to health.

Be careful not to confuse a subordinate conjunction with a preposition. Remember that a subordinate conjunction connects two complete ideas.

A. Complete each sentence with an adverbial clause.
The subordinate conjunction is given. **[Answers will vary.]**

1. We will eat dinner when ____[Mom gets home from work]____ .

2. Jason answered as soon as _____ .

3. He listened to the stereo after _____ .

4. When _____ , the birds fly southward.

5. They returned home after _____ .

6. The storm arose as soon as _____ .

7. Edward acted as though _____ .

8. Because _____ , I cannot recommend him.

9. He waited until _____ .

10. The expedition struggled on while _____ .

B. Complete each sentence with an adverbial clause.
Circle each subordinate conjunction. **[Sample answers are given.]**

1. The pizza finally arrived _[(after) we called again]_____ .

2. School was dismissed _____[(when) the fire alarm went off]_____ .

3. The car broke down on the highway ____[(after) we passed the intersection]____ .

4. _[(Because) I was so hungry,]_____ I ate two hamburgers and a large pickle.

5. _[(Because) we left it outside,]_____ the rain ruined the new rug.

6. _[(After) we visited the Petersons,]_____ we finally arrived home from vacation.

7. _[(Because) we had been gone so long,]_____ the milk in the refrigerator was sour.

8. _[(When) the time came for soccer,]_____ everyone was dressed in ratty clothes.

9. _[(After) I got home from practice,]_____ I opened my drawer, but there were no socks.

10. _[(While) Mom slept,]_____ Dad made me a delicious club sandwich.

Name _____

III. Reviewing Adjectival and Adverbial Clauses

A. Underline the dependent clause in each sentence. On the line, write whether it is adjectival or adverbial.

[adverbial]   1. Before you visit a Florida beach, you should become familiar with its creatures.

[adverbial]   2. People collect seashells because they are beautiful.

[adjectival]   3. Sea urchins, whose spines are sharp, are called the porcupines of the sea.

[adjectival]   4. A sea cucumber is a marine animal that looks like a cucumber.

[adverbial]   5. Until Pam studied seahorses, she didn't realize that the male incubates the eggs.

[adverbial]   6. When the ocean tide is low, you can see a variety of sea life.

[adjectival]   7. Sea turtles that can weigh 300 pounds come ashore to lay eggs.

[adverbial]   8. After I was stung by a Portuguese man-of-war, I was more careful where I swam.

[adjectival]   9. A blue crab, whose legs are blue, is used for food in the East.

[adverbial]   10. If you're hungry, you can make a tasty broth from coquinas.

B. Complete each sentence with an adjectival clause. **[Sample answers are given.]**

1. Our teacher, _____[whom we are all crazy about]_____, finally returned the test papers.

2. I enjoyed reading this book, _____[which I found buried in my drawer]_____.

3. The players, _____[who were evenly matched]_____, did not stop until noon.

4. The car, _____[which had just been to the mechanic]_____, broke down.

5. The Joneses, _____[who had a soccer game to attend]_____, left the party.

C. Complete each sentence with an adverbial clause. **[Sample answers are given.]**

1. _____[Before we went to class]_____, we decided to play volleyball.

2. Take the train _____[even though the bus is more direct]_____.

3. I ate everything in sight _____[before I went to the game]_____.

4. _____[While I am at camp]_____, I plan to read four novels.

5. We were stranded on the island _____[when everyone else went shopping]_____.

Name _____

112. Identifying Noun Clauses Used as Subjects

A noun clause is a subordinate clause used as a noun. Like nouns, noun clauses can have several functions in a sentence. A noun clause can serve as the subject of a sentence.

That reptiles fascinate people is shown by the report.

(That reptiles fascinate people is a subordinate clause that is the subject of the sentence.)

A. Underline the noun clause used as a subject in each sentence.

1. That pandas are adorable creatures is undisputed.

2. Whether pandas are endangered is also not questioned.

3. Why some pandas reproduce and others don't is being studied.

4. That female pandas can mate only three days each year is a biological fact.

5. That pandas are essentially solitary doesn't increase their odds of reproducing.

6. What scientists are learning about pandas in captivity may help keep pandas alive in the wild.

7. That female pandas give birth to twins is not new information.

8. Why the mother panda rejects one twin is a puzzle.

9. Whether the female selects the stronger twin is not known.

10. Whoever solves that mystery will help increase the number of pandas in existence.

B. Complete each sentence with a noun clause used as the subject. Remember that a clause has a subject and a predicate. **[Answers will vary. Sample answers are given.]**

1. [What we saw that November night] _____ was not clear at all.

2. [What Jane saw] _____ was perfectly evident.

3. [What he knew] _____ did not discourage him.

4. [That Grandma was from Missouri] _____ was a well-kept secret.

5. [Why Justin came home] _____ mystified everyone.

6. [How the children will be treated] _____ will be decided by the group.

7. [That teaching is a difficult job] _____ is evident to me.

8. [Who will go on the trip] _____ will be announced.

9. [That I like to play word games] _____ was not a surprise to Jay.

10. [Why the temperature is often cooler by the lake] _____ is the topic of my paper.

Phrases, Clauses, Sentences

123

113. Identifying Noun Clauses Used as Direct Objects

A noun clause may be used as the direct object of a verb.

Scientists know that the balance in nature is easily upset.

(That the balance in nature is easily upset is the direct object of the verb know.)

A. Underline the noun clause used as the direct object.

1. We know that all parts of an ecosystem are important.

2. Did you realize that harvesting a species of crab can lead to a decline in a species of bird?

3. Biologists know that horseshoe crabs come ashore in Delaware Bay to spawn in May.

4. They also know that shorebirds arrive to eat crabs' eggs.

5. The crabs' eggs provide whatever energy the birds have for their migration to the Arctic.

6. Lately biologists have noticed that the number of red knots, a shorebird, has declined.

7. Scientists think that the birds' food supply has dwindled.

8. They believe that commercial fishing is responsible for the decline in the number of crabs.

9. They have calculated that half the crab population in Delaware Bay is gone.

10. The U.S. Commerce Department proposed that we set aside an area in the ocean as a horseshoe crab reserve.

B. Complete each sentence with a noun clause used as the direct object. Remember that a clause has a subject and a predicate. **[Answers will vary. Sample answers are given.]**

1. The boy said ____[that his dog ate his homework]____.

2. She could not remember ____[what she had eaten]____.

3. We all knew ____[who was at the door]____.

4. Our teacher promised ____[that we would have no homework over the weekend]____.

5. Did they discover ____[what group had written the letter]____?

6. Kim proved ____[that she could pitch as well as anyone]____.

7. We should always do ____[what our mothers and fathers tell us]____.

8. Has anyone heard ____[that the dance has been cancelled]____?

9. Jerry tried to explain ____[how the accident happened]____.

10. All of us hope ____[that the rain will not spoil the picnic]____.

Name _____

114. Identifying Noun Clauses Used as Subject Complements

> A noun clause may be used as a subject complement.
>
> **A requirement for a senator is <u>that he or she must be thirty years of age</u>.**
>
> *(That he or she must be thirty years of age* is the subject complement that completes the meaning of the linking verb *is.)*

A. Underline the noun clause used as a subject complement.

1. A qualification for the presidency is <u>that the candidate must be a native-born citizen</u>.

2. Is this <u>what you understood about the qualifications</u>?

3. Constant fundraising is <u>what can take up a candidate's time</u>.

4. That candidate is <u>who I will vote for</u>.

5. Their greatest disappointment is <u>that they don't have time to study the issues</u>.

6. The demand of the voters was <u>that the lottery money be spent on schools</u>.

7. The question was <u>how test scores could be raised</u>.

8. The decision of the committee was <u>that the money would go for energy research</u>.

9. The senator's prediction was <u>that aid to foreign countries would decrease</u>.

10. A requirement is <u>that the country must improve its human rights record</u>.

B. Complete each sentence with a noun clause used as a subject complement. Remember that a clause has a subject and a predicate. **[Answers will vary. Sample answers are given.]**

1. A safety rule of biking is __[that you always use hand signals]__.

2. His chief difficulty was __[that he was too short]__.

3. My chief concern is __[that someone will get lost]__.

4. The pilot's first thought was __[how she could land the plane safely]__.

5. The advice of our coach is __[that stretching should come before running]__.

6. The survivor's only hope is __[that a boat will come by]__.

7. The question became __[who would win the prize]__.

8. The student's excuse will be __[that she was not given enough information]__.

9. The reason for the defeat was __[that the goalie didn't show up]__.

10. Mom's excuse was __[what you might expect on Mother's Day]__.

Name _____

115. Identifying Noun Clauses Used as Objects of Prepositions

> A noun clause may be used as the object of a preposition.
>
> **The spectators came upon what was an ancient racetrack.**
>
> (*What was an ancient racetrack* is the object of the preposition *upon*.)

A. Underline the noun clause used as the object of a preposition. Circle the preposition.

1. We had an excellent view of the race (from) where we stood.

2. The team's success will depend (upon) what training they have.

3. Last week the team studied (about) how previous relay teams trained.

4. The track coach is concerned (with) how runners pass the baton.

5. The runners were amazed (by) what they thought would be an easy maneuver.

6. Passing the baton well depends (upon) where you are in relation to the other runner.

7. During practice we talked (about) how a runner should receive the baton.

8. You don't look (at) where the runner behind you is.

9. You give the baton (to) whoever is there.

10. Our coach will give a pizza (to) whoever wins the heat.

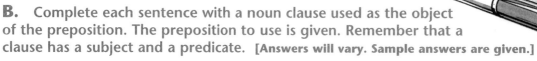

B. Complete each sentence with a noun clause used as the object of the preposition. The preposition to use is given. Remember that a clause has a subject and a predicate. **[Answers will vary. Sample answers are given.]**

1. You have no idea about ___[how our ancestors survived the cold climate]___ .

2. I am reading a book about ___[how people made sod houses]___ .

3. Give the package to ___[whoever turns up]___ .

4. The result of our education depends upon ___[how students and teachers work together]___ .

5. Marcy was delighted with ___[what the rabbit did]___ .

6. There has been some dispute about ___[who will wear the green dress]___ .

7. During the ride we talked about ___[whatever occurred to us]___ .

8. Great people rarely talk about ___[how they became famous]___ .

9. Many books have been written about ___[what the right diet is]___ .

10. She can give the assignment to ___[whoever comes in late]___ .

Phrases, Clauses, Sentences

126

116. Identifying Noun Clauses Used as Appositives

> A noun clause may be used as an appositive.
>
> **The theory that Surtsey is an island born from an underwater volcano intrigues me.**
>
> *(That Surtsey is an island born from an underwater volcano is an appositive that identifies the word that precedes it—theory.)*

A. Underline the noun clause used as an appositive in each sentence. Circle the word it modifies.

1. The (idea) that a new landform can be created seems like science fiction.

2. The (fact) that an island can be formed from an underground volcanic eruption is fantastic.

3. The people of Iceland accepted the (idea) that an island was growing off their southern coast.

4. (It) is interesting that scientists divide eruptions into six basic groups.

5. The (classification), how scientists identify various volcanoes, is based on violence of eruption and material erupted.

6. The (fact) that the eruption of Mount Pelee in 1902 killed more than 38,000 people is the reason that most violent eruptions are called Pelean.

7. We saw an (Icelandic eruption), what scientists consider the least violent type.

8. My sister's (wish) that she see a volcano erupt is possible

9. Dad kept his (promise) that he would take us to see Kilauea.

10. (It) is interesting that people want to see something so destructive.

B. Complete each sentence with a noun clause used as an appositive. Remember that a clause has a subject and a predicate. **[Answers will vary. Sample answers are given.]**

1. Joan kept her promise __[that she would meet us at the basketball game]__.

2. The motion __[that we have pop machines in the cafeteria passed]__.

3. The rumor __[that Jennifer was leaving spread quickly]__.

4. Her suggestion __[that the dog be trained was a good one]__.

5. The fear __[that she would not pass was groundless]__.

6. Trudy was upset by the report __[that named her the culprit]__.

7. The thought __[that boys are better scientists is wrong]__.

8. Dad's wish __[that we all play nicely came true]__.

9. My idea __[that we decorate the gym in the school colors was voted down]__.

10. Jack's assumption __[that everyone would vote for him was incorrect]__.

Name _____

117. Reviewing Noun Clauses

A. Underline the noun clause in each sentence. Write on the line how it is used. Use **S** for subject, **DO** for direct object, **OP** for object of a preposition, **SC** for subject complement, and **A** for appositive.

[DO] 1. This article says that a society lived in Peru a thousand years before the Inca.

[OP] 2. Such a discovery is exciting to whoever is interested in archaeology.

[SC] 3. The truth is that the Moche state extended 220 miles along Peru's coast.

[S] 4. That the Moche had a highly stratified society is shown by the burial tombs.

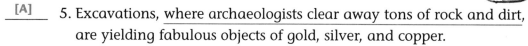

[A] 5. Excavations, where archaeologists clear away tons of rock and dirt, are yielding fabulous objects of gold, silver, and copper.

[S] 6. That these tombs were looted for more than four centuries is unfortunate.

[DO] 7. Archaeologists say that the Moche did not have a writing system.

[S] 8. Whatever we know about their activities is recorded on ceramic pots, textiles, and murals.

[SC] 9. The fact is that the Moche lived in one of the driest regions on Earth.

[DO] 10. Archaeologists say that the Moche had a complicated irrigation system.

[SC] 11. One idea is that bats were important symbols to the Moche.

[DO] 12. Archaeologists explain that bats appear in depictions of human sacrifice.

[A] 13. One find, what appeared to be a headdress with bats, supports this theory.

[SC] 14. One thing about each tomb is that it contained a very tall adult male.

[DO] 15. Archaeologists do not know why this man was buried with much smaller people.

B. Write sentences using each noun clause as indicated. **[Sample answers are given.]**

1. that those children study *(direct object)*

   [The teacher wanted primarily that those children study.]

2. when the Yankees won the World Series *(subject)*

   [When the Yankees won the World Series is the subject of a new movie.]

3. whether the clock is correct *(subject complement)*

   [The question is whether the clock is correct.]

4. whatever dangers threatened him *(object of a preposition)*

   [The animal escaped from whatever dangers threatened him.]

5. that she was seeking elective office *(appositive)*

   [The report that she was seeking elective office was true.]

Name _____

118. Reviewing Clauses

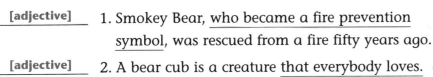

A. Underline the subordinate clause in each sentence. Write whether it is used as an adjective, an adverb, or a noun.

[adjective]   1. Smokey Bear, <u>who became a fire prevention symbol</u>, was rescued from a fire fifty years ago.

[adjective]   2. A bear cub is a creature <u>that everybody loves</u>.

[adverb]   3. <u>After the cub was rescued from the fire in New Mexico</u>, he went to a zoo.

[adverb]   4. <u>As a fire raged through Montana in 2000</u>, another cub was found.

[adjective]   5. The cub, <u>which was a black bear</u>, was found by a game warden.

[adverb]   6. The cub needed help <u>because his little paws were burned</u>.

[noun]   7. <u>What they should do with this cub after bandaging his paws</u> was not an issue.

[noun]   8. A wildlife official insisted <u>that this cub go back to the forest</u>.

[noun]   9. The plan was <u>that the cub be put into a hand-dug den to hibernate</u>.

[adjective]   10. The cub will be in the den with another orphaned cub <u>that rangers found</u>.

B. Combine each set of sentences into one sentence using an adjectival or an adverbial clause as directed. Use a subordinate conjunction to connect the clauses correctly. **[Sample answers are given.]**

1. *(adverbial)* Traffic was backed up for miles. A huge truck was on fire.

   [Because a huge truck was on fire, traffic was backed up for miles.]

   _____

2. *(adverbial)* I turned the corner. A gust of wind blew my hat off.

   [Just as I turned the corner, a gust of wind blew my hat off.]

   _____

3. *(adjectival)* Leonardo da Vinci made a mechanical lion. Leonardo da Vinci was an artist and inventor.

   [Leonardo da Vinci, who was an artist and inventor, made a mechanical lion.]

   _____

4. *(adverbial)* I was standing in a good spot. I had an excellent view of the Grand Canyon.

   [I had an excellent view of the Grand Canyon, as I was standing in a good spot.]

   _____

Phrases, Clauses, Sentences

CONTINUED

5. *(adjectival)* There are magazines piled on the table. Don't take any of the magazines.

[Don't take any of the magazines that are piled on the table.]

6. *(adjectival)* The Battle of New Orleans was fought in January of 1815. It lasted only twenty minutes.

[The Battle of New Orleans, which was fought in January of 1815, lasted only twenty minutes.]

7. *(adverbial)* John and Sue did all the work. We should be grateful to John and Sue.

[We should be grateful to John and Sue because they did all the work.]

8. *(adverbial)* Frank was vice president of the camera club. Frank organized many interesting programs.

[When Frank was vice president of the camera club, he organized many interesting programs.]

9. *(adjectival)* A new supermarket is opening here soon. The supermarket will provide jobs for many people.

[When the new supermarket opens here, it will provide jobs for many people.]

10. *(adverbial)* The skaters finally arrived home. They were cold, tired, and hungry.

[When the skaters finally arrived home, they were cold, tired, and hungry.]

C. Write sentences using these noun clauses as indicated. [Sample answers are given.]

1. where they had started *(object of a preposition)*

[They wanted to return to where they had started.]

2. that the contest be held at their school *(subject complement)*

[The teacher's dream was that the contest be held at their school.]

3. whether I will arrive in time *(subject)*

[Whether I will arrive in time is always in question.]

4. that we visit my aunt *(appositive)*

[The plan that we visit my aunt fell through.]

5. where the game was being played *(direct object)*

[My neighbor told us where the game was being played.]

119. Exploring Word Order in Sentences

> A sentence is in natural order when the verb follows the subject. A sentence is in inverted order when the main verb or an auxiliary comes before the subject.
>
> NATURAL ORDER
> **I heard what she said.**
>
> INVERTED ORDER
> **Did you hear what she said?**

A. Underline the complete subject once and the complete predicate twice. Put a check on the line if the sentence is in inverted order.

_____ 1. Emigrating from Japan, people settled in California during the 1880s.

[✔] 2. Did you know that many Japanese came to study?

_____ 3. Many others came and worked as farmers, tailors, gardeners, fishermen, and factory workers.

_____ 4. San Francisco was the destination of many Japanese.

[✔] 5. Across the Pacific Ocean came the immigrants.

[✔] 6. What did the new immigrants face in 1906?

_____ 7. The San Francisco earthquake was devastating!

_____ 8. Hundreds of city blocks burned.

[✔] 9. Over the city hovered smoke and gases.

_____ 10. More than 200,000 people took refuge in Golden Gate Park.

_____ 11. Soldiers came to keep order.

[✔] 12. There were hotels, mansions, theaters, and libraries to be rebuilt.

B. Rewrite each sentence as indicated.

NATURAL: **The early pioneers trudged across the continent.**
INVERTED: **Across the continent trudged the early pioneers.**

1. Just beyond the house stand two large evergreen trees.

   Natural: [Two large evergreen trees stand just beyond the house.] _____

2. Shall I promise to do better from now on?

   Natural: [I shall promise to do better from now on.] _____

3. A lonesome dog trotted around the corner.

   Inverted: [Around the corner trotted a lonesome dog.] _____

120. Working with Simple Sentences

> A simple sentence consists of one independent clause. Remember that an independent clause is a group of words that has a subject and a predicate and can stand alone.

A. Make sentences by matching the complete subjects in Column A with the complete predicates in Column B. Write the correct letter on the line. Use each letter once.

COLUMN A

__[a]__ 1. A cat's skeleton

__[d]__ 2. The exact number of bones

__[e]__ 3. The skeleton

__[h]__ 4. A cat's ears

__[f]__ 5. After eating or sleeping, a cat

__[g]__ 6. Long, thin, flexible leg muscles

__[i]__ 7. Owners sometimes

__[j]__ 8. Being a carnivore, a cat

__[c]__ 9. A cat's tail

__[b]__ 10. Pads on its paws

COLUMN B

a. has about 250 bones.

b. make a soft landing.

c. helps it stay balanced.

d. depends on tail length.

e. protects internal organs.

f. cleans itself.

g. enable a cat to run fast.

h. can lie flat on its head.

i. remove a cat's claws.

j. likes to eat meat.

B. Choose the best simple predicate to complete each sentence. Use each once.

| have written | read | borrowed | describes | named |
| imagined | enjoy | saw | appears | delights |

1. Authors throughout the ages ____[have written]____ about cats.

2. *Puss in Boots* ____[delights]____ both young and old readers.

3. A favorite nursery rhyme ____[describes]____ mittenless kittens.

4. The author of *Catwings* ____[imagined]____ flying cats.

5. In *Alice in Wonderland* a Cheshire cat ____[appears]____ from time to time.

6. We ____[saw]____ a play about Dick Whittington and his cat.

7. I ____[borrowed]____ a book about a cat that saw ghosts.

8. I ____[enjoy]____ reading poetry about cats.

9. Sometimes I ____[read]____ aloud to my cat, Jake.

10. My sister ____[named]____ her black cat Ichabod Crane.

121. Writing Compound Sentences

> A compound sentence contains two or more independent clauses. The clauses in a compound sentence are joined either by a comma and a coordinating conjunction or by a semicolon.
>
> **The day was cold, yet we still decided to go.**
>
> **The day was cold; we still decided to go.**

A. Make compound sentences by matching independent clauses from each column and writing the letter of your selection on the line at the left. Write a conjunction that makes sense, along with the proper punctuation, on the second line. **[Answers will vary.]**

COLUMN A

__[b]__ 1. Cars are easy to drive [, but]

__[j]__ 2. Dad bought a new SUV [, and]

__[i]__ 3. We like driving it [, but]

__[h]__ 4. The car is good for off-road driving [, but]

__[c]__ 5. Mom does not drive [, nor]

__[g]__ 6. She walks everywhere [, or]

__[f]__ 7. Riding a bike is good exercise [, and]

__[e]__ 8. My sister is sixteen [, and]

__[a]__ 9. Will she pay for gas [, or]

__[d]__ 10. Gas prices go up [, but]

COLUMN B

a. will her dad pay?

b. they are expensive to maintain.

c. does she want to.

d. people still want to drive.

e. she wants to drive.

f. it saves energy.

g. she rides her bicycle.

h. we live in a suburb.

i. we don't like buying gas for it.

j. it uses a lot of gasoline.

B. Complete each sentence with an independent clause. **[Sample answers are given.]**

1. The girls arranged the chairs, __[and the boys set up the tables]__ .

2. The assignment was difficult, but __[we all completed it]__ .

3. The crowd was silent; __[the pianist began to play]__ .

4. Finally the game began, and __[we trounced them]__ .

5. Take my advice, and __[you will succeed]__ .

6. I am not a musician, but __[I could have played better]__ .

7. The weeds we pulled were poison ivy; consequently, __[we all got a rash]__ .

8. I did not finish my chores; therefore __[I did not get paid]__ .

9. We spent the entire afternoon at the beach, and __[I got badly sunburned]__ .

10. We bought treats for the children, but __[Jason dropped his ice cream cone in the sand]__ .

122. Identifying Complex Sentences

A complex sentence contains one independent and one or more dependent clauses.

DEPENDENT CLAUSE | INDEPENDENT CLAUSE
If you visit Australia, | **you can visit the largest reef in the world.**

A. Underline the independent clause in each sentence. Write the word that begins each dependent clause on the line.

[Although] 1. Although the name suggests a continuous strip, Australia's Great Barrier Reef is more than 2,800 reefs.

[when] 2. A coral reef forms when colonies of plant and animal skeletons pile up.

[that] 3. Divers meet many sharks that seem more curious than dangerous.

[Because] 4. Because the waters are clear, divers can go 150 feet deep or more.

[which] 5. Biologists are finding new species of fish every year, which brings the total to about 2,000.

B. Underline the dependent clause in each sentence. Write the word that begins each dependent clause on the line.

[Because] 1. Because they look like plants, corals were wrongly classified.

[After] 2. After corals were studied further, scientists likened them to anemones and jellyfish.

[Because] 3. Because they eat other animals, corals are carnivores.

[If] 4. If you dive around the Great Barrier Reef, you are likely to see a sea turtle.

[that] 5. Some of the marks on a sea turtle's shell are from sharks that bite them.

C. Complete each sentence with a dependent clause. [Sample answers are given.]

1. Vegetables are good for you because __[they contain fiber]_____ .

2. The dog panted as if __[she had run a long way]_____ .

3. July 4 is the date when __[the band will march in the parade]_____ .

4. I have a suggestion that __[she will like]_____ .

5. We wondered how __[the machine worked]_____ .

6. Spring is the season when __[the trees bloom]_____ .

7. We should honor our school because __[we're proud of it]_____ .

8. Be sure to return those books if __[you go to the library]_____ .

9. I will finish my paper after __[I complete my research]_____ .

10. The game was forfeited because __[the other team didn't show up]_____ .

Name _____

123. Combining Sentences

A simple sentence consists of a subject and a predicate, either of which may be compound.
A compound sentence consists of two or more independent clauses.
A complex sentence contains one independent clause and one or more dependent clauses.

Combine each pair of sentences. Write at least two simple sentences, two compound sentences, and two complex sentences. After each of your sentences, write whether it is simple, compound, or complex. **[Sample answers are given.]**

1. The date of the festivities was announced. I cannot attend.
   [The date of the festivities was announced, but I cannot attend. compound]

2. Books are a great source of knowledge. They can broaden people's minds.
   [Because books are a great source of knowledge, they can broaden people's minds. complex]

3. Football is an exciting sport. I like hockey more than football.
   [Football is an exciting sport, but I like hockey more. compound]

4. Snakes are unusual animals. They are often misunderstood.
   [Because snakes are unusual animals, they are often misunderstood. complex]

5. The car sped around the corner. It skidded into a ditch.
   [The car sped around the corned and skidded into a ditch. simple]

6. Study in a quiet place. You will be able to concentrate.
   [If you study in a quiet place, you will be able to concentrate. complex]

7. The students assemble in the yard. They assemble there every morning.
   [The students assemble in the yard every morning. simple]

8. The aircraft carrier entered the harbor. People on the dock cheered.
   [As the aircraft carrier entered the harbor, people on the dock cheered. complex]

9. The students were cooperative all year. The class went on a trip to a theme park.
   [The students were cooperative all year; consequently, the class went on a trip to a theme park.

   compound]

10. The story is very interesting. It was written by Walter Dean Myers.
    [The story written by Walter Dean Myers is very interesting. simple]

124. Identifying Compound Complex Sentences

A compound complex sentence contains two or more independent clauses and one or more dependent clauses.

INDEPENDENT CLAUSE | DEPENDENT CLAUSE | INDEPENDENT CLAUSE

Many people go to the horse show that is held in Devon, **but I have never been there.**

A. Write on the line whether each sentence is simple, compound, complex, or compound complex. Underline all the independent clauses.

_____[simple]_____ 1. The horse has been one of the most useful animals for thousands of years.

_____[simple]_____ 2. Horses once were the fastest way to travel.

_____[simple]_____ 3. Hunters on horseback pursued animals and killed them for food.

_____[complex]_____ 4. When they settled the West, pioneers used horses.

_____[compound]_____ 5. Horses aren't used as much today for transportation; they have been replaced by "iron horses" and "horseless carriages."

_____[simple]_____ 6. Most horses have good memories and can be trained to obey commands.

_____[complex]_____ 7. The horse is suited to working and running because it has wide nostrils that help it breathe easily.

_____[compound]_____ 8. A horse wants to please its owner, and usually a strong bond exists between horse and owner.

[compound complex] 9. Many people watch horses that are trained by others, and they don't see the command signals.

[compound complex] 10. A horse that is well trained can do work, yet it can also be a fine companion.

_____[simple]_____ 11. Horses have been used in therapy for troubled youngsters.

[compound complex] 12. Horses truly are magnificent creatures, and it is appropriate that they have been appreciated for thousands of years.

B. Write three different types of sentences about the topic of science.
[Sample answers are given.]

simple sentence 13. [Science is my favorite subject.]

compound sentence 14 [Last year I entered a project in the Science Fair, and I won first prize.]

complex sentence 15. [Even though I am good in science, I will major in English in college.]

Name _____

125. Reviewing Phrases, Clauses, and Sentences

A. Write on the line how each underlined phrase is used: write **A** for prepositional, **B** for participial, **C** for infinitive, and **D** for gerund.

___[B]___ 1. The book <u>shelved in the children's section</u> is really an adult story.

___[A]___ 2. Stories <u>of adventure</u> appeal to children and adults alike.

___[A]___ 3. *Robinson Crusoe* is a great tale <u>of shipwreck and survival</u>.

___[D]___ 4. Daniel Defoe gained fame <u>by writing novels</u>.

___[C]___ 5. <u>To read *Robinson Crusoe*</u> is to take an amazing adventure.

B. Underline the dependent clause in each sentence and write on the line how it is used: write **A** for adjective, **B** for adverb, and **C** for noun.

___[C]___ 1. It was evident <u>that the trial would be lengthy</u>.

___[B]___ 2. <u>After the crime was committed,</u> the neighbors were outraged.

___[B]___ 3. The courtroom grew noisy <u>as the spectators tried to push in</u>.

___[B]___ 4. <u>Because no photographs are allowed,</u> the court artists sketched the defendants.

___[A]___ 5. Judge Jacob, <u>who is the most famous judge in Minneapolis,</u> presided over the case.

___[C]___ 6. <u>That the defendants were found not guilty</u> made many people sad.

___[C]___ 7. The important thing is <u>that they had a fair trial by their peers</u>.

___[A]___ 8. The detective <u>who questioned the witness</u> will write a book.

___[B]___ 9. The jurors asked for more information <u>when they couldn't decide on a verdict</u>.

___[C]___ 10. <u>Whether or not the verdict will be appealed</u> remains to be seen.

C. Identify each sentence: **A** for simple, **B** for compound, **C** for complex, **D** for compound complex.

___[A]___ 1. The Navy trains dolphins off the coast of California.

___[B]___ 2. A dolphin may look harmless, but it can be trained to kill.

___[C]___ 3. As it travels through the water, a dolphin makes very high-pitched sounds.

___[A]___ 4. By listening to the echoes, the dolphin avoids objects in its path.

___[D]___ 5. Many people believe the stories that are told about dolphins who save humans, but I am not convinced they are true.

CONTINUED

Phrases, Clauses, Sentences

D. Write a sentence of each type, as indicated. [Answers will vary. Sample answers are given.]

1. *compound sentence*

   [My sister plays the flute in the orchestra, and I play drums in the band.]
   _____

2. *complex sentence with an adverbial clause*

   [Because we both need practice space, Dad built a room above the garage.]
   _____

3. *simple sentence with a compound predicate*

   [Now we can sing and play to our hearts' content.]
   _____

4. *compound complex sentence*

   [Many people like the rock concerts that are held outside, but I can't stand the crowds.]
   _____

5. *simple sentence with a compound subject*

   [Jane, Joe, and the twins listen to music on the radio.]
   _____

Try It Yourself
On a separate sheet of paper, write five or six sentences about an animal you would like to study. Vary your writing by including different kinds of sentences.

Check Your Own Work
Choose a selection from your writing portfolio, journal, work in progress, an assignment from class, or a letter. Revise it, applying the skills you have learned in this chapter. The checklist will help you.

✔ Have you varied your sentences, using simple, compound, complex, and compound complex sentences when appropriate?

✔ Have you combined sentence parts correctly?

Phrases, Clauses, Sentences

Name _____

126. Using Periods, Exclamation Points, and Question Marks Correctly

> Use a **period** at the end of a declarative or imperative sentence.
>
> > **She is a good student. Learn the rules tomorrow.**
>
> Use a period after an abbreviation and after the initials in a name.
>
> > **At 8:00 P.M. the Rev. Catherine Scott will be at John F. Kennedy Hall.**
>
> An **exclamation point** is used after an exclamatory sentence and after most interjections.
>
> > **Ouch! The stove is hot. Watch out!**
>
> A **question mark** is used at the end of a question.
>
> > **Where are my shoes?**

A. Complete each sentence with the proper punctuation.

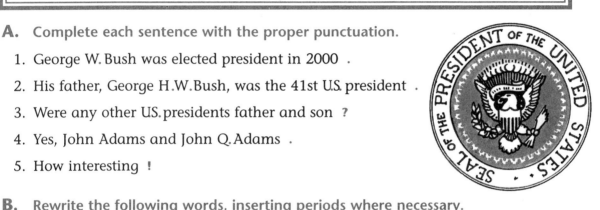

1. George W. Bush was elected president in 2000 **.**

2. His father, George H. W. Bush, was the 41st U.S. president **.**

3. Were any other U.S. presidents father and son **?**

4. Yes, John Adams and John Q. Adams **.**

5. How interesting **!**

B. Rewrite the following words, inserting periods where necessary.

1. Patricia Vogel, PhD **[Patricia Vogel, Ph.D.]**   6. Franz Fitzpatrick, Jr **[Franz Fitzpatrick Jr.]**

2. US Constitution **[U.S. Constitution]**   7. 10:30 AM **[10:30 A.M.]**

3. WC Fields **[W.C. Fields]**   8. 700 BC **[700 B.C.]**

4. Jan 11, 1982 **[Jan. 11, 1982]**   9. 35 in **[35 in.]**

5. John F Kennedy **[John F. Kennedy]**   10. J W Samuels, MD **[J. W. Samuels, M.D.]**

C. Complete each sentence with words that show a correct use of the period.
[Sample answers are given.]

1. The doorbell rang at _____ **[6:30 A.M.]** _____ today.

2. A man with a box in his hand said, "I am _____ **[José M. Soler]** _____, your new neighbor."

3. The letter carrier had delivered the package to his house on _____ **[Elm Rd.]** _____ by accident.

4. "_____ **[Mrs. Withers]** _____, I had to pay for the postage."

5. A package sent this way is said to be _____ **[C.O.D.]** _____, which stands for cash on delivery.

127. Using Commas Correctly

A reader pauses when he or she comes to a **comma.** There are many rules for using commas correctly; knowing these rules and using them correctly will make your writing clearer and easier to understand. A comma is used

1. to separate words in series of three or more:
   We ate cheese, bread, and lettuce.

2. to set off the parts of dates, addresses, and geographical names

3. to set off words of direct address, appositives, and parenthetical expressions:
   **Harry, I made the squad! Jan, my sister, did not. The try-outs,
   by the way, were brutal.**

4. to set off nonrestrictive phrases and clauses from the rest of a sentence:
   Our teacher, who was trained in nutrition, wants us to eat healthful snacks.

5. to set off long introductory phrases and clauses and when
   needed to make the meaning clear:
   As soon as our pet cat saw the squirrel race up the tree, she was out the door.

6. to set off a short direct quote and the parts of a divided quote
   (unless a question mark or exclamation point is needed):
   "Just who," Ms. Ward demanded, "ate all the jelly beans?"

7. before conjunctions such as *and, but, or, nor,* and *yet* when they are
   used to connect clauses in a compound sentence:
   The class was scheduled for Tuesday, but it was postponed until Thursday.

8. after the salutation in a friendly letter and after the close in all letters

A. Insert commas into each sentence correctly. Then write the
number of the rule for each comma use on the line.

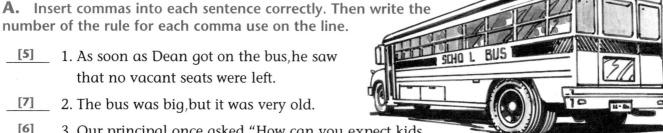

__[5]__ 1. As soon as Dean got on the bus, he saw
that no vacant seats were left.

__[7]__ 2. The bus was big, but it was very old.

__[6]__ 3. Our principal once asked, "How can you expect kids
to want to ride the bus when it looks like this?"

__[3]__ 4. That report, however, has not been confirmed.

__[3]__ 5. The Cramers, our next-door neighbors, have started walking.

__[4]__ 6. Woodrow Wilson High, which was named after our
twenty-eighth president, is just over two miles away.

__[7]__ 7. It was designed to hold 1,500 students, but now there are 2,100.

__[3]__ 8. John, can you believe the school that was built in 1996 is bursting at the seams?

__[1]__ 9. Kids who live close bike, skate, or carpool.

__[2]__ 10. Whoever thought our town of Rocky Creek, Oregon, would ever be overcrowded?

B. Insert the missing commas in the following sentences.

1. Alternative energy includes solar power, tidal power, and geothermal power.

2. Iceland, a volcanic region, has extremely high temperatures close to the surface.

3. Consequently, water piped from under ground can heat nearby homes, offices, and factories.

4. A pool in Reykjavik, Iceland's capital, is heated year-round by geothermal energy.

5. Tidal power has enormous potential, yet few plants exist today.

6. One such plant, located in Brittany, France, provides power for a town of 90,000 people.

7. On December 19, 1982, a solar-powered car began a 2,500 mile journey across Australia.

8. The car, called *The Quiet Achiever*, set out from Perth, Australia.

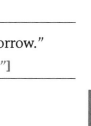

9. Indeed, that is a long way for a car running on sunshine to go.

10. It coasted into Sydney, Australia, on January 7, 1983, 20 days later.

C. Rewrite the following sentences, adding the missing commas.

1. "Kevin please hand me the map" said Vicki.

   ["Kevin, please hand me the map," said Vicki.]

2. Even Clara always a light packer brought two extra shirts a jacket and a scarf.

   [Even Clara, always a light packer, brought two extra shirts, a jacket, and a scarf.]

3. As soon as they got on the train started to move.

   [As soon as they got on, the train started to move.]

4. Arthur enjoying the cream pastries in Vienna Austria said "My diet starts tomorrow."

   [Arthur, enjoying the cream pastries in Vienna, Austria, said, "My diet starts tomorrow."]

5. On March 9 2001 the group reached Rome Italy.

   [On March 9, 2001, the group reached Rome, Italy.]

6. The trip to the ruins was scheduled for morning yet the students were too tired to go.

   [The trip to the ruins was scheduled for morning, yet the students were too tired to go.]

7. "I want" she said her eyes on the menu "pasta fruit salad and a lemonade."

   ["I want," she said, her eyes on the menu, "pasta, fruit salad, and a lemonade."]

8. After having lost the loser Ramon had to pay for lunch.

   [After having lost, the loser, Ramon, had to pay for lunch.]

9. Having arrived late the group missed the lecture.

   [Having arrived late, the group missed the lecture.]

10. After visiting Austria France and Italy the group decided that they wanted to go home.

    [After visiting Austria, France, and Italy, the group decided that they wanted to go home.]

128. Using Semicolons and Colons Correctly

Like a comma, a **semicolon** is a signal for a reader. A semicolon is a signal that two or more ideas will be connected. Use a semicolon

- to separate the principal clauses of a compound sentence when they are not joined by a conjunction
- to separate the clauses of a compound sentence that are joined by a conjunctive adverb (*nevertheless, moreover, therefore, then*)
- before *as* and *namely* when these words introduce examples
- to separate groups of words in a series when a comma would not do so clearly

A **colon** is a signal that a list or explanation is coming. Use a colon

- to introduce a list of items
- before a long quotation
- after the salutation in a business letter

Insert semicolons and colons where needed.

1. For some, an act of heroism lasts but a moment; for Albert Schweitzer, it lasted a lifetime.

2. By age 28, Albert was many things: pastor, musician, author, and professor.

3. He felt empty, but his life was to change; he soon found his life's mission.

4. He learned of the appalling problems in Africa: fierce animals; poisonous snakes; and diseases such as malaria, leprosy, and sleeping sickness.

5. He knew what he would do; namely, become a doctor and operate a hospital in Africa.

6. The first year was full of activity: gaining hospital experience, learning about Africa, and raising funds.

7. The Congo became Albert's home; he set up a clinic in the city of Lambaréné.

8. Albert had an able assistant in his wife; she was a trained nurse.

9. Albert and his wife worked for fifty years; the hospital grew and served ever more people.

10. Albert Schweitzer won a Nobel Peace Prize in 1952; it was a fitting tribute to a man who had nobly served so many.

Albert Schweitzer dedicated his life to helping those in need. How have you helped someone in need?

Punctuation

129. Using Commas and Semicolons Correctly

Be careful to use commas and semicolons correctly when joining clauses. A comma is used before the coordinate conjunction in a compound sentence.

It was sunny, yet the temperature was below zero.

A comma is also used to separate a dependent clause from the rest of a sentence.

After the rain stopped, we went hiking.

A semicolon is used to join two principal clauses not joined by a coordinate conjunction.

The troop was exhausted; they had hiked for hours.

A. Insert a comma or a semicolon on the line.

1. The White House is the president's house __[;]__ it is located in Washington, D.C.

2. It is a popular tourist destination __[,]__ yet little of it is open to the public.

3. The White House contains 132 rooms __[;]__ only five allow public access.

4. Although once called the Executive Mansion __[,]__ it is now known as the White House.

5. This name was not accurate at first __[,]__ because originally it was not white.

6. The mansion was made out of sandstone __[;]__ therefore, it was colored a pale gray.

7. It was burned in the War of 1812 __[;]__ white paint was used to hide the smoke stains.

8. George Washington never lived in the White House __[;]__ it had not been built yet.

9. He never lived in Washington, either __[;]__ nevertheless, the city is named after him.

10. Before being moved to Washington __[,]__ the government was headquartered in New York.

B. Create sentences by matching the clause or phrase from Column A with the appropriate clause or phrase from Column B. Write the correct letter on the line.

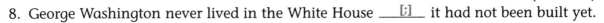

	Column A	Column B
__[d]__	1. Jack hurt his knee;	a. he commanded attention.
__[a]__	2. When Bob spoke,	b. however, we were still late.
__[e]__	3. Sid remained confident,	c. she had stayed up all night.
__[b]__	4. We left at 8:00 that morning;	d. nevertheless, he kept playing.
__[c]__	5. Maxine fell asleep;	e. even though he had never played before.

130. Using Quotation Marks Correctly

Quotation marks have two basic functions.
Quotation marks enclose dialogue and direct quotations. Sometimes a quotation includes another quotation. This is known as a quotation within a quotation and is marked with single quotation marks.

"When," asked my father, "did General Pershing say, 'Lafayette, we are here'?"

Quotation marks set off the titles of stories, poems, songs, magazine articles, television shows, and radio programs.
The titles of books, movies, plays, newspapers, magazines, and artwork are printed in italics. In handwriting, italics are indicated by underlining.

A. Insert quotation marks and underlining where necessary.

1. "Be quiet!" said Olive, "I'm reading the <u>Tribune</u>."

2. Joseph's favorite poem is "The Charge of the Light Brigade."

3. Thoreau is famous for <u>Walden</u> and the essay "Civil Disobedience."

4. "I lost my copy of <u>Great Expectations</u>," Oswald said.

5. "How long does 'Sixty Minutes' last?" Jacob asked.

6. "I thought it was fun," Al said, "when we sang 'Hail to the Chief.'"

7. "What time," asked Marge, "does the play <u>My Fair Lady</u> start?"

8. The teacher asked, "Have any of you read <u>Lord of the Flies</u>?"

9. The only show Sally is allowed to watch is "Sesame Street."

10. For his birthday Noam got a subscription to <u>National Geographic</u>.

B. Rewrite each sentence, adding punctuation where needed.

1. The monkeys said Josephine are my favorite animals at the zoo

    ["The monkeys," said Josephine, "are my favorite animals at the zoo."]

2. Twain wrote the novel Tom Sawyer and the short story The War Prayer

    [Twain wrote the novel <u>Tom Sawyer</u> and the short story "The War Prayer."]

3. Look exclaimed Mr Donahue my picture is in The New York Times

    ["Look," exclaimed Mr. Donahue, "my picture is in <u>The New York Times</u>!"]

4. Buzz Lightyear said Jane is my favorite character in Toy Story

    ["Buzz Lightyear," said Jane, "is my favorite character in <u>Toy Story</u>."]

5. The last time I saw him Harper told me he said I want to be a dancer

    ["The last time I saw him," Harper told me, "he said, 'I want to be a dancer.'"]

131. Using Apostrophes, Hyphens, and Dashes Correctly

There are three uses for the **apostrophe:**
- to show possession: **Ed's car, the Caseys' house**
- to show the omission of a letter(s) **(isn't)** or figures **('20s)**
- with *s* to show the plural of letters when not having an apostrophe would be confusing: **four i's in Mississippi** is clearer than **four is in Mississippi.**

Use a **hyphen** when writing the numbers twenty-one to ninety-nine; to separate parts of some compound words, as in *light-year;* and to divide a word of several syllables when it runs over at the end of a line.

Use a **dash** to indicate a sudden change of thought.
The test—it covers three chapters—is next week.

A. Insert apostrophes, hyphens, and dashes where needed. Add other punctuation as needed.

1. Don't think that anyone can run for the U.S. presidency !

2. The president and the vice president must be at least thirty-five years old .

3. They must also be natural-born citizens of the United States .

4. The first seven presidents weren't born U.S. citizens .

5. They were born subjects of England the United States didn't exist yet .

6. Presidents who've been elected to two terms are rare .

7. Few presidents only fifteen out of forty-two have done so .

8. Franklin Roosevelt he was Teddy Roosevelt's cousin was elected four times .

9. But Roosevelt's long reign twelve years prompted new legislation .

10. Now presidents may serve only two four-year terms .

B. Rewrite the following sentences, adding apostrophes, hyphens, dashes, and other punctuation as needed.

1. Youre still going to Dr. Salks house, arent you
   [You're still going to Dr. Salk's house, aren't you?]

2. Herberts keyboard it doesnt have any is or us is broken
   [Herbert's keyboard—it doesn't have any i's or u's—is broken.]

3. By midJanuary all of Jurgens relatives had gone back to Germany
   [By mid-January all of Jurgen's relatives had gone back to Germany.]

4. Julias birthday she will be thirty eight years old is tomorrow
   [Julia's birthday—she will be thirty-eight years old—is tomorrow.]

5. I didnt see the display of womens clothing
   [I didn't see the display of women's clothing.]

Name _____

132. Using Punctuation Correctly

Insert quotation marks, underlining, and other marks of punctuation where they are needed.

1. John Keats wrote, "A thing of beauty is a joy forever."

2. In Jack's bedroom hangs a print of Homer's famous painting Breezing Up.

3. "Ha! Ha!" laughed Richie, "I can solve that puzzle."

4. Sharon took me to see the movie Pearl Harbor.

5. "The Savannah," said Ben, "was the first American steamship to cross the ocean."

6. I like to read clever poems like "Ancient History" and "Advice to Travelers."

7. "Remember," said Mom, "the proverb 'A stitch in time saves nine.'"

8. Carrie chuckled, "Did they really think you were a senior citizen?"

9. "Where is the Golden Gate Bridge?" asked Jennifer.

10. The man replied, "You've hit the nail on the head."

11. Kelly's reading list includes poems, short stories, and novels.

12. A paragraph has the following parts: a beginning sentence that arouses interest, at least one middle sentence that tells about the topic, and an ending sentence that sums up the paragraph.

13. If the statement is true, write *yes* after it; if the statement is false, write *no* after it.

14. "Grab this rope!" shouted the lifeguard.

15. I missed the train to Seattle, Washington; moreover, I forgot my train ticket.

16. Alexander G. Bell became a U.S. citizen in 1882.

17. Edward Jenner, an English physician, introduced vaccination.

18. The United States is a land of farms, a land of cities, and a land of opportunity.

19. Besides writing books such as The Giving Tree, Shel Silverstein wrote funny poems.

20. Do you, Zach, drink eight glasses of water a day?

Name _____

133. Using Capital Letters Correctly

Use a capital letter for the following:

- the first word in a sentence
- the first word of a direct quotation
- the first word of most lines of poetry
- the titles of books, plays, poems, and full works of art
- proper names and adjectives
- a title when it precedes a person's name

- sacred books and the names of deities
- the pronoun *I* and the interjection *O*
- north, east, south, and west when referring to sections of a country
- abbreviations when capital letters would be used if the words were written out

A. Rewrite each item, capitalizing letters where necessary.

1. eva l. sloan, ph.d. _____[Eva L. Sloan, Ph.D.]_____

2. republican party _____[Republican Party]_____

3. ohio river _____[Ohio River]_____

4. private college _____[private college]_____

5. professor reiss _____[Professor Reiss]_____

6. fourth of july _____[Fourth of July]_____

7. jesus christ _____[Jesus Christ]_____

8. friday, may 3 _____[Friday, May 3]_____

9. doctor _____[doctor]_____

10. george bush _____[George Bush]_____

B. Circle all letters that should be capitalized in the following sentences.

1. benjamin franklin was an american author, scientist, and statesman.

2. he helped draft the declaration of independence.

3. of this, he said: "we must all hang together, or assuredly we will all hang separately."

4. he was a member of the pennsylvania assembly for twelve years.

5. after the revolutionary war, franklin oversaw the treaty with great britain.

6. the treaty was signed at versailles, france, on september 3, 1783.

7. in 1732 he published poor richard's almanac.

8. in it he coined many phrases, such as, "practice makes perfect."

9. he also wrote the autobiography of benjamin franklin.

10. his greatest legacy, however, is his part in drafting the u.s. constitution.

134. Abbreviating the Names of States

Each state and territory has a two-letter postal abbreviation. Both letters are capitalized and are not followed by a period. These abbreviations are normally used only in mailing addresses.

AL	Alabama	KY	Kentucky	ND	North Dakota
AK	Alaska	LA	Louisiana	OH	Ohio
AZ	Arizona	ME	Maine	OK	Oklahoma
AR	Arkansas	MD	Maryland	OR	Oregon
CA	California	MA	Massachusetts	PA	Pennsylvania
CO	Colorado	MI	Michigan	RI	Rhode Island
CT	Connecticut	MN	Minnesota	SC	South Carolina
DE	Delaware	MS	Mississippi	SD	South Dakota
DC	District of Columbia	MO	Missouri	TN	Tennessee
FL	Florida	MT	Montana	TX	Texas
GA	Georgia	NE	Nebraska	UT	Utah
HI	Hawaii	NV	Nevada	VT	Vermont
ID	Idaho	NH	New Hampshire	VA	Virginia
IL	Illinois	NJ	New Jersey	WA	Washington
IN	Indiana	NM	New Mexico	WV	West Virginia
IA	Iowa	NY	New York	WI	Wisconsin
KS	Kansas	NC	North Carolina	WY	Wyoming
		GU	Guam	VI	Virgin Islands
		PR	Puerto Rico	AS	American Samoa

A. Write the postal abbreviation for each state or territory.

[ME] 1. Maine   [NE] 6. Nebraska   [WV] 11. West Virginia

[NM] 2. New Mexico   [DE] 7. Delaware   [HI] 12. Hawaii

[IN] 3. Indiana   [CT] 8. Connecticut   [AK] 13. Alaska

[MS] 4. Mississippi   [LA] 9. Louisiana   [VI] 14. Virgin Islands

[KS] 5. Kansas   [VT] 10. Vermont   [MO] 15. Missouri

B. Write the name of the state for each postal abbreviation.

1. NJ [New Jersey]   6. MI [Michigan]   11. MN [Minnesota]

2. FL [Florida]   7. OH [Ohio]   12. OK [Oklahoma]

3. AL [Alabama]   8. NY [New York]   13. AR [Arkansas]

4. TN [Tennessee]   9. KY [Kentucky]   14. MT [Montana]

5. UT [Utah]   10. WY [Wyoming]   15. IA [Iowa]

Name _____

135. Reviewing Punctuation

A. Insert commas, periods, question marks, and exclamation points where needed.

1. Have you ever read *The War of the Worlds* ?

2. It is about Martians attacking Earth .

3. How scary !

4. It was written by H.G.Wells .

5. He is well known for his stories of fantasy, technology, and science fiction .

6. H.G.Wells also wrote *The Time Machine, The Invisible Man,* and *Ann Veronica* .

7. *The War of the Worlds* was performed on the radio by Orson Welles in 1938 .

8. What happened ?

9. Many people, believing it to be the news, thought Earth was really being attacked .

10. That's terrible !

B. Insert colons, semicolons, and quotation marks where needed.

1. Brook's father told her to do the following: mow, rake, and weed the lawn.

2. "But I'm tired," she pleaded.

3. Her father said, "Then you should not have stayed up all night."

4. She had rented some movies the night before; therefore, she was up very late.

5. Brook watched three movies: *Casablanca, Gigi,* and *Ben-Hur.*

6. "If you get started now," her father said, "you can finish by nightfall."

7. She was exhausted; nevertheless, she would do what he asked.

8. "When I was a boy," her father said, "we worked all day, or we didn't eat."

9. "Here we go again," she thought to herself.

10. Brook worked all afternoon; she finished just before dark.

C. Insert hyphens, apostrophes, and dashes where needed.

11. The fastest-growing tree on Earth is a member of the pea family.

12. One specimen grew thirty-five feet in a year.

13. The tallest tree—though not the largest—is the sequoia.

Punctuation

CONTINUED

149

14. Some oldgrowth specimens are more than 300 feet high.

15. The worlds largest tree is the redwood.

16. A redwoods weight can be more than 200 tons.

17. Its not the oldest tree, however.

18. One species of pine the worlds oldest tree can live 5,000 years.

19. These trees aren't necessarily the oldest living things on Earth.

20. Lichens plants made up of algae and fungus are also thousands of years old.

D. Circle the correct example of capitalization in each row.

21. (Harvard University)   world war II   Mexican Silver

22. Mathematics   (East Coast)   Sears tower

23. (Tuesday)   Third avenue   asian

24. republicans   (Lutherans)   aunt Helga

25. *Of Mice And Men*   memorial day   (spring in Paris)

26. Nile river   sir Isaac Newton   (October)

27. (Canadian border)   Pacific ocean   Lakeview high school

28. Dictionary   middle East   (Buddha)

29. bible   Gettysburg address   (*The Time Machine*)

30. Frederick the great   (Russian history)   President

Try It Yourself

On a separate sheet of paper, write six or seven sentences about what you will do after you have graduated from eighth grade. Be sure to punctuate your sentences carefully and correctly.

Check Your Own Work

Choose a selection from your writing portfolio. Revise it, applying the skills you have learned in this chapter. The checklist will help you.

✔ Do your sentences end with the correct punctuation?

✔ Have you used commas correctly?

✔ Have you used quotation marks before and after every quotation and around certain titles?

✔ Have you capitalized all proper nouns and adjectives?

✔ Have you used semicolons, colons, hyphens, and dashes where needed?

136. Deciding Which Internet Site to Use

When you use a search engine to locate information on the Internet, it is important to know what kind of Web site it has taken you to. The organization or group that sets up a Web site is called a host. The hostname domain, the three letters that end each address, will tell you what kind of site you are looking at. The seven hostname domains in common use are:

.com	Businesses and individuals use .com.
.edu	All educational institutions, which may include museums, use this ending.
.gov	These letters signify that the address belongs to a government agency.
.org	Addresses for nonprofit groups such as United Way end in .org.
.mil	The armed forces use these letters.
.net	This means a networking organization such as netscape.net.
.int	International organizations such as the International Red Cross use these letters.

A search engine is a handy tool for finding information. But sometimes you may wish you knew the URL (Uniform Resource Locator), or address, for a specific place like the Smithsonian Institution or the White House. It would save time if there were a giant directory of Web addresses, but none exists. Following are a few addresses that may be useful to you in doing research online.

For information on the federal government

- FedWorld is a gateway to links to federal government departments.
  http://www.fedworld.gov:80

- The White House Web site provides information on the activities of the current president and the executive branch of government.
  http://www.whitehouse.gov

- Each house of Congress has its own Web site. To reach the home page of a particular senator or representative, type his or her last name after the slash in the appropriate URL.
  - U.S. Senators: http://www.senate.gov/
  - House of Representatives: http://www.house.gov/

- Thomas, maintained by the Library of Congress, has links to the House, Senate, Congressional Record, and other federal departments.
  http://thomas.loc.gov

Research Skills

- The National Park Service is the system of more than 350 national parks, historic sites, historic parks, monuments, battlefields, seashores, rivers, and recreation areas.
http://www.nps.gov

For general information on United States history

- The Library of Congress, the national library of the United States, hosts a number of sites with documents, photos, and time lines of important events in American history, such as the construction of Washington, D.C.; Lincoln's assassination; and the women's suffrage movement.
http://www.loc.gov

- U.S. statistical information from the annual *Statistical Abstract* is available online; it includes census data, election results, federal budget data, and similar information about the people, business, and government of the United States.
http://www.census.gov/statab

- The Smithsonian Institution is operated by the federal government as a center of the arts and scientific research. It is made up of a number of museums, such as the Museum of the American Indian and the National Gallery of Art, as well as the National Zoo.
http://www.si.edu

- Internet Public Library is a source for information on many United States presidents. In the space between the slashes, type as one word the initials for the first and middle names of the President and his complete last name, for example, /rwreagan for Ronald Wilson Reagan.
http://www.ipl.org/ref/POTUS/   .html

- *National Geographic,* the magazine, offers information on United States and world human and animal cultures.
http://www.nationalgeographic.com

- Each year the Public Broadcasting System televises a number of programs of interest to students of United States history and government, programs on topics such as immigration, African Americans, the Civil War, and the development of jazz. This is the companion site for its programs.
http://www.pbs.org

For the news

- CNN Interactive, cable news site
http://www.cnn.com

- *The New York Times*
http://www.nytimes.com

- *Washington Post*
http://www.washingtonpost.com

For the 50 states

- In the space between the periods, type the two-letter postal abbreviation for the state whose home page you want to find. Do not leave any space between the letters and the periods.
  http://www.state. .us

For science information

- The National Air and Space Museum, part of the Smithsonian Institution, offers aerospace resources and exhibits.
  http://www.nasm.edu/

- The Franklin Institute Science Museum, founded in honor of Benjamin Franklin, has exhibits on many areas of science, including a giant model of the heart.
  http://www.fi.edu

- The National Aeronautics and Space Administration's site includes links to the home pages of the NASA Space Centers around the country.
  http://www.nasa.gov

- The National Audubon Society is an organization that encourages the protection of wild birds and promotes education about them.
  http://www.audubon.org

- The National Zoo's site lets you visit the animals.
  http://natzoo.si.edu

- The New York Botanical Garden is a good site for information on plants.
  http://www.nybg.org

Name _____

Review the URLs on pages 151–153, and then answer the following questions.

Which sites would you choose to investigate if you wanted information on the following topics? For each topic, choose as many sites as you think look promising. To practice being precise, write each URL exactly as it is shown, not the name of the host.

1. How the brain functions

   [http://www.fi.edu]
   _____

2. Information on current United States–China relations

   [http://www.cnn.com; http://www.nytimes.com; http://www.washingtonpost.com; student's local

   newspaper if it is a large daily with world news coverage.]

3. U.S. Department of Justice

   [http://www.fedworld.gov:80; http://thomas.loc.gov]

4. Information on how weightlessness affects humans

   [http://www.nasa.gov]

5. Total population of the United States

   [http://www.census.gov/statab]

6. Information on the park system in your state

   [http://www.state.   .us (Be sure students have entered the 2-letter state abbreviation correctly.)]

7. Nesting habits of bald eagles

   [http://www.audubon.org]

8. Photo to illustrate a report on Franklin D. Roosevelt

   [http://www.ipl.org/ref/POTUS/fdroosevelt.html (Students might also suggest the sites for the

   White House, the Smithsonian Institution, *National Geographic* magazine, and PBS.)]

9. Write the Web address for one of your two Senators.

   [http://www.senate.gov/*name*]

10. If your local newspaper has a Web site, write its URL here.

   [Answers will vary.]

Research Skills

Name _____

137. Choosing Research Tools

Writing a research paper involves a great deal of work. You have to choose a subject, narrow its focus to a single topic, do the necessary research, and then write it up. Using your time efficiently during the research process can make a great deal of difference in having a manageable project. One way to be efficient is to decide before you begin which reference tools you will need to consult. Following is a brief review of different reference tools.

- **Computer catalog:** the media center or library's central reference tool for locating books in the library

- **Dictionary:** listing of words and their meanings; print

- **Thesaurus:** listing of synonyms and antonyms for words; print

- **Encyclopedia:** information in the form of articles about people, places, events, and things; print, CD-ROM, online

- **Almanac:** published yearly; up-to-date facts on a variety of subjects from the major news stories in the United States and the world to sports records and the population of major U.S. and world cities; print. Much of the statistical information on the United States comes from federal government agencies.

- **Atlas:** book of maps; may be maps of the United States only or of the world; may also contain other interesting geographical information about a country or continent in text form; print

- **Biographical dictionary:** basic information about famous people—full name, birth date, death date, if no longer living; accomplishments of the person; may be subject specific such as famous women or African Americans; print, CD-ROM, and Internet search

- **Guides to periodical literature:** listing of articles in magazines (not newspapers); print, online

- *Books in Print:* listing of all the books that are currently being published in the United States; some guides may also list books that are no longer being published; print, online in some libraries

- *Statistical Abstract:* compilation of statistical information about the United States such as the annual budget of the federal government, population of each state and of major cities, election results, number of people employed in certain industries, and so on; published by the federal government annually; print, CD-ROM, online at the Census Bureau Home Page

Read each of the topics below and decide which reference tool you would use to find the information. For some topics you may decide that several reference works would be useful. List them all and then circle the one that you would probably consult first.

1. Check information about a book's year of publication and publisher for your bibliography _[Books in Print]_ _____

2. Number of students in public schools in the United States in 1990 _[Statistical Abstract,_ __ **either in book format or online at the Census Bureau Web site]**

3. Information on Langston Hughes **[Encyclopedia; biographical dictionary, print, CD-ROM,** __ **online; Internet search]**

4. Major industries in Mexico **[Atlas, encyclopedia, Internet search]** _____

5. A synonym for the word _talk_ **[Thesaurus]** _____

6. A magazine article about Civil War battles **[Guide to periodical literature (The item asks** __ **specifically for a magazine article; students may also suggest searching the Internet for Web sites** __ **of magazines to find articles.)]**

7. The meaning of the word _synthetic_ **[Dictionary]** _____

8. Information on lizards **[Encyclopedia, Internet search]** _____

9. A map showing land use in the United States **[Atlas, encyclopedia]** _____

10. A list of manned space flights since 1960 **[Almanac, encyclopedia, Internet search]** _____

[First choices may vary. Challenge students to review their reasoning to make sure that their choices are the most efficient and the most likely to get results quickly. For example, searching on the Internet to find information about Langston Hughes might not be more efficient than going to the media center or library to use the encyclopedia—either in print or on CD-ROM.]

138. Using the Statistical Abstract of the United States

The **Statistical Abstract of the United States** is the national data book. It is filled with statistics about the United States—the government, people, industries, schools, elections, parks, incomes, health care, and similar topics. You will find information on the 50 states, all the counties in the United States, and major metropolitan areas. For example, there is a table comparing the ten fastest growing states and their percent of population change from 1990 to 2000.

The *Statistical Abstract* uses tables, charts, graphs, and maps to show data. Sometimes the data is for one year only, and sometimes the information spans a number of years to indicate trends over time. The *Statistical Abstract* also includes discussions of such issues as immigration policies, explanations of how statistical information was obtained, and definitions of certain terms as they are used in the *Statistical Abstract*.

Some information is updated annually, and some is revised after the decennial census of the American people. The Census Bureau in the U.S. Department of Labor compiles and publishes the *Statistical Abstract* in print format, on CD-ROM, and at its Web site, www.census.gov/statab.

At one time the federal government published in a print version the *Historical Abstract of the United States, Colonial Times to 1957*. Some of the information in this volume is used to show trends in the yearly editions of the *Statistical Abstract,* such as the change in land areas in the United States from 1790 to 2000. However, much of the early data about the United States, starting with the 1790 census, is available only in the print volume of the *Historical Abstract* in libraries. Both the *Historical Abstract* and the *Statistical Abstract* can be very helpful when you are doing research for papers in United States history, government, and economics.

The following is part of the table of contents of the *Statistical Abstract of the United States*. Read the table of contents and then indicate where in the *Statistical Abstract* you would look for the information listed below it.

Research Skills

> **Sec. 1. Population** (Tables 1–76)
> Immigration
> Population estimates, projections
> States, metro areas, cities
>
> Population characteristics
> Marital status and households
> Religion
>
> **Sec. 2. Vital Statistics** (Tables 77–150)
> Births
> Life expectancy
>
> Deaths
>
> **Sec. 3. Health and Nutrition** (Tables 151–238)
> Health expenditures, insurance
> Health facilities, workforce
>
> Health measures
> Food consumption, nutrition
>
> **Sec. 4. Education** (Tables 239–328)
> Education projections
> School building conditions
>
> Internet access
> Degrees conferred
>
> **Sec. 5. Law Enforcement, Courts, and Prisons** (Tables 329–379)
> Crime arrests, and victimizations
> Courts
>
> Juveniles, child abuse
> Prisoners and inmates
>
> **Sec. 6. Geography and Environment** (Tables 380–414)
> Land and water
> Air quality
>
> Hazardous waste sites
> Climate
>
> **Sec. 7. Parks, Recreation, and Travel** (Tables 415–451)
> Book purchasing
> NCAA sports
>
> Leisure activities
> Travel
>
> **Sec. 8. Elections** (Tables 452–489)
> Vote results
>
> Campaign finances
>
> **Sec. 9. State and Local Government Finances and Employment** (Tables 490–531)
> Government units
> State government finances
> Local government finances
>
> Finances for large cities and counties
> Employment and payroll

1. What presidential candidates spent in the 2000 election

   [Section 8. Elections: Campaign finances]

   _____

2. Number of schools that have Internet connections

   [Section 4. Education: Internet access]

   _____

3. How Americans spend their time
   [Section 7. Parks, Recreation, and Travel: Book purchasing, Leisure activities, Travel; possibly NCAA sports to see if attendance at games is one of the tables]

4. What Americans eat

   [Section 3. Health and Nutrition: Food consumption, nutrition]

5. List of hazardous waste sites

   [Section 6. Geography and Environment: Hazardous waste sites]

6. Structure of the federal court system

   [Section 5. Law Enforcement, Courts, and Prisons: Courts]

7. Tax revenue of your state government

   [Section 9. State and Local Government Finances and Employment: State government finances]

8. Number of people employed in hospitals
   [Section 3. Health and Nutrition: Health facilities, workforce]

9. Number of citizens of Hispanic descent
   [Section 1. Population: Population characteristics]

10. Birth rates over the last 100 years
    [Section 2. Vital Statistics: Births]

    _____

Sentence Diagrams

A diagram is a visual outline of a sentence. It shows the essential parts of the sentence (subject, verb, object, complement) and the relationship of the other words and constructions to those essentials.

Diagramming Simple Sentences

The main line of a diagram is a horizontal line.

- The verb is written on the center of the diagram line.

- The subject is written in front of the verb with a vertical line separating it from the verb. This vertical line cuts through the horizontal line.

- The direct object is written after the verb with a vertical line separating it from the verb. This vertical line touches the horizontal line but does not cut through it.

Modifiers of the subject, verb, and direct object are written on slanted lines under the appropriate word. Note the way in which prepositional phrases are indicated.

Yesterday many excited children played noisy games in the park.

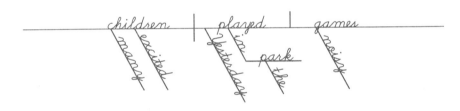

A subject complement is indicated by a slanted line pointing back to the subject between the verb and the complement.

Mrs. Mitchell is a good teacher. She is always very kind.

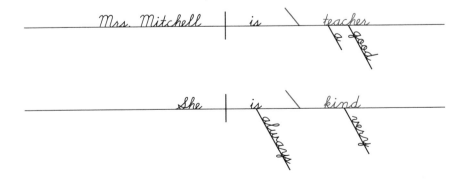

CONTINUED

An indirect object is placed under the verb.

The babysitter read the children a scary story.

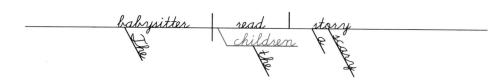

An appositive goes in parentheses after the noun it renames or describes.

My family visited Tokyo, the capital of Japan.

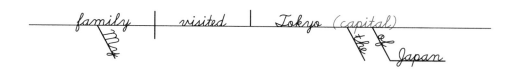

A participial phrase works like an adjective. It goes under the word it modifies.

The boy playing the tuba fell down. Shouting angrily, Tom helped him.

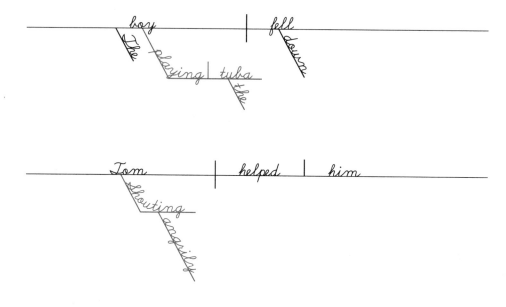

A gerund phrase works like a noun. It goes above a noun position in a diagram.

Playing the piano is my favorite hobby.

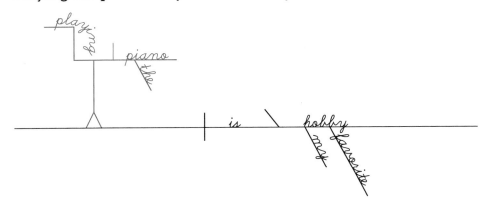

I remember meeting your cousin.

An infinitive phrase used as a noun goes above a noun position in a diagram.

To win the game was my intention.

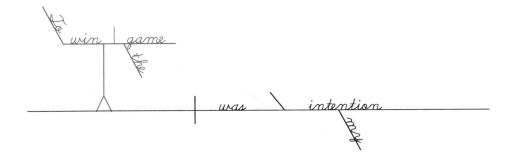

I like to see good movies.

Compound subjects, compound predicates, and compound direct objects are diagrammed in similar ways—on parallel lines with the conjunction on a broken line between the words it joins. Add modifiers to the appropriate words.

Bob and Joanne designed and built the children's playhouse

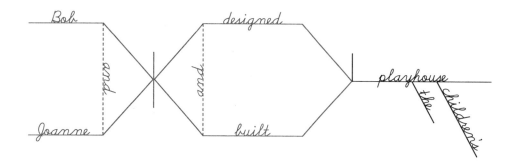

The children and their parents ate chocolate cake and vanilla ice cream.

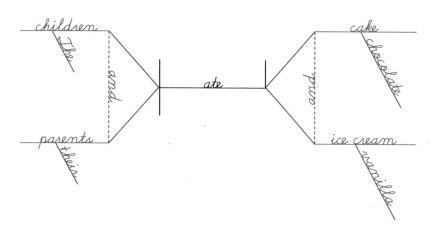

Diagramming Compound Sentences

A compound sentence contains two or more independent clauses. Each clause is diagrammed according to the form for a simple sentence. When both independent clauses have been diagrammed, place the conjunction on a horizontal line between the verbs and connect it to the main diagram lines with broken vertical lines.

The longest cave in the world is Mammoth Cave, but the deepest cave is in France.

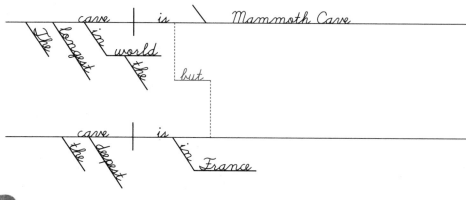

If a semicolon is used instead of a conjunction, place an X on the line between the clauses.

Snow fell during the night; the field lay under a soft white blanket.

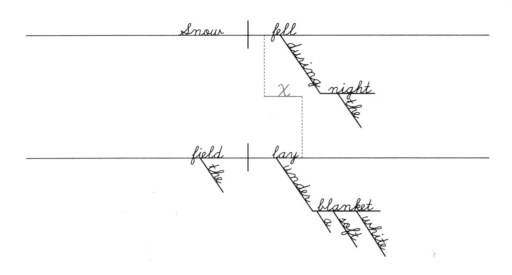

Try It Yourself
Diagram each of these sentences on a sheet of paper.

1. The weather was perfect yesterday; the sun shone brightly.

2. Cindy and her family visited the White House, the home of the president.

3. The boy and his mother washed and polished their old car.

4. Cheering loudly, the students ran from the building and swarmed into the street.

5. Selling insurance is his job, but playing the drums is his hobby.

1.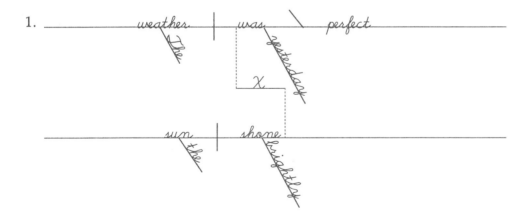

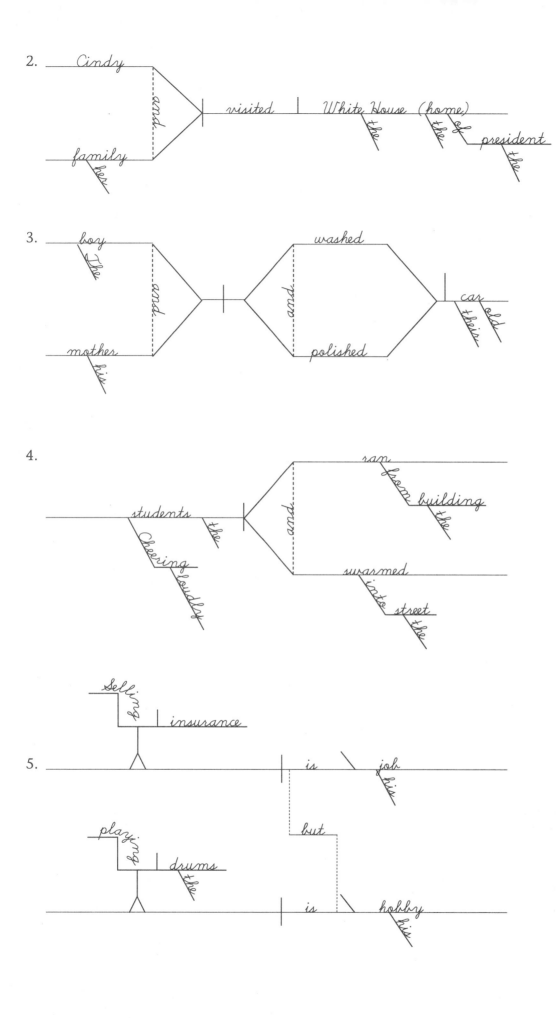

Handbook of Terms

A

adjective A word that describes a noun or pronoun.

> Some descriptive adjectives come from proper nouns and are called proper adjectives. A proper adjective begins with a capital letter: *American* history.

> The adjectives *a, an,* and *the* point out nouns. They are called articles.

> Demonstrative adjectives point out specific persons, places, or things.
> - *This* and *that* point out one person, place or thing.
> - *These* and *those* point out more than one person, place, or thing.
> - *This* and *these* point out persons, places, or things that are near.
> - *That* and *those* point out persons, places, or things that are far.

> Possessive adjectives show possession or ownership. The possessive adjectives are *my, your, his, her, its, our, your,* and *their.*

> Numeral adjectives indicate exact numbers: *ten, twenty-five, third, twelfth.*

> Some adjectives indicate number but not exact number: *many, few, several, some.*

> An adjective usually comes before the noun it modifies: *sunny* morning, *hot* chocolate.

> An adjective that follows a linking verb is a subject complement. A subject complement completes the meaning of the verb and describes the subject of the sentence: The night was *dark* and *cold.*

> An adjective that follows a direct object and completes the thought expressed by a transitive verb is an object complement: Mary considered the test *difficult.*

> *See also* **comparison.**

adverb A word that modifies a verb, an adjective, another adverb, a participle, a gerund, or an infinitive.

> An adverb of time answers the question *when* or *how often:* It rained *yesterday.* We *usually* eat lunch at noon.

> An adverb of place answers the question *where:* Toshi bent his head *forward.* Sit *here* by the gate.

> An adverb of manner answers the question *how* or *in what manner:* Jason draws *well.* She dances the waltz *gracefully.*

> An adverb of degree answers the question *how much* or *how little:* The boy is *very* tall. Gaelic is *seldom* spoken in that part of Ireland.

> An adverb of affirmation asserts something: The music is *certainly* beautiful.

> An adverb of negation expresses the negative of an alternative choice or possibility: The door is *not* locked.

(continued on next page)

A conjunctive adverb is used to connect two independent clauses. The principal conjunctive adverbs are *consequently, however, moreover, nevertheless, therefore,* and *thus:* Jill had studied journalism; *therefore,* the newspaper editor hired her.

A relative adverb does the work of an adverb and a relative pronoun: Louisville is the city *where* I was born. The principal relative adverbs are *when, where,* and *why.* These adverbs usually follow a noun of time or place and may be replaced by a prepositional phrase that contains a relative pronoun: Louisville is the place *in which* I was born.

Interrogative adverbs are used in asking questions: *Where* was she born?

Nouns that express time, distance, measure, weight, value, or direction can function as adverbs by modifying verbs: Every *Sunday* we attend church. The room measured 144 square feet.

Equally means "as" when it modifies an adjective or adverb. The correct forms are *equally good, equally well, equally great,* and so forth. Never use *as* between *equally* and the adjective or adverb.

Use *anywhere, everywhere, nowhere, somewhere* instead of *any place, no place, every place, no place, some place.*

See also **comparison.**

apostrophe A punctuation mark (') used in the following ways:
- to show ownership: the *cook's* hat, the *girls'* horses
- to replace letters or numbers left out in a contraction: *wasn't* for *was not;* the blizzard of *'93* for the blizzard of *1993*
- with *s* to show the plural of lowercase letters: Mind your *p's* and *q's.*
- with *s* to show the plural of uppercase letters if omitting it would cause confusion: *A's, I's, S's*

articles The adjectives *a, an,* and *the. A* and *an* are the indefinite articles. An indefinite article refers to any of a class of things: *a* banana, *an* elephant. *The* is the definite article. The definite article refers to one or more specific things: *the* bananas in the bowl, *the* elephants in the zoo.

The repetition of the article in a sentence changes the meaning of the sentence: *A* blue and white jacket hung on the hook. (one jacket) *A* blue and *a* white jacket hung on the hook. (two jackets)

C

capitalization The use of capital letters. Capital letters are used for many purposes, including the following:
- the first word of a sentence: *The* bell rang.
- proper nouns and proper adjectives: *Betsy Ross's American* flag
- an abbreviation if the word it stands for begins with a capital letter: *Rev.* for *Reverend.*
- the first word and the name of a person addressed in the salutation of a letter: *Dear Marie,*
- the first word in the complimentary close of a letter: *Yours truly,*

- the principal words in the titles of books, plays, pictures, and most poems: A T*ale of T*wo Cities, *R*omeo and *J*uliet, *Mona Lisa,* "*Fire and Ice*"
- the first word of a direct quotation: Mother said, " *It's* time for my favorite television program."
- proper nouns and proper adjectives: *C*hina, *C*hinese checkers
- titles when used in direct address as substitutes for the names of persons: Thank you, *Professor.*
- North, East, South, West when they refer to a section of the country or the world: the old *West.* They are not capitalized when they refer to direction: He drove *west* on Main Street.
- the pronoun *I,* the interjection *O*
- names referring to deities or to sacred books: *God,* the *Bible*
- two-letter state postal abbreviations: *MA, NY, CA*

clause A group of related words that contains a subject and predicate and is used as part of a sentence.

An independent clause expresses a complete thought.

A dependent clause does not express a complete thought and cannot stand alone. A dependent clause, together with an independent clause, forms a complex sentence.

- An adjectival clause is a dependent clause used as an adjective: The roses *that he bought* were yellow. Adjectival clauses are usually introduced by relative pronouns: *who, whom, which, whose, that.*
- An adverbial clause is a dependent clause used as an adverb: *After we had canoed down the river,* we went to a clambake on the beach. Adverbial clauses are usually introduced by conjunctions such as *although, as, after, because, before, for, since, that, though, unless, until, where, where,* and *while.*

A restrictive clause points out or identifies a certain person, place, or thing. A restrictive clause cannot be omitted without changing the meaning of a sentence: The girl *who runs the fastest* will win the prize.

A nonrestrictive clause adds to the information about a person, place, or thing, but it is not necessary to the meaning of the sentence: New York, *which is the located on the eastern seaboard,* has many fine museums. A nonrestrictive clause is separated from the rest of the sentence by commas.

A clause can be used as a noun.

- A noun clause may be used as the subject of a sentence: *That some mushrooms are poisonous* should be kept in mind.
- A noun clause may be used as the direct object of a sentence: The bus driver told us *where the amusement park was.*
- A noun clause may be used as a subject complement: This camcorder is *what I wanted.*
- A noun clause may be used as the object of a preposition: We were amused by *what we saw.*
- A noun clause may be used as an appositive clause to explain the noun or pronoun that precedes it: The prediction *that the storm would bypass our farm* was encouraging.

colon A punctuation mark (:) used in the following ways:

- after the salutation in a business letter: Dear Sir:
- before a list or an enumeration of items: We bought the following: eggs, limes, bread.
- before a long direct quotation

comma A punctuation mark (,) used to make reading clearer. Among its many uses are the following:

- to separate words or groups of words in a series: elephants, giraffes, hyenas, and monkeys
- to set off parts of dates, addresses, or geographical names: January 1, 2003; 321 Spring Road, Atlanta, Georgia; Paris, France
- to set off words in direct address: Josie, I'm so pleased that you called me this morning.
- after the words *yes* and *no* when they introduce sentences: Yes, I agree with you completely.
- to set off direct quotations, unless a question mark or explanation point is required: "We have only vanilla and chocolate today," he said in an apologetic tone.
- to separate clauses connected by the conjunctions *and, but,* and *or:* She called his name, but he didn't answer her.
- after the salutation and closing in a social or friendly letter: Dear Mrs. Porter, Dear Ben, Sincerely yours,
- to set off parenthetical expressions—words or groups of words that are inserted in a sentence as comments or explanatory remarks but are not necessary to the thought of the sentence: The time, I think, is up.
- after long introductory phrases and clauses: As the band marched down the street, the class cheered and applauded.
- to separate nonrestrictive phrases and clauses from the rest of the sentence: Chicago, which is the biggest city in Illinois, is not the state capital.

comparison The act of comparing. Many adjectives and adverbs can be used to compare two or more persons, places, or things.

Adjectives

- An adjective in the *positive* degree describes one or more persons, places, or things: The cat is *quiet.* The dogs are *powerful.*
- An adjective in the comparative degree compares two persons, places, or things. Form comparative adjectives by adding *–er* to the positive degree or by putting *more* before the positive degree: *quieter, more powerful.*
- An adjective in the superlative degree compares three or more persons, places, or things. Form superlative adjectives by adding *–est* to the positive degree or by putting *most* before the positive degree: *quietest, most powerful.*

Adverbs

- Form the comparative degree by adding *–er* to the positive degree or by putting *more* before the positive degree: *faster, more carefully.*

- Form the superlative degree by adding *–est* to the positive degree or by putting *most* before the positive degree: *faster, most carefully*.

Farther refers to distance: She went *farther* into the forest. *Further* denotes an addition: *Further* research is necessary. Both *farther* and *further* are used as adverbs and as adjectives.

When comparing persons, places, or things use *as . . . as* in positive statements: Her face is *as* dirty *as* her hands.

When comparing persons, places, or things use *so . . . as* in negative statements: Jeff is not *so* tall *as* Carlos.

complex sentence A sentence that contains one independent clause and one or more dependent clauses: *If you want to win, you must jump higher.*
- An independent clause expresses a complete thought: *You must jump higher.*
- A dependent clause does not express a complete thought and cannot stand alone: *If you want to win.*
- A dependent clause may precede, follow, or be contained within an independent clause.

compound complex sentence A compound sentence that contains two or more independent clauses and one or more dependent clauses: *Many students go to the Jobs and Careers Show that is given at the public library twice a year, but Glenn has never attended it.*

compound sentence A sentence that contains two or more independent clauses: *Usually Jane drives to work, but today she took the train.*
- The clauses in a compound sentence are usually connected by a conjunction or by a conjunctive adverb.
- A semicolon may be used to separate the clauses in a compound sentence.

compound subjects, predicates, objects In a simple sentence or a clause, the subject, the predicate, and the direct object may be compound: *Ivan* and *John* argued with the grocer. The baby *walks* and *talks* well. Wear your *hat, scarf,* and *gloves.*
- Compound subjects connected by *and* usually require a plural verb: Ontario *and* Nova Scotia *are* provinces of Canada.
- If the subjects connected by *and* refer to the same person or thing or express the same idea, the verb is singular: Bacon and eggs *is* his favorite breakfast.
- Compound subjects connected by *and* and preceded by *each, every, many a,* or *no* require a singular verb: Every boy and girl here *wants* to graduate.
- When two or more subjects of different person or number are connected by *or* or *nor*, the verb agrees with the subject nearest to it: The children or the teacher *is* in the auditorium. The ladders, the paint brushes, or the paint *is* in the garage.

conjunction A word used to connect words, phrases, or clauses in a sentence. The most common conjunctions are *and, but,* and *or.*

(continued on next page)

Coordinate conjunctions connect subjects, predicates, direct objects, and clauses of the same rank and function: Joshua *and* Leanne cut *and* pasted the words *and* pictures on the posters. It poured all day, *and* a cold wind blew.

Correlative conjunctions are coordinate conjunctions used in pairs: *Neither* Tom *nor* Laurie left the party early.

Conjunctive adverbs connect two independent clauses: The meal was expensive; *however,* I wasn't surprised.

Subordinate conjunctions connect an independent and a dependent clause: He missed gym class *because* he was sick.

Without is a preposition and introduces a phrase; *unless* is a conjunction and introduces a clause.

Like is a preposition and introduces a phrase; *as* and *as if* are usually conjunctions and introduce clauses.

contraction Two words written as one with one or more letters omitted: *doesn't* for *does not, I've* for *I have.* An apostrophe is used to show the omission of a letter or letters.

D

dangling participle A phrase or clause that is positioned in a sentence so that it seems to modify a word that it doesn't make sense for it to modify: *Running for the bus,* the curb tripped Roberta. Rewrite the sentence so the phrase or clause modifies the correct noun or pronoun: Running for the bus, *Roberta* tripped on the curb.

dash A punctuation mark (—) used to indicate a sudden change of thought: The boy jumped—indeed, soared—over the hurdle.

demonstrative pronoun A pronoun that points out a definite person, place, or thing. *This* and *these* are used for objects that are nearby; *that* and *those* are used for objects that are distant.

A demonstrative pronoun may be used as an adjective to modify a noun or as a pronoun to take the place of a noun: Is *this* book yours? Is *this* yours?

direct object The receiver of the action of a verb: Nathaniel gave the *baby* to her mother. An object pronoun can be used as a direct object: Nathaniel gave *her* to her mother.

E

exclamation point A punctuation mark (!) used after an exclamatory sentence and after an exclamatory word or phrase: More than one thousand people attended the wedding! Wonderful! What a celebration!

G

gerund A verb form ending in *–ing* that has the properties of a noun and a verb.

- Like a verb, a gerund may have an object: Teresa loved *playing the flute*. It may be modified by an adverb or by an adverbial phrase: She enjoyed *singing loudly*. *Mining in the Rockies* became a favorite hobby.
- Like a noun, a gerund may be used as a subject, a direct object, a subject complement, the object of a preposition, or an appositive: *Practicing* will make you a better player. I enjoy *swimming*. Her hobby is *sewing*. Start *by pressing* this key. Your sport, *snowboarding*, is too dangerous for me.

A gerund has the same form as a present participle. A participle is used as an adjective; a gerund is used as a noun.

H

hidden infinitive An infinitive in which *to* is not expressed.

- An infinitive is used without *to* after verbs of perception, such as *hear, see, know, feel, behold:* We felt the waves *rock* the boat.
- An infinitive is used without *to* after verbs such as *let, dare, need, make, bid, help:* The outline helped her *memorize* the speech.
- An infinitive is used without *to* frequently after the preposition *but* and the conjunction *than:* Dad does nothing but *work* every weekend. I would much rather do manual labor than *be* unemployed.

See also **infinitive** *and* **split infinitive**.

hyphen A punctuation mark (-) used to divide a word at the end of a line whenever one or more syllables are carried to the next line.

The hyphen is also used in the words for compound numbers from twenty-one to ninety-nine and to separate the parts of some compound words: *soldier-statesman, half-baked plan.*

I

indefinite pronoun An indefinite pronoun refers to any or all of a group of persons, places, or things.

Indefinite pronouns such as *anyone, anything, everybody, no one, nobody, nothing, one, somebody,* and *something* are always singular and require a singular verb. Possessive adjectives and pronouns that refer to these pronouns must be singular: Somebody left *her* coat on the bus. Everyone in this class works hard for *his* or *her* grades.

Indefinite pronouns such as *all, both, few, many, several,* and *some* are generally plural. Possessive adjectives and pronouns that refer to these pronouns must be plural: *Few* look to *their* left before turning.

indirect object The noun or pronoun that tells to whom or for whom the action in a sentence is done: I gave *him* a present. He baked *Martha* a cake.

infinitive A verb form, usually preceded by *to*, that has the properties of a noun, an adjective, or an adverb.

An infinitive may have an object or be modified by an adverb: His aim was to join *the army*. You are expected to respond *quickly*.

(continued on next page)

Like a noun, an infinitive may be used as a subject, a direct object, a subject complement, or an appositive: *To learn* a second language is my intention. Everyone must try *to understand*. Jenny's goal is *to act*. The mountaineer's goal, *to reach* the summit, was admirable.

Like a noun, an infinitive may be used as the object of a preposition. The prepositions that usually take the infinitive are *but, except,* and *about:* The show is about *to begin*.

An infinitive is used as an adjective when it modifies a noun or pronoun: This was his chance *to win*.

An infinitive is used as an adverb when it modifies a verb, a participle, an adjective, or an adverb: He was eager *to play* the game.

An infinitive may be used in the present or the perfect tense.

- The present infinitive is used when the action takes place at the same time as expressed by the main verb or after the time expressed by the main verb: We have *to discuss* it.
- The perfect infinitive is used only when the action has been completed by the time expressed in the main verb: Neil Armstrong is known *to have stepped* on the moon.
- A present infinitive following *ought* indicates obligation or necessity You *ought to heed* your father's advice.
- A perfect infinitive following *ought* indicates that the action did not take place: He *ought to have written* a month ago.

An infinitive may be active or passive: *to ask* (active); *to be asked* (passive).

See also **hidden infinitive** *and* **split infinitive**.

interjection A word that expresses a strong or sudden emotion. An interjection may express delight, disgust, pain, agreement, impatience, surprise, sorrow, wonder, etc. An interjection is grammatically distinct from the rest of the sentence: *Oh! Shh! Ouch! Wow!*

interrogative pronoun A pronoun that is used to ask a question: *who? whom? whose? which? what?*

N

noun The name of a person, place, or thing.

There are two main kinds of nouns: proper nouns and common nouns.

- A common noun names any one member of a group of persons, places, or things: *queen, city, church.*
- A proper noun names a particular person, place, or thing. A proper noun is capitalized: *Queen Elizabeth, London, Westminster Abbey.*
- A collective noun names a group of persons, places, or things considered as a unit. A collective noun usually takes a singular verb: The *crew* is tired. The *herd* is resting.
- A concrete noun names something that can be seen or touched: *brother, river, tree.* Most nouns are concrete.
- An abstract noun names a quality, a condition, or a state of mind. It names something that cannot be seen or touched: *anger, idea, spirit.*

A noun can be singular or plural.

- A singular noun names one person, place, or thing: *boy, river, berry.*
- A plural noun names more than one person, place, or thing: *boys, rivers, berries.*

The possessive form of a noun expresses possession or ownership. The apostrophe (') is the sign of a possessive noun.

- To form the possessive of a singular noun, add *'s* to the singular form: *architect's*
- To form the possessive of a plural noun that ends in *s*, add an apostrophe (') to the plural form: *farmers'*
- To form the possessive of a plural noun that does not end in *s*, add *'s* to the plural form: *children's*

An appositive is a noun that follows another noun. It renames or describes the noun it follows: Kanisha Taylor, the *president* of our class, will make the first speech.

O

order in a sentence The sequence of the subject and verb in a sentence expresses its order.

- When the verb in a sentence follows the subject, the sentence is in natural order: The *settlers planted* the seeds.
- When the main verb or the helping verb in a sentence comes before the subject, the sentence is in inverted order: Across the plain *marched* the tired *soldiers.*

P

participle A word that does the work of both a verb and an adjective.

- Like a verb, a participle may have an object and may be modified by an adverb or an adverbial phrase: *Having driven* for hours, we finally caught sight of the city skyline.
- Like an adjective, a participle modifies a noun or a pronoun: The poems *written* by Geoffrey Chaucer are in Middle English.

Participles are either present or past in form; they may be active or passive: *singing* (present active), *being sung* (present passive), *having sung* (past active), *having been sung* (past passive)

See also **dangling participle** *and* **participial adjective.**

participial adjective An adjective that is derived from a verb but is not a true participle. A participial adjective has the following characteristics:

- It is descriptive in character and occupies the usual position of an adjective—before a noun or after a linking verb: Fix the *broken* window. She is *known* as a skilled weaver.
- It may or may not have an object.

period A punctuation mark (.) used at the end of a declarative or an imperative sentence and after initials and some abbreviations.

phrase A group of related words that forms a single unit within a sentence. A phrase can be prepositional (introduced by a preposition), participial (introduced by a participle), infinitive (introduced by an infinitive), or gerund (introduced by a gerund).

- An adjectival phrase is used as an adjective and modifies a noun: The book *on the table* is mine. The girl *singing with the band* is my sister.
- An adverbial phrase is used as an adverb and modifies a verb, an adjective, or an adverb: The children played *in the park.*

See also **prepositional phrase.**

possessive adjective *See* adjective.

possessive pronoun A pronoun that shows possession or ownership by the speaker; the person spoken to; or the person, place, or thing spoken about: *mine, yours, his, hers, its, ours, theirs.* A possessive pronoun takes the place of a noun and its possessive adjective.

predicate The part of a sentence that tells something about the subject. The predicate consists of a verb and its modifiers, objects, and complements, if any: Jason *laughed.* Nikki *ate breakfast.* They *have run through the tall grass.*

preposition A preposition is a word that relates a noun or a pronoun to some other word in the sentence. The noun or pronoun that follows the preposition is the object of the preposition: The huge mountain lion leaped *through* (preposition) the tall *grass* (object of the preposition).

Some words may function as prepositions or as adverbs:

- A preposition shows the relationship between its object and some other word in the sentence: Megan sat *near* the door.
- An adverb tells how, when, or where: My friend is always *near.*

prepositional phrase A phrase that is introduced by a preposition. A prepositional phrase contains a preposition and an object: *off* (preposition) the *grass* (object of the preposition).

- An adjectival phrase is used as an adjective and modifies a noun: The cabin *in the woods* burned down.
- An adverbial phrase is used as an adverb and modifies a verb: The river flows *into the sea.*

pronoun A word that takes the place of a noun or nouns.

A personal pronoun names:

- the speaker (first person): *I, mine, me, we, ours, us*
- the person spoken to (second person): *you, yours*
- the person, place, or thing spoken about (third person): *he, she, it, his, hers, its, him, her, they, theirs, them*

A personal pronoun is singular when it refers to one person, place, or thing. A personal pronoun is plural when it refers to more than one person, place, or thing.

The third person singular pronoun can be masculine, feminine, or neuter.

A pronoun may be used as the subject of a sentence. The subject pronouns are *I, you, he, she, it, we,* and *they.*

A subject pronoun can replace a noun used as a subject complement.

A pronoun may be used as the direct object of a verb. The object pronouns are *me, you, him, her, it, us, them.*

An object pronoun may be used as the object of a preposition.

A pronoun that follows the conjunction *than* or *as* must be a subject pronoun if the word with which it is compared is a subject: John (subject) is happier than *I* (subject). It must be an object pronoun if the word with which it is compared is an object.

When a sentence contains a negative, such as *not* or *never,* use *anyone* or *anything* rather than *no one* or *nothing.*

See also **contraction, possessive pronoun,** *and* **reflexive pronoun.**

Q

question mark A punctuation mark (?) used at the end of a question: What time is it?

quotation marks Punctuation marks (" ") used before and after every direct quotation and every part of a divided quotation: "Let's go shopping," said Michiko. "I can go with you," Father said, "after I have eaten lunch."

Quotation marks enclose titles of short stories, poems, magazine articles, television shows, and radio programs. Titles of books, magazines, newspapers, movies, and works of art are usually printed in *italics* or are underlined.

R

reflexive pronoun A reflexive pronoun ends in –*self* or –*selves.* The reflexive pronouns are *myself, yourself, himself, herself, itself, ourselves, yourselves,* and *themselves.* A reflexive pronoun often refers to the subject of the sentence: She saw *herself* in the mirror.

A reflexive pronoun can also be used to show emphasis: I *myself* cooked the entire dinner.

relative pronoun A pronoun that connects a dependent clause to the person, place, or thing it modifies: Hal, *who* grew up in Indonesia, now lives in Boston.

The relative pronouns are *who, whom, whose, which,* and *that.* Use *who* if the pronoun is the subject of the dependent clause: Sue, *who* helped me, is my cousin. Use *whom* if the pronoun is the object of the dependent clause: Sue, *whom* you know, helps me study.

S

semicolon A punctuation mark (;) used as follows:

- to separate the clauses of a compound sentence when they are not separated by a conjunction: The bicycle was broken; the wheel was damaged.

(continued on next page)

- to separate the clauses of a compound sentence that are connected by a conjunctive adverb: Helga plays the violin; however, she can barely read music.
- before *as* and *namely* when these words introduce an example or an illustration: Three famous composers of classical music are called the three B's; namely, Bach, Beethoven, and Brahms.

sentence A group of words that expresses a complete thought.

A declarative sentence makes a statement; it is followed by a period: *The sun is shining.*

An interrogative sentence asks a question; it is followed by a question mark: *Where is my pen?*

An imperative sentence gives a command or makes a request; it is followed by a period: *Go to the store. Please pick up the papers.*

An exclamatory sentence expresses strong or sudden emotion; it is followed by an exclamation point: *What a loud noise that was!*

A sentence is made up of a subject and a predicate.

- The subject names a person, a place, or a thing about which a statement is made. The simple subject is a noun or pronoun without any of its modifiers: The *man* is riding his bike.
- The complete subject is the simple subject with all its modifiers: *The tall, athletic young man* is riding his bike.
- The predicate tells something about the subject. The simple predicate is a verb without any of its modifiers, objects, and complements: Teresa *waved.*
- The complete predicate is the verb with all its modifiers, objects, and complements: Teresa *waved to the child from the window.*

A simple sentence contains one subject and one predicate. Either or both may be compound. *See also* **compound subjects, predicates, objects.**

See also **complex sentence, compound complex sentence, compound sentence, order in a sentence, predicate,** *and* **subject.**

split infinitive An infinitive in which an adverb separates the words of the infinitive: She decided *to immediately cancel* her subscription. Rewrite the sentence to reposition the adverb: She decided *to cancel* her subscription *immediately.*

subject The person, place, or thing that a sentence is about: *Daniel* spoke. The *prairie* was dry. The *cup* broke into pieces.

subject complement A word that completes the meaning of a linking verb in a sentence. A subject complement may be a noun, a pronoun, or an adjective: Broccoli is a green *vegetable.* The prettiest one was *she.* The sea will be *cold.*

V

verb A word that expresses action or state of being.

A verb has four principal parts: the present, the present participle, the past, and the past participle.

- The present participle is formed by adding *–ing* to the present.
- The simple past and the past participle of regular verbs are formed by adding *–ed* to the present.
- The simple past and the past participle of irregular verbs are not formed by adding *–ed* to the present.

The tense of a verb shows the time of its action.

- The simple present tense tells about an action that happens again and again; I *play* the piano every afternoon.
- The simple past tense tells about an action that happened in the past: I *played* the piano yesterday afternoon.
- The future tense tells about an action that will happen in the future; the future tense is formed with the present and the auxiliary verb *will:* I *will* play in the piano recital next Sunday.
- The present progressive tense tells what is happening now; the present progressive tense is formed with the present participle and a form of the verb *be:* He *is eating* his lunch now.
- The past progressive tense tells what was happening in the past; the past progressive tense is formed with the past participle and a past form of the verb *be:* He *was eating* his lunch when I saw him.
- The present perfect tense tells about a past action that is relevant to the present: I *have lived* here for six years now.
- The past perfect tense tells about a past action that happened before another past action: I *had lived* in Memphis for a year before I moved here.
- The future perfect tense tells about an action that will be completed by a specific time in the future: I *will have finished* dinner by the time you get here.

A transitive verb expresses an action that passes from a doer to a receiver. The receiver is the direct object of the verb: The dog *ate* the bone.

An intransitive verb has no receiver of the action. It does not have a direct object: The sun *shone* on the lake.

Some verbs may be transitive or intransitive according to their use in the sentence: Chita *played* the harp. Joel *played* at Notre Dame.

A linking verb links a subject with a subject complement (a noun, a pronoun, or an adjective). Linking verbs are not action verbs; therefore, they do not have voice.

- The verb *be* in its many forms *(is, are, was, will be, have been,* etc.) is the most common linking verb.
- The verbs *appear, become, continue, feel, grow, look, remain, seem, smell, sound, stay,* and *taste* are also considered to be linking verbs.

In the active voice, the subject is the doer of the action: Betty *wrote* a poem. In the passive voice, the subject is the receiver of the action: The poem *was written* by Betty.

The modal auxiliaries *may, might, can, could, must, should,* and *would* are used to express permission, possibility, ability, necessity, and obligation.

(continued on next page)

A verb phrase is a group of words that does the work of a single verb. A verb phrase contains one or more auxiliary, or helping, verbs *(is, are, has, have, will, can, could, would, should,* etc.) and a main verb: She *had forgotten* her hat.

A subject and a verb must always agree.

- Singular subjects must have singular verbs. The third person singular of the simple present tense ends in –s or –es: I *run.* You *run.* He *runs.*

- Plural subjects must have plural verbs. A plural verb does not end in –s or –es: We *run.* You *run.* They *run.*

- Use *am* with the first person singular subject pronoun: I *am* a soccer player.

- Use *is* with a singular noun or a third person singular subject pronoun: Paris *is* a city. She *is* a pianist. It *is* a truck.

- Use *are* with a plural noun, the second person subject pronoun, or a third person plural pronoun: Dogs *are* good pets. You *are* the winner. We *are* happy. They *are* my neighbors.

- Use *was* with a singular noun or a first or third person singular subject pronoun: The boy *was* sad. I *was* lucky. It *was* a hard job.

- Use *were* with a plural noun, a second person subject pronoun, or a third person plural subject pronoun: The babies *were* crying. You *were* a good friend.

- A phrase or a parenthetical expression between the subject and the verb does not affect the verb: A *crate* of bananas *was* hoisted off the boat.

- A collective noun requires a singular verb if the idea expressed by the subject is thought of as a unit: The orchestra *plays* tomorrow.

- A collective noun requires a plural verb if the idea expressed by the subject is thought of as individuals: The family *are* living in Georgia, Virginia, and the Carolinas.

- Some nouns are plural in form but singular in meaning and require a singular verb. These nouns include *athletics, civics, economics, ethics, mathematics, measles, molasses, mumps, news, physics.*

- Some nouns are used only in the plural and require a plural verb. These nouns include *annals, archives, clothes, eaves, goods, pincers, pliers, proceeds, scissors, shears, slacks, spectacles, thanks, tongs, trousers, tweezers, whiskers.*

In sentences beginning with *there,* use *there is* or *there was* when the subject that follows is singular: *There is* no cause for alarm. Use *there are* or *there were* when the subject is plural: *There were* many passengers on the bus.